LANDMARK VISITORS GUIDE

India:
Kerala &
The South

Christopher Turner

Published by
Landmark Publishing Ltd
Waterloo House, 12 Compton, Ashbourne
Derbyshire DE6 1DA England

Since 1993 Christopher Turner has spent three months of each year in India. He knows Kerala and its surrounding areas intimately and has produced, as part of the research for this title, the first-ever comprehensive street map of Kovalam (included on pages 28/9 and 30).

This Landmark Visitors Guide to India: Kerala and The South is the author's third guide book to the sub-continent. A fully revised new edition of his best-selling guide to Goa is now in preparation.

Christopher is the author of London Step-by-Step, which won the 1985 Guidebook of the Year Award. He has recently completed a new guide to Edinburgh, together with his updated guide to Bruges. His guides to Goa, Edinburgh and Bruges are also published by Landmark Publishing.

The author wishes to express his thanks to VK Pradeep for his invaluable advice and assistance in all matters and, for their generous hospitality: Somak Holidays, the Taj Group of Hotels, and the Casino Group of Hotels.

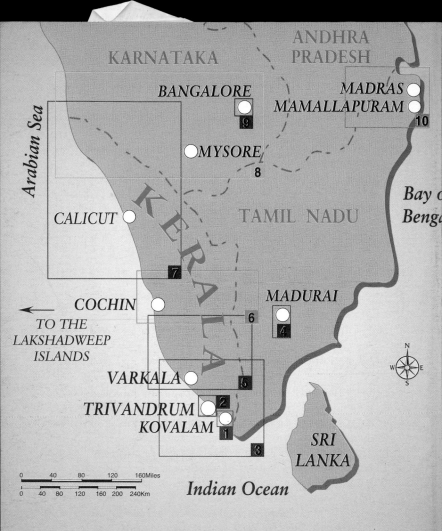

SOUTHERN INDIA

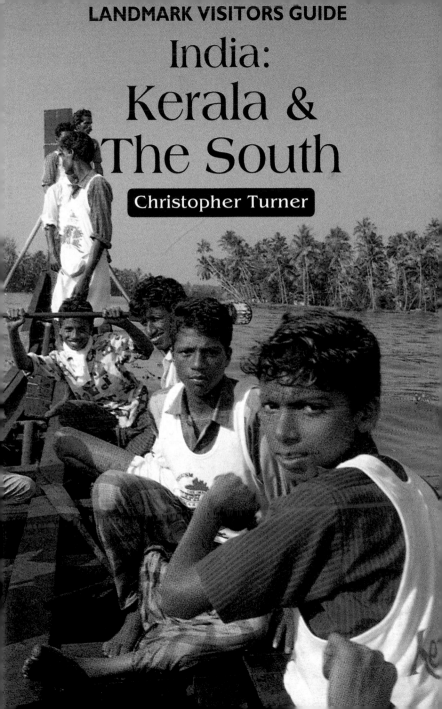

LANDMARK VISITORS GUIDE

India:
Kerala &
The South

Christopher Turner

CONTENTS

INTRODUCTION

Welcome to Kerala and the South

Acres of vivid green palm trees, golden beaches, backwaters where the only sound is the occasional splash of the boatman's pole, the Chinese fishing nets of Cochin, the trumpeting of elephants, the celebratory fireworks at Hindu festivals – these are the sights and sounds of Kerala that visitors will remember long after returning home.

Since direct charter flights from London to Trivandrum began in 1995, Kerala has become extremely easy and economical for western holiday-makers to reach. With hot sunshine, warm seas, and barely a cloud in the sky from December to April, this exotic south Indian state has understandably become a popular winter-sun destination.

Above: *The intense blues and greens of Kerala's backwaters can almost be blinding.*

To the west, Kerala's coastline, the fabled Malabar Spice Coast, borders the Lakshadweep Sea, whilst to the north the Deccan Plateau, and to the east the Western Ghats, proclaim Kerala's borders with the adjoining states of Karnataka and Tamil Nadu.

Kovalam and Varkala, Kerala's most popular beach resorts, are explored intensively in this book, as they are where many holidaymakers will spend most of their time. Nevertheless, it will be hard to resist making at least an occasional excursion to the ancient Hindu temples and palaces in the vicinity, or to visit the charming state capital of Trivandrum. A popular day trip is to Cape Comorin, the most southerly point in India, where three seas meet. A little further afield, in Tamil Nadu, the world-famous temple of Madurai, with its towering *gopura*, is another popular destination.

Having fully described these locations, this book then leads the visitor northward via the Quilon-Alleppey backwaters to Cochin, Kerala's largest city, which retains many venerable buildings, including Asia's best-preserved synagogue, a Dutch palace, and the church in which Vasco da Gama was buried.

In central Kerala, the delightfully temperate tea-producing centre of Munnar and its pastoral surroundings are explored, followed by the Periyar Wildlife Sanctuary, where wild elephants are more likely to be seen by tourists than anywhere else in India. A brief detour can then be made to the cool hill resorts of Tamil Nadu, terminating at Ooty which is usually approached by a steam-driven 'toy train', designed for amazingly steep gradients. Returning to Kerala's coast and continuing northward, Cannanore, so far neglected by tourists, is a connoisseur's discovery, with superb beaches, luxurious villas and a fascinating Muslim quarter.

Running almost in a straight line just across Kerala's border with Karnataka are the exquisite Hoysala temples of Belur and Halebid, the delightful city of Mysore, with its fairytale royal palace and, on its outskirts Tipu Sultan's capital of Shrirangapatam and the Jain temple city of Shravana Belgola with its enormous figure of Gomateshvara, the largest monolithic statue in the world. North east of Mysore lies Bangalore, the country's 'silicon valley', where visitors can gain a sense of India's modern development as well as enjoying the city's attractions, which include a near perfect climate.

Because many visitors to southern India arrive at Madras airport, this city and its 'Golden Triangle' incorporating Mamallapuram, with the unique Shore Temple, and Kanchipuram, the city of 104 temples, are also described.

This Landmark Guide to Kerala and the South caters for all Kerala visitors, from the independent traveller, who wants to miss nothing within reasonably easy reach, to the holidaymaker who prefers to spend most of his or her time lazing on the beaches or around the hotel swimming pools of Kovalam and Varkala. But perhaps the most endearing aspect of a Kerala holiday is the friendliness of the local people, cheerful waves and huge smiles framing gleaming white teeth are usually followed by the genuinely concerned question 'How do you find Kerala?'. Your answer is unlikely to be anything but complimentary.

History

The present state of Kerala was established in 1956, when all existing state boundaries were revised by the Indian government on a linguistic basis. Every region (*taluka*) of Kerala had to be Malayalam speaking, which meant that the most southerly part of the Malabar Coast, where the inhabitants spoke Tamil, was incorporated within Tamil Nadu.

Myth and early history

Little is known with certainty about Kerala's early history. According to ancient writings in the Sanskrit and Malayalam languages, Kerala was created by Parasurama, the sixth incarnation of Vishnu. By permission of the sea god Varunan, Parasurama flung his spear from Cape Comorin into the sea, which receded at the point where it fell: the reclaimed land became Kerala. The formation of the state of Goa is also attributed to a similar action by Parasurama which suggests that a dramatic recession of the Arabian Sea from India's west coast actually did occur at some time in prehistory.

Parasurama is also accredited with personally consecrating the temple at Padmanabhapuram, which he designated the first capital of Kerala. The god then appointed Bhanu Vikrama king, and established the supremacy of the Brahmin caste throughout the state; its members later elected Keya Perumal as king, whose dynasty was to rule for many years. King Keralan, who reigned 12 years, proved to be a successful and popular monarch, and it has been suggested that his name may have inspired that of the state; most, however, believe that Kerala simply means 'land of the coconut tree'.

Kerala prospered under Kulasekhara Perumal, due primarily to the introduction of technological advances. His reign also saw the remarkably sudden collapse throughout India of the Buddhist and Jain religions in favour of a return to Hinduism, which had never completely disappeared. It has been estimated that 25 Perumals became kings of Kerala; every one was elected, although not necessarily for life, and all came from outside the kingdom.

Archaeological finds indicate that progress in south India from the early stone age to the iron age took several thousand years, and it was not until the 4th century BC that routes between south Indian settlements were formalized; land communication with north India, however, remained virtually non-existent until the British laid out roads and railways in the 19th century.

It would appear that coastal trading with Malabar, as Kerala was known for most of its history, began in the 1st century BC when, presumably, the cyclical nature of the monsoon winds, essential for powering sailing craft, was discovered by western merchants. Greek and Roman traders first made the arduous crossing from Africa to Kerala, eager for its valuable spices, pepper in particular. Written accounts of some of these voyages, notably by Greek sailors and Ptolemy (in the 2nd century), have survived together with Roman coins. Jews fleeing from

Above: Gleaming white coral beaches proliferate on the Lakshadweep Islands.
Below: The Secretariat of Madras, located within Fort St George.

Roman occupied Palestine followed, some of them settling in Kerala. During this early trading period, Jainism and to a lesser extent Buddhism were the prime religions of Kerala, but by the 3rd century BC, Hinduism had regained its former ascendancy.

By tradition, Christ's disciple St Thomas ('Doubting Thomas') landed near Cranganore in 52 AD to spread the gospel in Malabar. Converts became known as Syrian Christians as St Thomas came from Syria. Although many fervently believe this tradition to be true, and such a mission was certainly possible, there is no evidence that St Thomas ever visited India. A stone cross in a Kerala church allegedly carved personally by the saint has been scientifically tested and found to be of more recent origin than the 1st century. In 643, Malik Ibn Dinar, a disciple of Muhammad, brought Islam to India, building the country's first mosque on the Kerala coast. The Emperor Cheraman Perumal, the last of the Perumal rulers, is believed to have been an early convert, allegedly making a pilgrimage to Jeddah, where he met the Prophet.

From 800 until 1102, Kerala formed the major part of the Chera Empire, but when this disintegrated, local chieftains – the Zamorin of Calicut, the Kolathiri of Cannanore, the Raja of Cochin and the King of Travancore (the Venad dynasty from the 10th century) – divided the region between them. However, by the end of the 15th century, the Zamorin ruled half of Malabar. Due to its remoteness and the impenetrability of the Deccan plateau to the north, Kerala escaped 'foreign' invasions, never being subjugated by either the Delhi Sultanate (1206-1526) or the Great Moguls (1526-1707), both of which were Muslim. For this reason, Hinduism has remained supreme throughout most of the state apart from its coastal strip. The same applies to adjacent Tamil Nadu, and it is in these two states that ancient Hindu temples and ceremonies are more numerous than elsewhere in India.

European rediscovery

As far as Europeans were concerned, the Malabar coast was ignored after the fall of the Roman Empire until its rediscovery when Vasco da Gama landed near Calicut in 1498. The relatively short routes to Malabar via the Persian Gulf and Red Sea, which had been followed by the Romans and Greeks, were no longer available to Europeans as they were blocked by the Ottoman Empire. The Portuguese navigator found a direct, albeit lengthy, trade route from Europe to India by sailing round the southern tip of Africa.

Arabs had continued to trade with Kerala throughout the centuries and many had settled on the Malabar coast, particularly around Calicut and Cranganore, where they were welcomed and permitted to follow the Islamic religion. The Calicut Muslims, known as Mappilas, acted as negotiators between merchants from Arabia and local producers. Cannanore, however, was the only city in Kerala to be ruled by Muslims, the Arakkal family, who had converted to Islam voluntarily. Vasco da Gama's exploratory voyage was soon followed by another, led by a more commercially-minded compatriot, Pedro Cabral, who discovered that Kerala's government had degenerated to feudalism, and lacked a central authority. He proved to be a tactless negotiator, making extravagant demands, including the prohibition of trade with Arabs. Cabral was given short shrift by the Zamorin, whose fleet chased the Portuguese from Calicut waters and made hastily for Cochin, where he was given a better reception, being welcomed by the Cochin Raja as a prospective ally against his Zamorin rival.

Portuguese trading and aggression

Vasco da Gama returned to Calicut in 1502, his fleet sinking Arab merchant ships on route. Once again, however, the Portuguese were unable to reach a trading agreement with the Zamorin, this time because they demanded that the Mappila Muslims should be banished from the area, a condition that the Zamorin was naturally unwilling to accept. The reason for this demand was not commercial but religious, the Roman Catholic hatred of Muslims and Jews then having reached its zenith, as expressed by the re-establishment of the Inquisition. The Kolathiri, also rivals of the Zamorin, did, however, agree to supply the Portuguese with spices. After mounting a vicious punitive attack on Calicut, Vasco da Gama proceeded southward to Cochin, where he presented the Raja with gifts, in return being granted an exclusive trading agreement. The Zamorin was infuriated by this treaty and insisted that the Portuguese should be expelled; his fleet subjugated Cochin and a garrison was established. However, after he had returned to Calicut with his main force, three Portuguese squadrons led by Albuquerque reinstated the Cochin Raja, who permitted them to build a fort. In 1509, Albuquerque, now Portuguese Viceroy, defeated the Zamorin and built a fort at Calicut. Thereby Portugal, which maintained trading supremacy on the Malabar coast for 150 years, effectively became the first foreign power to colonize a part of Kerala, even though its influence rarely extended far from the ports. Soon, however, Portugal's main Indian base was to be transferred further north, to Goa, and the importance to them of Kerala receded.

Disputes between the Portuguese and the Zamorin continued for almost a century, and new combatants, the Kunjalis, fought both for control of Calicut. In 1600, the Kunjalis were finally defeated by the Zamorin. The Portuguese became increasingly corrupt, and were greatly weakened when Philip II of Spain incorporated their country into his domain, taking virtually no personal interest in India. Their administration generally proved to be inefficient, and fierce rivalry within the Roman Catholic church led to disharmony. In spite of introducing many new crops from America the Portuguese never won popularity.

Arrival of the Dutch

Another European power was now seeking an Empire: the Dutch, who in 1604 formed an alliance with the Zamorin, the aim of which was the eventual expulsion of the Portuguese from Kerala. In 1663, the Dutch took Cochin and Cannanore from the Portuguese and subsequently made a treaty with the Kolathiri, under which they were granted a trading monopoly.

The Protestant Dutch were almost as intolerant of Roman Catholicism as were the Portuguese of the Muslims and Jews: initially, all Catholic priests were expelled from their areas of control and Jesuit buildings were demolished or converted to armament stores. Unlike the Portuguese, however, for reasons of self interest, no attempt was made to convert Hindus to Christianity. Wars with England in the 17th century weakened the Dutch, and this, combined with their colonization of Indonesia, led eventually to their complete abandonment of India. Before this occurred a rapprochement was reached with the Portuguese, to whom the Dutch returned all their former possessions on the Malabar coast with the exception of Cochin. Although the Dutch showed little interest in educating the indigenous population, they did revive trade and introduced more advanced agricultural techniques, together with salt harvesting and dyeing. The Dutch were far less corrupt than the Portuguese, and their administration was fairer.

Arrival of the English

In 1625 an Englishman, Captain Keeling, negotiated the first trading agreement between the East India Company and the Calicut Zamorin, who the company assisted in expelling the Portuguese from Cranganore and Cochin. By the mid-17th century, the Company had established a fort at Madras, which enabled them to halt French expansion of trade on the east coast from their base at Pondicherry. In 1662, Charles II married the Portuguese Princess Catherine of Braganza, part of her dowry being the then insignificant island of Bombay; peace between England and Portugal was thereby ensured. Another royal marriage, between Mary, niece of Charles II, and the Dutch Prince William of Orange, in 1677, similarly brought to an end the wars between England and the Netherlands.

Internal disputes

Fighting in Malabar during the last quarter of the 17th century was primarily confined to internecine disputes between the Zamorin and the Raja of Cochin, disputes which spanned a period of 500 years. In 1680, the Kolathiri broke up over a family feud, and their territory disintegrated into small principalities. At the same time, a vassal of Aurangzeb, the last Great Mogul, occupied the southern part of Travancore, which was administered from Trivandrum; however, he was soon assassinated and the brief period of Mogul rule in Kerala ended. During the reign of Raja Marthanda Varma (1729-58), Travancore expanded its domain northward to the Periyar River, and great improvements were made to the royal palaces and temples in Trivandrum. A canal was also constructed, linking the backwaters between Ashtamudi and Kayamkulam lakes. The Raja dedicated his kingdom to Sri Padmanabha Swami, becoming the god's 'servant'. The sacred nature of this title proved highly beneficial to the Raja and his successors, all of whom would adopt it.

Muslim invasions

Hyder Ali, a Muslim, had taken over the powerful state of Mysore (now Karnataka), which adjoined Kerala to the north, and was encouraged by his fellow Muslim, the Ali Raja of Cannanore, to invade Kerala. His invasion was successfully accomplished in 1766, and as a reward for his assistance, Ali Raja was appointed governor of all the Muslim conquests. This gave the East India Company the opportunity to bring their troops into north Malabar to assist the Zamorin in repelling Hyder Ali's force. However, further invasions continued until the final defeat by the English of Hyder Ali's son and successor Tipu Sultan, who died in the Battle of Seringapatam in 1799. The Mysore army never reached Travancore as Tipu had planned, but for the first time in centuries, most of Kerala was controlled by a centrally-based authority, rather than a plethora of numerous administrative units.

Although Tipu laid out a network of roads in north Kerala and modernized the taxation and monetary systems, he ruined Kerala's economy as trading came to a standstill, and the reserves of gold and silver disappeared, almost certainly ending up in the Mysore coffers. In addition, the Hindu and Muslim communities, which had previously lived together harmoniously, took sides and became intolerant of each others religions.

British administration

At the time of Tipu's defeat, the English were already in control of Malabar, which they divided into north and south sectors in 1793. The administration, originally from Bombay, was transferred to the Madras Presidency in 1800. Throughout India, in the late-18th and early-19th centuries, the East India Company gradually gained control of the country by making treaties with each maharaja in turn, under which they were given a monopoly of trading rights in exchange for protection and administration. The maharaja and his *diwan* (prime minister) remained nominally in control, but in reality all decisions of importance were subject to the Company's approval.

Undoubtedly, with the rapid decline of the Moguls, India was in a chaotic state at the time, only the Maharashtras being powerful enough to put up any resistance to the English army, and a significant number of maharajas were content to 'delegate' effective control to the Company in return for security from invasion by hostile neighbours. Those who cooperated, and most did, were treated with all due respect, and their possessions and customs were

Below: Tea-picking in the hills around Munnar.

untouched. Nevertheless, it cannot be disputed that this 'protection racket' was one of the most cynical in history.

As might be expected, there were several revolts against the English: in Kerala, those of the Raja of Kottayam, Paliath Achan (Cochin), Velu Thambi (Travancore) and Kurichaya (Wynad) being the most notable, but all were put down with relative ease as communications had improved and troops could be brought more quickly from one garrison to another. By the mid-19th century, the East India Company controlled all India apart from Goa, which was to remain Portuguese until 1961, and Pondicherry, a French outpost from where a handful of small, separate enclaves in south India were also administered; one of them, Mahe, although located within the Kerala boundaries, is currently designated Union Territory and administered directly by the national government.

India provided a vast controlled market for British goods, and this did much to facilitate the progress of the industrial revolution. In addition, its raw materials were exploited by the British, who controlled their production and marketing.

Absorption within the British Empire

For more than 150 years, India's overlords were members of the East India Company; however, following the Indian Mutiny of 1857, which had few repercussions in Kerala, the Company was disbanded and India became the 'Jewel in the Crown' of Queen Victoria's empire; to encourage cooperation, India's citizens were given, in theory, equal rights with those of the United Kingdom.

Even before the Mutiny, the British had founded universities at Madras, Calcutta and Bombay, with the aim of creating a subservient middle class that would be able to assist their administrators and at the same time absorb British ideology. Unlike their Portuguese and, to a lesser extent, Dutch predecessors, the British took little interest in religious conversion, and interfered with neither Hindus nor Muslims. Excesses such as the immolation of women (a north Indian Rajput speciality) and slavery were eventually outlawed, but it was not until Independence that any governmental attempt would be made to abolish the iniquitous caste system. Some alleviation of the 'untouchables' misery did, however, result from the 1936 proclamation by which they were permitted to enter Hindu temples for the first time. One unforeseen result of creating a middle class was the fostering of Indian nationalism, which led to the foundation, in 1885, of the Indian National Congress, together with numerous societies and 'scurrilous' publications.

Organized rebellion

The peasant Muslims of Kerala were in almost permanent revolt against the British during the second half of the 19th and the early years of the 20th centuries. The freedom movement was particularly strong in Kerala, and in 1919 a Keralan committee of the National Congress convened at Trichur. Two years later, the Malabar Rebellion took place in line with other similar revolts throughout India. During this rebellion the 'Wagon Tragedy' occurred when 61 Indian political prisoners suffocated while being transported by the British from Trivandrum to Coimbatore.

Inspired by the Mahatma Gandhi's principle of non-violent resistance, civil disobedience campaigns were mounted in the 1930s, and the British authorities retaliated by outlawing the Congress Party. The nucleus of the party then split into militant and non-militant wings; members of the former, who had become impatient with Gandhi's pacific views, would form the Communist Party of Malabar in 1939. India supported Britain in both World Wars, but Gandhi and Pandit Nehru made it clear throughout the Second World War that they expected India to be granted independence when it ended. Both Indian leaders, amongst others, suffered imprisonment, and Gandhi threatened self-starvation on several occasions in the constant battle for Indian freedom.

Independence

After the war ended in 1945 and with the election of Clement Attlee's Labour government, arrangements were made for Indian independence, which came into effect in August 1947.

At the time of Independence, Malabar comprised three states, which were, from north to south, Malabar, Cochin and Travancore. All were administered from Madras, and continued to be so until 1 November 1956, when the boundaries of the present state of Kerala were established. In 1949, Cochin and Travancore had been combined to form a single state ruled by a Rajapramuk, formerly the Maharaja of Travancore; the Cochin Raja lost his power and was awarded a pension. Trivandrum became the capital of the new state.

By the 1956 act, all Indian titles were abolished and the Maharaja of Travancore was replaced as head of state by a governor. Following elections in 1957, Kerala became the first and only state in India to be ruled by communists, and in 1996 this party came to power once more. In practice, Kerala's communists tend to follow left of centre socialist principles rather than those of communism in the generally accepted sense.

The future

Kerala has not industrialized, remaining primarily dependent on agriculture for its income.

Like virtually all the agricultural regions of the third world, where no money is available for modern equipment or state subsidies, there is a great deal of poverty. Commercial establishments of any size are virtually restricted to Trivandrum, Calicut and the twin cities of Cochin/Ernakulam. Insufficient electrical power is a problem that Kerala shares with other southern Indian states, particularly when the north-east monsoon rains have been unable to provide power for the hydro-electric stations. Until this has been overcome, no industrial or commercial expansion of note seems possible.

Fortunately, a safety valve exists overseas, in the Gulf States, where many Keralans carry out menial tasks in order to be able to send home a wage that is munificent by Indian standards. There is a high price to pay however, as the workers are rarely accompanied by members of their families, and must accept, particularly if non Muslim, a culture that is alien to them.

Tourism

Much is expected from the development of tourism to increase wealth within Kerala itself, and great importance is placed on the new international airport under construction at Cochin, together with the imminent opening of the Konkan railway, which will provide a direct link between Kerala and Bombay, via Karnataka and Goa. At present, most tourists in Kerala keep to the southern extremity of the state, at the beach resorts of Kovalam and Varkala which flank Trivandrum, and here as elsewhere in Kerala, there is a great shortage of European-style medium grade hotels. Development of new resorts is envisaged, particularly in north Kerala, but beaches from where swimming is safe and pleasurable are somewhat restricted, and draconian measures would have to be taken in order to clean up those that do exist so that they became acceptable to western tourists. Greater scope for development at present would seem to be along the backwaters, particularly if tastefully designed resort hotels (in the manner of the existing Coconut Lagoon) were able to offer ayurvedic treatment and provide fast boat trips to a nearby beach.

One simple act would remove a major obstacle to western tourism; a reduction in the high liquor licence fee, which makes it difficult for most establishments, even on Kovalam beach, to supply alcohol of any type unless they are able to 'persuade' the police to turn a blind eye. There is even an absurd movement in Kerala, led by Catholic priests and Muslim women (strange bedfellows) to ban alcoholic drinks altogether – and this is in a state that desperately needs western tourists!

Another hindrance to tourism,

Geography, Flora and Fauna

Covering an area of almost 40,000 square miles (102,400 sq km), with the Lakshadweep Sea to one side and the Western Ghat heights to the other, Kerala is 375 miles (600km) long, but only 47 miles (75km) wide at its broadest point. Between the coast and the higher mountains, Kerala's fertile soil is well watered by the monsoon rains, which fall in two three-month periods, and by the 41 rivers that make their way westward from the mountains to the sea. The alluvial deposits from the rivers, combined with great coastal storms, have created Kerala's most unusual natural feature, the famous backwaters, which stretch south-ward from Cranganore almost as far as Kovalam. Fortunately for Kerala, all its river estuaries have been bridged, as they are nowhere near as wide as Goa's, some of which can still only be crossed by ferries.

Approximately 25 per cent of Kerala remains aforested and, in spite of the ubiquitous palm tree, more than 500 species of tree have been recorded. Rice and coconuts are the main crops, but on the higher ground grow the more valuable coffee, tea, cocoa, rubber, pepper and cardamom. Tropical fruits are also abundant, in particular pineapples and bananas, including the rare red-skinned variety, which grows around Trivandrum and is said to be good for the health. More exotic fruits such as mango, jackfruit and durian are in season throughout the summer, when few tourists are around to taste them. As throughout much of India, bougainvillea is the most commonly seen bloom, al-though fruit trees supplement this with their blossom in the early spring. In the hills around Munnar can be seen the spectacular flowering kurinji, which carpets the uplands for miles around – but only once every twelve years: the next occasion will be in 2004!

Kerala brims with exotic wildlife; tigers, leopards, elephants, lion-tailed macaque monkeys, ibex, and many more. Unfortunately, few visitors see any of these secretive, mostly nomadic creatures, in spite of the abun-dant Wildlife Sanctuaries that have been established. Even monkeys rarely approach the tourist areas (apart from Periyar), and never the beaches, and the green parrot, so numerous in north India, apparently gives the south a miss. A visit to Periyar gives the best chance of observing wildlife, particularly elephants, but even here sightings cannot be guaranteed. Most visitors have to be satisfied with cows, goats, black crows, egrets and sea eagles.

which applies throughout India, is the imposition of a visa on tourists, which must be obtained before departing for India. Many other countries equally desperate for tourism, such as Sri Lanka, waive this requirement completely whilst others issue visas on arrival as a formality. It has been estimated that abolishing the visa requirement would at least double India's tourism – virtually overnight.

The present administrators of tourism in Kerala are most enthusiastic and go-ahead, and given the beauty of the state, its superb winter climate and the absurdly low prices, a bright tourist future must surely await its friendly, happy people.

The people of Kerala, their language and religions

Although most Keralans are racially Dravidian, many of them still have traces of earlier, Austric blood. Anthropologists believe that the Austrics of Kerala came from the same stock as the Australian aboriginies, and some of their common distinguishing features, such as broad noses with flared nostrils, can be observed. Most Dravidians are darker skinned than the Aryans of north India and become even darker when exposed to sunshine, which they therefore tend to avoid.

A series of communist-run state administrations since 1957 are accredited with gaining for Kerala a literacy rate of 90% (India's average is 50%), low infant mortality and zero growth in population, and it is hard to disagree, no other believable reason having been proposed. Unfortunately, the Keralan language, Malayalam, requires a lot of tongue-work, and many pronounce English in the same way, which makes it quite unintelligible, the resulting sound resembling not so much Peter Sellers speaking Indian English as Peter Sellers gargling. Malayalam is very difficult for foreigners to pronounce, mainly due to some unusual vowels, and Roman transliteration is no great help. Remember that double letters indicate that a consonant should be emphasized or a vowel lengthened. *Th* is always pronounced as a light *t*, never *th* as in *thing*.

The innate politeness of the average South Indian means that truthfulness is not defined in precisely the same way as it is in the west. An answer to a question must please or placate, but it need not necessarily be factual. Never suggest an answer to a question; for example, do not ask 'Is this the bus to Trivandrum?' but say 'Where is this bus going?'. If there is any suggestion of doubt, confirm with someone else – and someone else...

The reason for Kerala's mixture of religions has been explained in the History section above; fortunately, little strife occurs between followers of the different faiths. At present, around 60 per cent of Keralans are Hindu, 20 per cent Muslim and 20 per cent Christian. Muslims are concentrated in the northern coastal areas of Cannanore and Calicut, Christians remain strong in Cochin, whilst in the tourist areas and Trivandrum most are Hindu. Only a handful of Jews remain (in Cochin), most having emigrated to Israel.

Hinduism

Many Westerners come into contact with Hinduism for the first time during their holiday in Kerala, where around two-thirds of the population is Hindu. It is one of the most complicated of the world's religions, and much study and tuition is necessary before it can be properly understood.

Hinduism evolved from Vedism, a form of nature worship introduced by the Indo/Europeans to the Indus valley (now in Pakistan) when they settled there about 1,200BC. Although is is supported by many holy books, which are primarily narratives of epic events, Hinduism is not a doctrinaire religion, and no all-powerful body exists to pronounce dogma. Because of this, Hindus are eclectic, tolerant, and wide-ranging in their beliefs. To precisely define a Hindu is, therefore, impossible; many followers claim that Hinduism is more a philosophy than a religion in the accepted sense. Hindi, incidentally, is the name of India's official language and not directly connected with any religion.

Most non-Hindus are surprised to discover that, in spite of numerous 'gods', Hinduism is, like Judaism, Christianity and Mohammedanism, a monotheistic religion. Brahmin, The Almighty, is revered as 'one that is all', and the gods that Hindus worship represent different aspects of him. Similarities with the adoration of their patron saints exhibited by Roman Catholics have been noted.

The trinity of primary gods comprises Brahma (not to be confused with Brahmin) the creator, Vishnu the preserver and Shiva the Destoyer and reproducer. When represented in human form, each has four arms.

Although Brahma is always depicted somewhere in Vishnu and Shiva temples, few Indian temples are primarily dedicated to him, probably because his work as creator of the world is finished. Brahma's consort, Sarawati, goddess of learning, is also depicted with four arms; she rides a peacock, and holds a *vina* (mucical instrument).

Vishnu as himself rather than one of his earthly incarnations is usually shown bearing a quoit and a conch shell; occasionally he holds a club and a lotus flower in his other hands. A more complex but popular depiction of Vishnu illustrates him floating on the ocean, his vessel formed of coiled serpents; Brahma emerges from a lotus blossom growing from the god's navel. Laxmi (or Lakshmi), Vishnu's consort, sits at his feet; she is the goddess of wealth, and was created from the ocean. Closely associated with Vishnu is his vehicle, the half man/half bird Garuda. Vishnu is accredited with nine incarntions on earth (avatars).

Throughout India, Vishnu is primarily worshipped in two of his earthly incarnations: Krishna and Rama. Krishna's life is documented towards the end of The Mahabharata epic. When depicted, he is blue in colour, which is why birds with blue plumage, such as pigeons and peacocks, are regarded as sacred. Krishna is often shown trampling serpents and playing a flute or holding a lotus blossom.

Vishnu, as Rama, is the subject of the epic poem *The Ramayana*; he is usually shown carrying a bow and sheaf of arrows. The monkey Hanuman, who assisted Rama, generally appears in Vishnu temples as a secondary god.

As the member of the trinity of gods who has the powers of destruction and reproduction, Shiva (meaning auspicious) inspires great awe and trepidation amongst Hindus, who therefore wish to placate and please him. By tradition, he dwells in the Himalayas. When depicted in human form, Shiva has a third eye and wears a tigerskin; he may be holding an antelope, a trident, a noose or a drum. More commonly, Shiva is symbolized by a *lingam*, usually a carved block of stone. This takes the form of a phallus, a reference to the god's reproductive powers. Shiva's vehicle, the bull Nandi (joyous), normally guards the shrine in Shiva temples. Followers of Shiva are known as Shaivites.

Parvati, goddess of beauty, and Shiva's consort, is the most revered of all Hindu goddesses. In her form as Durga, ten-armed and riding a tiger, or as the even more terrible Kali, with a protruding tongue and demonic appearance, she is also the most feared and inspired the murderous thugee cult of the nineteenth century. It appears that Parvati now accepts more responsibility for cosmic violence than Shiva himself.

Shiva and Parvati have two children: Kartikkhaya, god of war, whose vehicle is a peacock, and Ganesh (or Ganpati), the elephant-headed god of learning, whose vehicle is a large rat. Ganesh, with his endearing, slightly comical appearance, is the best-loved of all the gods. He possesses none of the violent traits of his parents or brother, preferring to pacifically eat the sweets and fruits of which he is so fond, and with which his followers so liberally provide him.

A precept of most Hindus is that all creatures are reborn continuously until a perfect life has been led. The form of

Ayurvedic Medicine

Few visitors to Kerala will not be tempted, at least once, by the ayurvedic treatment centres, most of which are simply massage parlours. Ayur means the science of life, and ayurvedic treatment has been practised in Kerala for more than 1000 years. Some swear by its efficacy, but others, particularly amongst the younger Keralans, regard it as little more than unscientific mumbo-jumbo. In the tourist areas of Kerala, however, ayurvedic is now very big business, and some resort hotels have been set up specifically for it. Courses can last up to a month, and various ailments are dealt with – at a not inconsiderable price. Enthusiasts regarding the prospectuses may well be persuaded that they can achieve immortality, as long as sufficient courses are taken!

Apparently, anyone may practise ayurvedic treatment without qualifications, and this means, of course, that a number of charlatans proclaim themselves to be specialists. Always ensure that the practitioner is bona fide. Most who try ayurvedic treatment will limit their experience to massage which, even if not particularly therapeutic, will always be relaxing. The recipient of the massage must be completely naked, which is why men will only massage men and women only women; this is not Thailand, and there is no likelihood of any hankey-pankey.

Apparently, the most responsive ailments to ayurvedic massage are rheumatism and arthritis. Warmed, medicated oil is applied to the body and gently rubbed into the skin by the palms of the hands. It is claimed that massaging improves the blood circulation, and warming of the skin stimulates the nervous system. Deep (painful) massage is not part of the usual ayurvedic treatment, and massaging with feet is only necessary when special treatment of joints is required.

each reincarnation may be higher or lower, depending on the deeds performed in the previous existence. Moksha, the reward for a perfect life, is relief from this onerous cycle, ie non-existence.

Traditional Dances and Martial Arts

Kerala's traditional dances, with the vivid make-up and exotic costumes of its exponents, appeal to foreign tourists more than any other art form in the state. Foremost in popularity is

Kathakali, in which the mute actors transmit, through facial expressions and hand movements, the words sung by those behind them. Make-up is all important, and takes much training and many hours to apply. Designs are standard, only varying according to the characters represented. Originally, performances lasted all night but are now usually reduced to around three hours. They take place in all the tourist areas and it is sometimes possible to watch make-up being applied.

Even more colourful are the make-up and headgear of the **Teyyam** dancers. *Teyyam* is a corruption of *deivam*, meaning God, and this ritual dance evolved in the Brahma temples of north Kerala. It is performed exclusively by male members of what were the lower castes and tribes. Cannanore and Kasargod are the districts where Teyyam dancing is most commonly performed.

Kalarippayattu, Kerala's traditional martial art, dates from the 12th century, and has recently been revived. In the feudal period, the separate principalities that then made up Kerala were constantly at war with each other, and *kalaris* (gymnasiums) were set up, where *payattu* (training for combat) took place. The fighters were employed by the ruling families as mercenaries and remained an important feature of Kerala society until they were disbanded by the English East India Company in 1792. Performances are held for tourists from time to time, consisting of a formalized training session on the use of various weapons including sticks, daggers and swords. It is apparent that much of the footwork and postures have since been adopted by Kathakali dancers.

Food and Drink

Most visitors to Kerala from the United Kingdom will have had some experience of Indian cuisine, but very few of the dishes with which they are familiar will appear on the local menus. Never expect to see, for example, dhansaks, bhoonas, balti, vindaloos or dishes described as Chicken Madras or Bombay. Incidentally, Indians refer to chillis as being spicy, not hot. Although beef can on occasions be found in the more expensive hotels, it is rarely available anywhere else. Mutton is also a rarity in south India, and should always be avoided as it will be bony, fatty and tough. Pork will never be seen anywhere in India outside Goa. Non-vegetarians are therefore restricted to seafood and chicken, but this should prove no hardship as tasty and remarkably varied vegetarian dishes are a speciality of south Indian cuisine. Undoubtably, some of them are difficult to obtain in the 'international land' of Kovalam and Varkala, the cuisines of which are dealt with separately elsewhere.

It seems that the majority of Keralans eat little else but rice with dhal or rice with fish (any fish) curry. Fish curry is rarely eaten in the west, but is without doubt the most reliable meal to order in Kerala, as well as the cheapest. Just about all curries are cooked with coconut milk as in Thailand, Sri Lanka and Malaysia, and if this is required specify 'Kerala style'. Some north Indian specialities are offered in the better restaurants, particularly tandooris, which are usually more successful with chicken than with fish. Kerala style pappadums are exceptional, being small, fluffy, light and tasting slightly of the coconut oil in which they are cooked. Order them with everything.

Fruit is much more plentiful and cheaper in Kerala than it is in Goa and fresh fruit juices are never watered down (as they usually are in Goa). Strangely, breakfast causes more problems for westerners than any other meal. Kerala bread is rather sweet, and 'toast' is usually just warm bread, so request it is 'well cooked'. Indians are used to eating eggs unaccompanied by bread, toast or butter, so when ordering, it is wise to insist that all are brought together at the same time. Tea will be another problem; it is usually too strong for western tastes and waiters have great difficulty in comprehending that cold (not hot) milk, served separately, is

required. Black tea and coffee are much easier, although instant coffee is ubiquitous. Those used to the efficient service provided by Indian waiters (usually Bangladeshi) in the west are in for a surprise. It does seem at times that there is a mass rehearsal in progress for the part of Manuel in an Indian version of Fawlty Towers.

Ensure that your order is comprehended by asking the waiter to repeat what you have requested – and listen carefully. When the food arrives, make sure that nothing has been forgotten before the waiter bids you farewell forever (this particularly applies to room service in a hotel). Pappadums and pickles (when available) are frequently forgotten and it is most unusual to be given a full complement of cutlery.

Never, ever, ever, ever drink water unless it is poured from a sealed bottle, and insist that the waiter opens the bottle for you – some tops are fiendishly difficult to unscrew. Luxury hotels usually provide filter water, which is quite safe, but always check first.

Eat as frequently as possible in the restaurants of the top hotels, where the food is safer and far more interesting than in the majority of restaurants, and well worth the extra rupees.

Some Keralan and south Indian specialities that are generally unknown outside India, together with a few basic translations, are listed in the FactFile.

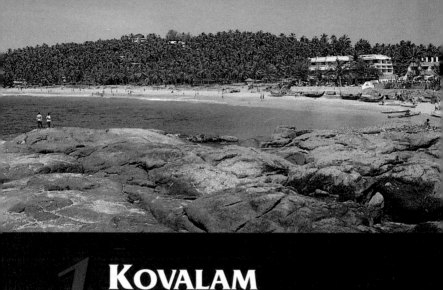

1 KOVALAM

Few of Kerala's visitors fail to spend some time at Kovalam; indeed, to many of them, this beguiling coastal resort *is* Kerala. Almost half a century has passed since that engaging travel writer, Rupert Croft-Cooke, in his *In Search of Nirvanha* enthusiastically described the charms of Kovalam's coastal scenery, possibly the first published reference in an English book to the small village. At that time, its beaches were entirely the preserve of fishermen, and most of the surrounding land was owned by the Maharaja of Travancore.

With the commencement, in 1995, of charter flights direct from London to Trivandrum, just a 20-minute drive away, Kovalam has been placed firmly

Above: *Kovalam's Eve's Beach.*

on the tourist map. Many now compare this resort's characteristics with those of Goa when selecting their winter sun holiday destination. The major difference is that Goa's tourists tend to congregate according to their wealth and age in specific locations along the entire coastline of the state, whilst Kovalam (and to a far lesser extent Varkala) are the only beach resorts so far developed in Kerala, and the tourist mix is therefore much greater.

Apart from the far north and far south of Goa, largely the preserve of backpackers, most Goan beaches are long and straight, with flat paddyfields immediately behind them; Kovalam's, however, comprise three relatively small bays, separated by picturesque headlands and backed by steeply rising ground, verdant with palm trees. Lighthouse Beach, Kovalam's most popular, is lined from end to end with a higgledy piggledy mix of restaurants, 'boutiques', souvenir shops, carpet emporiums, tour agents and fax/telephone outlets. There is, therefore, a 'resort' feel to Kovalam that exists nowhere else in India. Easy access to major temples gives Kovalam a more exotic, Hindu ambience than Goa, where the most important buildings, particularly the churches, are Portuguese and the dominant religion along its coastal strip is Christian.

Most are surprised to learn that Kovalam's tourist development preceded that of Goa. A few hippies had discovered its beaches in the 1960s but never arrived in vast numbers. However, as early as 1972, the Indian Tourist Development Corpora-

tion (ITDC) built a group of cottages at the south end of Kovalam beach, which is now incorporated in the **Ashok Hotel** complex.

Arrival

After passing through immigration clearance at Trivandrum airport (much less of an ordeal than at Goa), all tourists on package holidays will be met, of course, by their tour operators' representatives. Most independent travellers wanting to go straight to Kovalam will require a taxi, which is best booked and paid for at the airport office, where prices are fixed and passengers cannot be cheated. This office is found by turning left immediately after leaving the terminal building. It is however possible to reach Kovalam much more cheaply by public transport, as a bus runs from the airport to Trivandrum, though there is no direct bus from the airport to Kovalam. At the terminus, walk a short distance ahead to another bus stop, which faces the Luciya Continental Hotel, and take the local bus to Kovalam Junction. From here, it will be necessary to hire an auto-rickshaw or taxi to reach the resort's hotels and guest houses. Alternatively, some will prefer to continue from Kovalam Junction on the bus to its terminus at Kovalam Bus Stand, which is located above Eve's Beach as, a short walk away, the area's brand new Tourist Information Centre

KO

To Trivandrum

VELLAR JUNCTION

KOVALAM VILLAGE

KOVALAM JUNCTION

GV Raja Road

- Post Office

Andathura Temple Road

Kovalam Beach

- Taxis/Autos

(146)
(145)
(144)
(143)
(142)
(141)
(140)
(139)
(138)
(137)
(136)
(135)
(133)
(134)
(131)
(132)
(129)
(130)
(128)
(126)
(125)
(127)
(116)
(117)
(118)
(119)
(120)
(121)
(123)
(124)
(122)
(113)
(112)
(111)
(110)
(109)
(115)
(114)
(108)
(107)
(106)
(105)
(104)
(103)
(1)
(2)

Eve's (Ha... Beach...

- Bus Stand
- Taxis/Autos

Lakshad...

(Deta...
K...

| 0 | 100 | 200 | 300 | 400m |
| 0 | 100 | 200 | 300 | 400yds |

ALAM

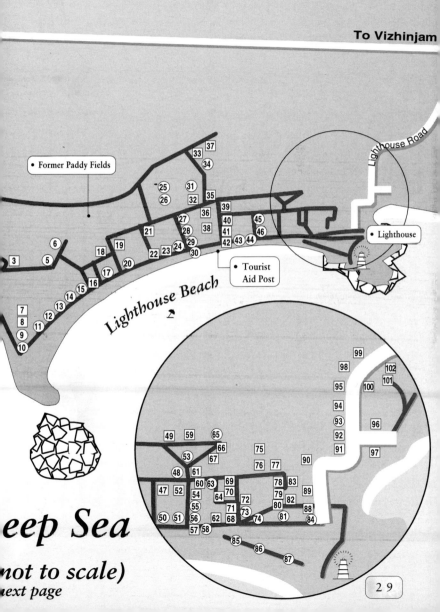

- Former Paddy Fields

Lighthouse Road

- Lighthouse

- Tourist Aid Post

Lighthouse Beach

eep Sea

(not to scale)
next page

KEY

1. Santhiyil Tourist Home
2. Sea Rock Hotel
3. Linchu Holiday Resort
4. Sea Face Hotel
5. Royal Retreat Cottages
6. Thushara Cottages
7. Dream House Hotel
8. Damaskar Inn Hotel
9. Sea Shore Restaurant
10. Dwaraka Restaurant
11. Telecom
12. Begum Restaurant
13. Garzia Restaurant
14. Leo Restaurant
15. Palm Beach
16. Neelakanta Hotel/Restaurant
17. My Dream Restaurant
18. Lal Tourist Home
19. Wilsons Tourist Home
20. Pappakutty Beach Resort
21. Sumangali Hotel
22. Achutha Hotel/Restaurant
23. Hawah Beach Hotel/Restaurant
24. Flamingo Restaurant
25. Kailas Restaurant
26. Lonely Planet Restaurant
27. Surya Restaurant
28. White House
29. Jeevan House
30. Coral Reef Restaurant
31. Vegetarian Restaurant (unnamed)
32. Hari Lekshni Guest House
33. Silent Valley Inn Hotel
34. Green Valley Cottages
35. Syam Nivas Guest House
36. Sandy Beach Hotel
37. Silent Valley House
38. Apsara Hotel
39. Neptune Hotel
40. Volga Palace Guest House
41. Blue Diamond Guest House
42. Sunset Guest House/Restaurant
43. Sea Fish Restaurant
44. Velvet Dawn
45. Simi Cottages
46. Sea Sand Home
47. Sea View Palace Hotel
48. Park Lane Hotel
49. Sreeva s Bombay Lodge
50. Crab Club Restaurant
51. German Bakery
52. Palm Garden Hotel

53. Shells Restaurant
54. Ajith House Hotel
55. Green Pease Restaurant
56. Woodstock Restaurant
57. Orion Hotel/Restaurant
58. Amma's Restaurant
59. Green Lane Sergeant Guest House
60. Sangeeth/Sri Nivas Guest House
61. Chaitra Nivas Guest House
62. Kavitha Hotel
63. Goldfish Restaurant
64. Taj Guest House
65. Sreevas Shangri-La
66. E.A. Nisha Hotel
67. Sea Breeze Guest House
68. Thomas House Guest House
69. Day's Wish Guest House
70. Rolling Stones Lodge
71. Holiday Homes
72. California Guest House
73. Flora Home
74. Sindhu Restaurant
75. Peacock Hotel
76. Appy Nivas Guest House
77. Pink Flowers Guest House
78. Golden Sands Hotel
79. Vinu Guest House
80. West View Guest House
81. Cashnova House
82. Seablue Guest House
83. Hilton Hotel
84. Sea Flower House
85. Shivas Moon Restaurant
86. Travancore Restaurant
87. Serenity Restaurant
88. Paradise Rock Hotel
89. Samudra Tara/Castle Rock hotels
90. Seaweed Hotel
91. Saibaba Resorts
92. New hotel (unnamed)
93. Sun House/Medicus
94. Thiruvathira Hotel
95. Nisha Hotel
96. Aparna Hotel
97. Rockholm Hotel
98. Nice House Hotel
99. Eden Seaside Resort
100. Amritham Beach Resort
101. Varmas Beach Resort
102. Palmshore Hotel
103. Moon Cottage Guest House/Restaurant
104. Mermaid Restaurant
105. Moonlight Tourist Home

106. Raji House
107. Merry Land Tourist House
108. Avudathura Temple
109. Men's Hairdressers
110. Devi Holiday Inn
111. Lobster House Restaurant
112. Upasana Hospital (Clinic)
113. Swagath Holiday Resort
114. Neo Park Hotel
115. Raja Hotel
116. Kovalam Police Station
117. Ketmac Beach Hostel
118. Hotel Blue Sea
119. Deepak Hotel
120. Hotel Holiday Home
121. Palm Garden Hotel
122. Telecom Centre (State)
123. Treveni (Beer Off License)
124. Sunshine Guest House
125. Sea View Restaurant
126. Tourist Information Centre
127. Government Guest House
128. Kovalam Ashok Beach Resort
129. Ashok snack bar
130. Ashok Kovalam Grove Hotel
131. Mosque
132. Dolphin Restaurant
133. Lobster Pot Restaurant
134. New Seafood Restaurant
135. Bright Resort
136. Samudra Hotel
137. Sea Food Restaurant
138. Indian Institute of Hotel Management
139. Hotel Green Park
140. Poem Number 1 Restaurant
141. The Fat Fish Restaurant
142. The Alice Restaurant
143. New hotel (Unnamed)
144. Sands of Dee
145. Alitalia Beach House
146. Kadaloram Beach Resort

☐ Hotel/Guesthouse

◯ Other

provides a room booking service and up-to-date information.

Virtually every visitor to Kovalam stays in close proximity to one of its beaches rather than in Kovalam Village, which is located on a high escarpment about a mile (2kms) from the sea, and possesses virtually nothing of interest. Each of the beach areas has its own characteristics, but all lie at the foot of a cascade of vivid green coconut palms. Four steep roads descend to the beaches from the main Trivandrum/Vizhinjam highway but, apart from this highway, they are only linked by footpaths which means that much of Kovalam's accommodation, particularly behind Lighthouse Beach, cannot be reached directly by motor vehicle. Fortunately, most establishments will arrange for boys to carry baggage.

Lighthouse Beach and **Eve's Beach** are really one and the same, although at first glance they appear to be separated by a low rocky outcrop, probably the remains of what was once a promontory. Formerly, the two beaches shared the same name: Ambalam (Temple) Beach, a reference to a festive procession, which took place between two small temples behind the beach, or Vavaduthura (Absolved Sins) Beach. The latter name commemorates a traditional ceremony held on the beach, during which local people gathered on the night of the new moon during March/April, to mark the absolution of their ancestors' sins by casting gifts for them into the sea. The official name of the beach remains Avaduthura, the initial letter V having been dropped, but it is rarely used. A new name, Hawah Beach, evolved in the 1960s.

Hawah means *Eve* in the Malayalam language, a reference to the young western ladies who bathed here topless – and sometimes bottomless – much to the horror of the locals, who nevertheless came in droves to be horrified. Tourist police now patrol Kovalam's beaches primarily, it would seem, to dissuade today's tourists from giving an encore. Apparently, prior to these sensational events, very few Indians, with the exception of fishermen ever visited the beach.

In 1968, however, the lighthouse was constructed at the south end of the beach, which then became generally known as Lighthouse Beach. It now appears that the Tourist Department has decided on Eve's Beach for the stretch north of the outcrops where also the beach abruptly changes direction, and becomes Lighthouse Beach for the southern stretch.

Eve's Beach

The north end of Eve's Beach is reached by descending the short but very steep road from the Bus Stand. On one side are souvenir stalls whilst the other side is government owned, most of it strewn with rubbish.

On reaching the sands, immediately on the right stands **Sea View**, one of the best beach restaurants in Kovalam, although not the cheapest: tiger prawns, for example, will always be fresh and the genuine article. The restaurant's location might perplex many, as no more buildings will be seen on Eve's Beach between here and its southern end; the reason for this is that the land to the south is government-owned, a gift from the Maharaja of Travancore, and no building has been permitted. Perched above the beach, on the rocky promontory, can be seen the **Government Guest House**.

A path follows Eve's Beach through the trees southward. However, animal lovers might prefer to give this a miss as it is just off this path that a small clearing has been selected for the inhumane destruction of stray dogs. Further along, open land directly behind the beach provides the site of **Gramam**, the Kerala Village Fair, held annually 14-23 January from late afternoon through the evening. Traditional Kerala houses are recreated, craftsmen can be observed at work, and local delicacies may be sampled. At nightfall, performances of Kathakali and Teyyam temple dancing, together with other cultural events, are held in an open air theatre.

Another steep road descends to Eve's Beach at **Hotel Sea Rock**, which marks the beginning of Kovalam's built-up beach area. From here southward, a variety of tourist establishments line the remainder of Eve's Beach and practically all of Lighthouse Beach, which bends round the corner.

Adjoining Sea Rock is one of Kovalam's newest hotels, **Sea Face**, opened in 1995. In the mid-price bracket, not only does this hotel directly overlook the beach, but it is fronted by a private swimming pool, and has its own generator to overcome power cuts. The well-appointed rooms are all provided with satellite TV, and some are air-conditioned. More rooms, including a private suite and a new integral restaurant to provide additional dining facilities to the poolside, were added in 1997. Many will find Sea Face to be the ideal Kovalam location.

On Eve's Beach, in addition to Sea View, already described, **Sea Face Hotel**, **Sea Shore**, a rare example of a two-storey restaurant, and **Dwaraka** can be recommended for their food.

Beaches

Kerala's beaches are washed by the Arabian Sea. Their sands vary from dark to almost white, but none is of powder-like coral (these only exist in India on the Lakshadweep and the Andaman and Nicobar Islands). Following a rough sea, black sand can on occasions be deposited on Kovalam's beaches; this eventually disappears, but can take some time; Lighthouse Beach is generally the most affected.

Few of Kerala's beaches offer very extensive stretches of shallow water for bathing, and some, but not Kovalam's, shelve quite steeply. Along virtually the entire coastline of the state the sea appears to have progressed from Africa with barely a ripple disturbing its surface until the beaches are reached. Then, as if filled with exultation at finally making it to India, the waters rear up to form a six-foot (2-m) high wave – just at the point where the depth of the sea has comfortably reached the average bather's chest level. Either a gigantic leap or a dive through the foam is now enforced on the bather. Young children should not be allowed near the **Big Wave** zone, and poor swimmers should take care as there is a significant drag back after the wave has crashed.

Fortunately, each of Kovalam's beaches offers a degree of escape from Big Wave, by courtesy of the rocky headlands that define them. By keeping to the north side of the rocks, an area of relative calm will usually be found. Those who wish to spend a great deal of time in calm water, or who are accompanied by young children that like to do so, will obviously be tempted to choose accommodation with a swimming pool. Currently, only nine of Kovalam's hotels have pools: the Ashok, Samudra, Blue Sea, Bright Resort, Green Park, Raja, Kadaloram, Sea Face and the new Linchoos. Fortunately, most of these establishments permit non-residents to use their pools for a daily fee.

A handful of boats are located on Eve's Beach beside the rocky promontory that stutters out to sea; these, as at Kovalam Beach, are primarily intended for tourist excursions, although a few are still used for fishing. It is in front of the rocks that some of the calmest waters in Kovalam for swimming can be found. Signs forbid clambering over the rocks, primarily because some are dangerous. Many who risk the scramble from here, however, will wish they had not as litter abounds and the few fishermen still operating insist on using the rocks as a toilet: the authorities seem powerless to dissuade them. From the opposite, lighthouse side of the headland, it is much easier to climb the rocks, from where the views are undoubtedly worth the effort involved.

Lighthouse Beach

It will have been noted that a cluster of hotels overlook the sea at the south end of Eve's Beach, but Lighthouse Beach, which follows around the corner, boasts little accommodation with sea views. Practically all its hotels and guest houses are scattered behind the beachfront itself, and must be approached from narrow lanes which criss-cross the area

between the beach and the former paddyfields. The beachfront is occupied primarily by restaurants. Though many will relish having a direct view of the sea from their room, there are certainly disadvantages including strong cooking aromas, the loud music churned out by restaurants' audio equipment, the noise of Big Wave crashing in, heat from the uninterrupted sunshine, the multitude of kitchens, and the booming beat of Techno music, favoured by the youngsters, who hold all-night parties from time to time on Lighthouse Beach.

The names of some Kovalam guest houses are changed regularly at the beginning of each season, partly due to the whim of a new owner, but partly to deliberately confuse – especially if a bad reputation has been established. Some have been closed by the police in recent years as they had become little more than brothels, and it is not surprising that the proprietors have decided to re-christen them. Undoubtedly, a few houses of ill- repute still survive, but tourists are unlikely to be troubled by their existence. A graver problem is child prostitution, single male visitors to Kovalam often being approached directly by youngsters of both sexes, or by their pimps, particularly on the beach at night. A polite refusal is the best response.

Opposite: Kovalam's Lighthouse Beach

The sugar-candy lighthouse, at the south end of the beach, serves as Kovalam's emblem; painted in alternate red and white stripes, its cheerful presence augments the lively nature of the scene. Hardly an empty space survives on the elevated walkway of rock and sandbags which serves as a 'promenade'. The mix of outlets is certainly vivacious and colourful and, to an extent, of course, vulgar; it will not suit everyone but, as will be seen, beaches of a quite different, more tranquil nature are only a short stroll away. Few, however, will fail to be enchanted by Lighthouse Beach at night, when the illuminations of the various establishments impart a fairytale magic. During one of the not infrequent power cuts, much of the electric lighting is replaced by candlelight, and the scene becomes even more entrancing. On busy fishing nights, pinpricks of light from the boats on the horizon merge with the canopy of stars to provide a mirror image of the beach.

It is as well to explore the establishments along Lighthouse Beach initially in the morning or evening as between 11.00am and 4.00pm the sand in front of them becomes unbearable to stand on. Slip-on shoes with thick soles, and which cannot be penetrated by the intensely hot grains of sand are recommended – most sandals are useless, in spite of their name. Only by the water's edge is the sand cool enough to walk on barefoot in comfort for much of the day, and most will find it preferable to make hasty sorties from the shore to a previously selected restaurant, rather than emulate a fakir.

Cuisine on the beaches

The Lighthouse Beach restaurants are more variable in standard than those of Eve's Beach, but the fish will always be fresh, and is by far the best bet.

As elsewhere throughout India, prices are never displayed outside a restaurant, only on menus at the table. Fish is often not priced at all as much is dependent on the morning's catch; when shown a mouth-watering display of tiger prawns or lobster, for example, always determine the price before ordering, or the bill might provide a nasty shock; the days of exotic seafood at give-away prices have long gone.

Due to the enormous cost of a licence in Kerala, no beach restaurant at Kovalam has ever sold alcohol legally, although beer is usually available, often served without a label and defined on the bill as 'minerals'. Two years ago the restaurant-owners decided to stop paying the heavy bribes demanded by the police in order to turn a blind eye, and no alcohol whatsoever was supplied, Eventually, a compromise was reached, and beer became available once more; but this is India, and who knows what the future holds!

At the height of the season, the restaurants have difficulty in coping with the demand, and long delays can be expected at the more popular establishments.

Noise can also be a problem. Warning signs are oversize loud speakers or a stage for live shows. Seats at the tables are either of plastic, or the much more attractive wicker; the latter may be good for lounging, but are most uncomfortable for dining purposes due to the reclining angle of their backs – choose plastic chairs every time when about to eat a meal.

Dining beneath the stars, with toes burrowing in the soft sand, rather than the prospect of a gourmet experience, is for many the prime reason for patronizing the Lighthouse Beach restaurants. Tandooris are seldom genuine as the chicken or fish is rarely marinated in advance, and the local fish tends to be rather coarse-textured and unsuitable for clay oven cooking, which dries it up too much. In order to overcome this, a boiling garlic sauce can be ordered to moisten the dish, which is then known as a 'sizzler' – the sizzling noise as it is served is more spectacular than the flavour.

A fairly recent introduction to the menus of the Lighthouse Beach restaurants is mussels. All are gathered daily from the local rocks; they are huge and, unlike the large varieties generally offered in northern Europe (most of them farmed in Holland) they still taste of the sea. In spite of the expense, many tourists will want to try tiger prawns and 'lobster' (really crayfish) at least once. However, to ensure that they are genuine and fresh it is advisable to order them from one of the better quality restaurants, preferably a day in advance.

General information regarding food in Kerala can be found in the Factfile. In addition to fish, the vegetarian specialities referred to are the chief glory of Kerala cuisine. Unfortunately they can seldom be found on Kovalam's beaches; in 1997 only one vegetarian restaurant, referred to later existed.

The map of Kovalam takes into consideration projected alterations for the 1997/98 season.

Circular route from Lighthouse Beach

The circular route now described in detail begins at the beachfront promenade, from which a few short incursions are made inland. As the lighthouse is reached, Lighthouse Road is followed before returning to explore the network of pathways behind the seafront. It finally peters out at the steep road that begins at the Sea Rock Hotel, and which is then ascended to its junction with the main road. This is then followed in the direction of Kovalam village for a short distance before returning to the bus stand above Eve's Beach, where the route ends.

Phoning from the beach

A small **communications centre** marks the beginning of the Lighthouse Beach establishments. Fax and international telephone calls may be made from here: although the rates will be higher than those charged by state-operated venues they are still much cheaper than those of the hotels. The centre remains open 24 hours a day, which is useful for overseas calls as rates for these are reduced after 11.00pm (5.30pm in the UK).

Restaurants at the beach

It is at this, the north end of the beach, that most of the better quality restaurants are to be found; particularly recommended are **Garzia** and **Leo**, both quite small, but with their tables and chairs spilling out on to the sand when required. Leo employ the beach's most personable 'barkers' who, good-humouredly, virtually dare passers-by not to occupy their tables – even if none are spare. **Neelakanta** is probably the most reliable of the larger restaurants, but unfortunately only wicker chairs are available. What appears to be a prison block immediately behind Neelakanta in fact provides holiday accommodation.

Currency exchange

The path beside the Pappukutty complex leads to **Wilson's Tourist Home**, unremarkable apart from being, in 1997, the only establishment in the Lighthouse Beach area licensed to exchange money. Rates are a few rupees lower than the banks offer. Several touts stroll around Wilson's offering a slightly better rate and, as they want repeat business, are unlikely to cheat – but be careful, and remember that their services are illegal.

Pappukutty is the most modern hotel development on Lighthouse Beach; at least its main block is, the other buildings vary from it significantly in amenities and tariffs. For the 1997/98 season the owner plans to open up the hotel grounds to the sea by demolishing the long-established Santaner restaurant, which may then reopen elsewhere on the beach. He also intends to apply for a licence to change money. The **Achutha Restaurant** has a charming manager, but indifferent food and service. Above its kitchen are two recently constructed rooms, with superb views over the beach – but bear in mind the disadvantages of beachfront accommodation referred to above. In the multi-storey block to the rear, there is accommodation of varying standard, all in the lower price bracket.

Flamingo is the largest restaurant on the beach; it is also the least tranquil. Apparently, its proprietor believes that trade increases in tandem with the decibels emitted from his huge loudspeakers. If the loud, repetitive beat of 'techno' is considered a good accompaniment to fish curry, this is the place. Behind the **Coral Reef Restaurant**, **Jeevan House** offers extremely basic accommodation, which, nevertheless, seems to be popular with some tour operators. Those seeking south Indian vegetarian food can follow the narrow path beside Coral Reef and turn left at the main path to the Lonely Planet restaurant.

Tourist Aid Post

Just south of Coral Reef, a kiosk juts out on to the sand; this accommodates the **Tourist Aid Post**, which was established in 1996. Information regarding transport, accommodation and tours available here is rather limited in scope. The path immediately before **Sunset Restaurant** leads to some basic guest houses which are of no particular interest, except that **Neptune** holds Kathakali dance performances in the evening, and visitors are permitted to observe the dramatic makeup of the artists being applied (top floor). The Sunset Restaurant is immediately followed by two restaurants, **Sea Fish** and **Velvet Dawn** and a collection of 'boutiques'; the latter overlook some waste land which, naturally, has become one great rubbish tip. **Crab Club Restaurant**, on the other side of the plot, has the benefit of another view of the rubbish.

Adjacent to the Crab Club Restaurant, beside another

short path, the **German Bakery** is an extremely popular venue. On the first floor, European-style (but not particularly German) pastries may be purchased. The apple crumble, delicately flavoured with cinnamon, and served in huge portions is outstanding. On the second floor is the only restaurant (continental) on Lighthouse Beach located above beach level. Views are superb, and the terrace provides excellent opportunities for photographers. **Orion** – guest house and restaurant – lies on the other side of the path.

At this point, the promenade rises slightly, and accommodates the **Kavitha** and **Thomas House** guest houses.

Three restaurants curve in front of the promenade, following the contours of the shore. One of the best on Kovalam Beach, **Travancore**, plans to move here for the 1997/98 season. This restaurant actually supplies pickles and strong filter coffee, rather than the ubiquitous instant version.

Lighthouse Beach ends with the rocky promontory ahead, on which stands the lighthouse. Here is to found another section of beach that also suffers less from 'Big Wave'.

On the other side of the headland are further beaches, all of which can be reached easily. Lighthouse Road, the third road connecting the two main beaches with Kovalam Village, was origi-

Potters at a wheel in the Kerala Village Festival behind Eve's Beach, Kovalam

nally laid out to give access to the lighthouse, but not extended to the beach itself until 1996. Only its first section is particularly steep, and direct access to the hotels by motor vehicle has encouraged the development here of some of the best medium grade accommodation in Kovalam, much of which is fully booked in the high season by UK tour operators.

Vizhingam Lighthouse

The entrance to **Vizhinjam Lighthouse** will be found on the way to these hotels. Opening times for visitors are posted by the gate, but there seems to be no objection to anyone walking around the complex, from where the views over Lighthouse Beach are exceptional.

Paradise Rock, the first hotel on Lighthouse Road, is exceptionally popular, and has so far resisted package tour bookings. The **Samudra Tara** (*samudra* means sea, and this hotel should not be confused with the luxury Samudra Hotel operated by KTDC), has been divided recently into Samudra Tara and Castle Rock – for legacy reasons. Its front rooms have sea view balconies, but those at the rear are somewhat dingy, and only one of them is air-conditioned. Next door, **Seaweed** also has some rooms with sea view balconies, while others look across the pleasant, leafy courtyard; the hotel's roof restaurant, **Lucky Coral**, has earned a good reputation. A new hotel is under construction, on the same side of the road, but no details are yet available. **Sunil House**, which follows, adjoins Dr. Babu's highly recommended ayurvedic clinic. **Thiruvathira,** primarily a restaurant with accommodation, has not been adopted by tour operators.

Facing Thiruvathira, a short road leads off Lighthouse Road to the rear of Aparna and, facing it, **Rockholm**, a hotel that has built up a name in Kovalam for exceptionally good, if slightly pricey, food; for much of the season it is advisable to reserve a table for dinner. The hotel and its dining terrace overlook the secluded bay immediately south of the lighthouse headland, and most rooms have private balconies. Satellite television may be viewed in the public lounge. The road continues past the Rockholm, and, after passing through a gate, leads to the grounds of the Palm Shore Hotel (formerly Palma Nova), which descend to an attractive sandy bay. The beach here is well-maintained, and shade from the sun is provided by vertical palm-matting shelters, which may be hired.

A return to Lighthouse Beach leads to the main entrance of the **Aparna Hotel**, built as a pagoda, with all its rooms having sea view balconies. The **Amritham Beach Resort** is followed by **Varma's Beach Resort**, where the en-suite bathrooms are extremely well-fitted, some even having a bath, a rarity in

Kovalam's smaller hotels. All Varma's bedrooms (two air-conditioned) have sea view balconies, and there is direct access to the beach. Almost opposite, **Eden Seaside Resort**, a more basic type of establishment, is popular with youngsters. Facing this is the main entrance to **Palm Shore Hotel**, which possesses 24 rooms (some air-conditioned) each of which overlooks the cove already referred to. Good food is served from either the indoor or the rooftop restaurants.

The headland

All the small beaches below the hotels on the south side of Lighthouse Road are connected, but they lead southward to a rocky headland – and fishermen. It is the custom in India for fishermen to excrete along the shoreline, thus simplifying their ablutions and ensuring that waste is removed by the tide. Those who have visited Goa are unlikely to have come across this problem as most Goan houses have access to a toilet which, even if it is not fitted to a sewage system, will be cleared by the family pig. Unfortunately, a similar system appears to exist nowhere else in rural India, and only beaches that are disregarded by fishermen are likely to be pleasant to walk along. For the same reason, care should also be taken on the rocky promontories of fishermen's beaches. One final word of warning on the same subject –

do not approach a fisherman crouching at the water's edge with a view to having a pleasant chat; he will not be pondering on the chance of a good day's catch, something far more private occupies him. Keep well away.

Because the terrain is so steep there is only one path leading northwards from Lighthouse Road to the network of tracks behind Lighthouse Beach. This narrow pathway begins beside the **Samudra Tara** hotel on Lighthouse Road.

Accommodation

Kovalam now has approximately 2,000 beds in all categories, most accommodation being situated behind Lighthouse Beach. It should be remembered that package tour operators now enthusiastically book a great deal of Kovalam's accommodation in advance for the entire season, particularly that in the mid-price range. This has inevitably led to a rise in all tariffs, and made it even more difficult for the individual traveller to find comfortable rooms than before, particularly in the frenetic Christmas/New Year period, when outrageous rates are demanded for the most basic accommodation. Unless they have been able to pre-book their rooms, holidaymakers are advised to stay elsewhere in Kerala during this period. By the middle of January, things have eased somewhat, and this is a much better time to arrive.

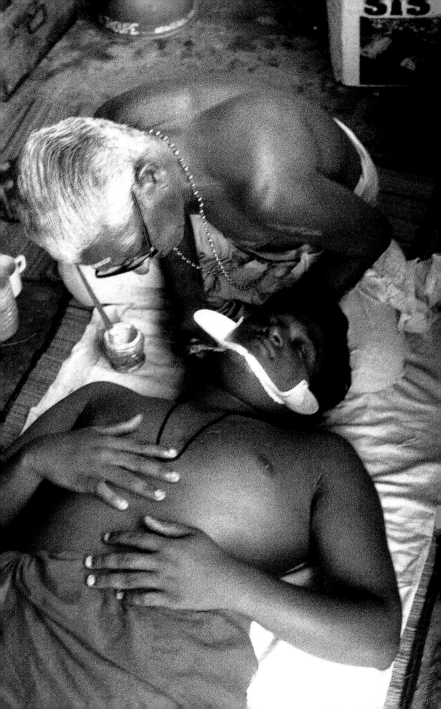

None of the accommodation in this area aspires to 3-star hotel standard, but most is perfectly acceptable.

Bring a torch

Behind Lighthouse Beach, Kovalam has evolved in a particularly haphazard way, which in certain respects adds to its charm: smart guest houses, houses with letting rooms, and a handful of restaurants straggle along a maze of lanes, some of them barely visible through the palm trees. Many pathways are narrow and steep, and practically all are unlit; this, in addition to the frequent power cuts, is a good reason for bringing or purchasing an effective torch – broken ankles are not unknown amongst Kovalam's tourists.

The grandly named **Hilton Beach,** opened in 1997, is the first hotel to be seen, on slightly elevated ground, right of the path. Rooms are surprisingly few in number, but very large. A swimming pool is envisaged, which will be shared with clients of the Hilton's sister hotel, Golden Sands. From **West View,** ahead, a narrow track leads downhill to **Flora Home,** a small, economically-priced but clean guesthouse. In front of this path leads southward (left) to the beach, after passing **Sindhu** and **Cashnova House,** two small guest houses. In the other direction, the same path curves eastward from **Flora Home,** to **California** guest house, joining the main path at **Day's Wish** and almost completing a circle.

From the California guest house, another path leads northward, providing access to **Rolling Stone's Lodge** and **Taj,** a small guest house, which has no connection with the Taj Group of luxury hotels. The main path is rejoined at the **Goldfish Restaurant,** which lies just north of Day's Wish.

Returning to West View, the main path skirts **Golden Sands Hotel,** then descends, turning abruptly northward towards **Peacock Hotel,** another recently-opened small hotel. This, together with the Hilton and Golden Sands, is indicative of the trend at Kovalam, where young and not so young backpackers are being squeezed out as higher standard and much higher-priced accommodation becomes the norm.

From Goldfish Restaurant, which lies just north of the Peacock Hotel, the path continues northward in a virtually straight line between **Chaitra Nivas** and **Sangeeth/Sri Nivas,** rambling complexes that provide very basic accommodation.

Open land to the right is then crossed by paths that form a triangle, the apex of which is occupied by **Shells Restaurant.** Several adequate, if not luxurious hotels and guest houses are situated ahead. In an anti-clockwise direction from Shells they are **Sea Breeze** (off the main

Opposite: Making up for Kathakali dancing takes several hours

path), **E.A. Nisha, Sreevas Shangri-La, Green Lane Sergeant** and **Sreevas Bombay Lodge**. At Sreevas Bombay Lodge, although the main path continues ahead, it is more interesting to take the path that runs diagonally westward, passing the **Park Lane Hotel**, before returning to Shells Restaurant. Immediately ahead, a short path leads to Lighthouse Beach, passing **Palm Garden Hotel, Ajith House Hotel, Green Pease Restaurant** (restaurant only), **Woodstock Restaurant** and **Orion Hotel/Restaurant**.

The northbound path in front of Shells Restaurant runs behind the **Sea View Palace Hotel** before ending at **Neptune Hotel**; between them, another short path leads to the beach, passing **Simi Cottages** and **Sea Sand Home**. Almost opposite Neptune is **Sandy Beach Hotel**, dreary and extremely basic, even though it has featured in at least one tour operator's brochure.

A right turn at Neptune leads to the main path, which was left earlier at Sreevas Bombay Lodge; this is the only northbound path running behind the north section of Lighthouse Beach, and it continues with a few twists and turns, eventually joining the road from Sea Rock Hotel. However, a minor path branching right at **Syam Nivas**, and indicated to Green Valley Cottages, is attractive and worth following. It passes what were until recently paddyfields, but which are now being planted with more lucrative coconut palms. All the paths bordering the former paddyfields are steeply elevated as, during the monsoon, a great deal of water had to be conserved for the rice. At some points, the paths, which are unfenced, stand cliff-like almost six feet (2m) above the paddyfield ground level, and a torch is virtually obligatory in this area at night. Towards the end of this short path, **Green Valley Cottages** and **Silent Valley Inn** adjoin, both with restaurants overlooking the lush, tropical scenery: the peaceful contrast with the vivacious beachfront, just a short stroll away, is most appealing. On higher ground, rising behind Silent Valley Inn, stands **Silent Valley House**.

Returning to the main path, **Hari Lekshmi** is a small but spotlessly clean guest house, currently run by a young English lady, who operates a paperback lending library at reasonable rates. Almost adjoining, is what for many years was the **Lonely Planet** vegetarian restaurant, the only establishment of its type at Kovalam. Standards were variable, but *masala dosas* usually proved to be acceptable as long as 'crispy' was specified, and *thalis* were reasonably satisfying. In 1997, however, Lonely Planet's lease expired, and the restaurant is to move to another location nearby. It is expected that a new vegetarian restaurant will take its place. Further north along the footpath, **Kailas Restaurant** formerly specialized in staging Kerala cultural shows on Sunday evenings, and it is here that **Lonely Planet**, under the same management as Kailas, is expected to reopen for the 1997/98 season: Kailas will then move to the site behind it, but the situation regarding the cultural shows is uncertain.

Avaduthura Temple

From the main path, a step descends to the former paddyfields, which may be crossed diagonally by a raised track. This leads to the Avaduthura Temple before continuing parallel with the road from Sea Rock hotel; few buildings are passed, and the rural scenery creates a most attractive walk. Buffalo and gleaming white egrets abound, and the occasional working elephant is likely to be seen tethered to a tree. Just below the temple, a stall sells soft drinks, confectionery and fruit, including locally grown red bananas.

Those who omit this diversion will continue northward along the path, passing the rear of the walled **Sumangali Hotel**, which is attached to the rear of the Achutha. A route leads beside these hotels to the Achutha Restaurant on the beach, but the aromatic rubbish heap at the rear of the Sumangali must first be negotiated.

The main path continues northward for a short distance before turning sharply left at a helpful, family-run **travel agency**. Immediately left is the **currency exchange** operated by Wilsons; this overlooks waste land, which is kept free of litter through the efforts of the proprietor of the **Lal Hotel**, passed on the east side. Several short tracks lead to Lighthouse Beach, but the main path turns diagonally north eastwards towards **Royal Retreat** and **Thushara**, two small but very smart guest houses, both newly built and very popular with tour operators. The rear of Sea Face is visible to the left, followed, to the right, at the bend in the path, by the brand new **Linchu Holiday Resort**, planned to open for the 1997/98 season, complete with swimming pool. It is said that no more new hotels will be permitted behind Lighthouse Beach. Let us wait and see!

Auto-rickshaws

The path joins the branch road from Sea Rock Hotel to Kovalam village just beside the **Santhiyil Tourist Home**. Immediately ahead lies the path skirting Eve's Beach; it is also the gathering point for a collection of auto-rickshaw drivers, the greediest to be found in south India, and that's saying something. Even though tariffs are fixed by law, they will not budge below, for example, an extortionate 25 rupees to drive the short distance up the steep hill to where the branch road meets the main road – all of 100 yards (100 m)! Unless desperate, ignore them; a taxi, in any case,

Above: Swimming pool and gardens of the Kadaloram Beach Resort, probably the most relaxed hotel in Kovalam. *Below left*: 'Messing about in boats' is a favoured hobby of village youngsters on the outskirts of Trivandrum. *Below right*: The splendid swimming pool of the Samudra Hotel, Kovalam

will cost little more. Certainly never go all the way with them to Trivandrum as there are plenty of buses. Apparently the Tourist Department is attempting to gain control of this situation by state legislation.

The road is extremely steep for its entire length. A branch on the right leads to the **Avaduthura Temple**, via a group of mid-range restaurants and guest houses: **Moon Cottage Restaurant** (with accommodation behind), **Mermaid Restaurant, Moonlight Tourist Home, Raji House** and **Merry Land Tourist House**. After this, the road peters out at the temple, before continuing as a path through the former paddyfields referred to above. Returning to the road junction and proceeding northwards, the only hairdresser (for men only) in the vicinity of either Eve's Beach or Lighthouse Beach is passed; immediately opposite stands **Devi Holiday Inn**. Ahead on the corner to the right are the **Lobster House Restaurant** and **Swagath Holiday Resort**. The latter has splendid views from its rooftop and is well regarded, although some might find its steep approach from the beach a disadvantage.

Upsana Hospital

Between Lobster House and Swagath, the **Upasana Hospital** (open Monday to Saturday 9.00am to 10.00am and 4.00pm to 8.00pm ☎ 480632), is in fact not a hospital but a clinic. Its presiding physician, the London qualified Doctor Chandrasenan, is the only medical practitioner located close to Kovalam's beaches, and provides an excellent and reasonably-priced service. It is likely, however, that in order to obtain his prescriptions a trip will have to be made to Kovalam village, where the nearest pharmacy is located.

Ketmac Beach Hostel overlooks the bus stop, and next to it stands **Hotel Blue Sea**, which possesses one of Kovalam's few swimming pools. The hotel's main building, of great character, includes a rooftop room with a large private terrace. Most guests, however, are accommodated in circular thatched cottages clustered around the grounds. The proprietors run $2^{1}/_{2}$ hour covered boat trips on the 4 mile (7 km) long, tranquil **Vellayani Lake** just north of Kovalam, which give the opportunity of sampling Kerala's renowned backwaters without travelling far from the beaches.

More hotels follow: **Deepak, Holiday Home, Palm Garden, Sunshine** and **Seaview**, all of them far enough from the beaches for their patrons to need buses — at least for the return uphill slog – and as buses don't run late at night, those dining at the beachfront restaurants must budget for taxis or auto-rickshaws. Two short terraces of shops punctuate the hotels. **Traveni**, the last shop in the second terrace, is a state-owned off-licence, but only beer is sold albeit at a cheaper price than elsewhere in Kovalam; the beers are all graded by alcoholic strength, but there rarely seems to be an extensive selection; one usually available is a musty beer called 'Charger', which tastes like corked wine and should definitely be avoided. Traveni is not really worth a special trip unless purchasing in quantity and with access to a refrigerator.

The state-operated communications centre, formerly in the same terrace, relocated further up the hill in 1997. It is now a long and tiring walk from the beaches, but there is a bus stop nearby. Whilst it is cheaper to telephone and fax from here than from the private centres, it closes at 11.00pm, just when the cheap rate for overseas calls begins.

In the other direction from the road junction (towards the sea), the rather venerable **Raja Hotel** has been well refurbished, and a swimming pool is planned for the 1997/98 season. Only here is it possible to buy foreign liquor, i.e. spirits, by the bottle in Kovalam. These are obtained from the usual dingy type of bar favoured by Indians, who seek anonymity whilst surreptitiously sipping their 'sinful' drinks. Almost opposite the Raja, the **Neo Park Hotel** is very basic and primarily aimed at visiting Indians. Downhill, towards Eve's Beach, souvenir shops and tourist agencies line the approach to the small square

where the buses terminate. A new hotel was under construction between them at the time of writing, but no details were available.

Tour of Kovalam Beach and the area to the north

From the square, the main road swings northward to Kovalam Beach passing, left, the drive to the main entrance of the Kovalam Ashok Beach Resort. A more attractive route to this complex, however, follows the coast, via the Tourist Information Office. The drive begins on the side of the square where the buses are stationed, at a gateway which appears to be private but is not. This is often manned by a forbidding looking troupe of soldiers when an important minister is in residence at the Government Guest House, but the drive is never closed. Just past a large health clinic is Kovalam's Government of India **Tourist Information Centre**, built in 1997 (☎ 480085). It should be the best place in Kovalam from where to arrange accommodation, transport and tours not only in the south but throughout India.

An offshoot of the drive curves left towards the **Government Guest House**. Built in 1986, the block is superbly sited, all rooms having balconies overlooking the rocky coastline. Unfortunately, the absurdly low-priced rooms are rarely available to tourists as, understandably, the establishment is very popular with guests of the Indian government; make enquiries at the Tourist Information Office as much in advance as possible. In spite of the building's modernity, its numerous staff seem quite unable to keep the rooms clean or free of mosquitoes – and the hot water systems in the bathrooms rarely work. Few western tourists will find the breakfasts enjoyable. Those who stay at other Government Guest Houses in Kerala will find similar deficiencies – a notable exception being that at Calicut.

An elephant owned by the Ashok Hotel will be seen tethered opposite Halcyon Castle, its function being to provide short rides for tourists.

The Ashok

Halcyon Castle, built in the 19th century as accommodation for his guests by the Maharaja of Travancore, has been converted into four suites by the Ashok. High ceilings and vintage furniture give a period atmosphere to the enormous rooms, but there are no views to speak of. Expect to pay around $US400 per night. Ahead lies the main entrance to the **Kovalam Ashok Beach Resort**, to give the complex its full name. This is, undoubtedly, the finest of all Kovalam's hotels, even though the high tariff tends to attract a rather elderly clientele, and the atmosphere is in consequence rather staid. As may be expected, it is very much cheaper to stay at the Ashok if it is booked as part of a package holiday before leaving home. Charles Correa, the internationally acclaimed Goan architect, was appointed by the government to design the core of this luxury hotel on the south headland of Kovalam Beach, and it opened in 1976. The obtrusive presence of its buildings had been minimized somewhat by existing palm trees, but environmentalists were not pleased. Recent additions to the hotel cannot be seen from the beach, and therefore have been less controversial.

Charles Correa's work, known respectively as Beach View and Beach View Cottages, is laid out on the terraced headland that overlooks Kovalam Beach. Every block is now partly hidden by palm trees, and few rooms have an uninterrupted beach view in spite of the names. Close to the entrance vestibule are the 24-hour coffee shop, swimming pool and Shells Restaurant, where lunch and dinner are served, the superb food being undoubtedly the best to be found in Kovalam. Although expensive by Indian standards, prices are still less than those demanded for a typical 'Indian take-away' in the west – as long as alcoholic beverages are avoided. The Ashok Hotel is the only establishment in Kovalam where imported drinks can be obtained, but all its drink prices are outrageous, e.g. 100 rupees for a local beer, 400 rupees for a one peck (60ml) measure of Scotch.

Sea View

To the west, forming a virtually separate hotel, stands the most recently built part of the complex, Sea View, opened in 1995. Here there can be no quibble: all rooms are the last word in luxury, and possess mesmerizing views from their balconies of the sea foaming over the rocks below. At dusk, the sun sets immediately ahead, and sea eagles glide effortlessly above the shallows; it is hard to think of a better place in all India from which to sip a drink before dinner (poured from a personally imported, duty-free bottle, of course). Sheer magic! Sea View has its own swimming pool and restaurant, the **Osheen**, which serves breakfast in the morning and Chinese cuisine in the evening.

Kovalam Beach

A descent by lift from the hotel's main building to the lower level enables visitors to wind through the grounds to the beach below. Immediately behind the beach, a sunbathing area is reserved for clients of the hotel, with parasols and loungers provided; non-residents can pay for daily use of the facilities, but there is no pool. To the rear, an open air **snack bar** is also run by the hotel. Here, south Indian specialities such as *uddapam*, *masala dosa* and *idli*, hard to find elsewhere in Kovalam, are

good and the prices not excessive – considering the quality and location.

Behind this restaurant, the road from the bus station's square finally peters out and becomes a track. Behind the Ashok snack bar is the older section of the Ashok complex, **Kovalam Grove**, constructed in 1972. This has its own swimming pool, and offers considerably cheaper tariffs than the more modern sections of the Ashok hotel, but its rooms cannot be called luxurious, and upgrading must surely be imminent.

Building-free zone

Most tourists are surprised that no buildings, apart from a mosque, exist on Kovalam Beach, a west-facing crescent of sand curving between two headlands on which stand, respectively, the Ashok and the Samudra hotels. The reason for this is that, as at Eve's Beach, the Government of India was presented with the land by the Maharaja of Travancore, and will not permit development. The squat, white mosque dates from 1976; its early 19th-century predecessor had been damaged in a storm, and it was decided to rebuild – daringly, the same exposed site was chosen. Still remaining, immediately behind the mosque, are the ruined cottages of fishermen who were expelled from Kovalam in the 1970s. How strange that the Indian government, apparently so keen on protecting the unspoilt nature of Kovalam's beaches, has not removed these eyesores after two decades! The sea at Kovalam Beach frequently appears to be calmer than at Lighthouse Beach and, once again, the area beside the south headland suffers less from 'Big Wave'. It is here that fishing boats take tourists on excursions – usually either fishing or to watch the dolphins; ascertain in advance roughly what the rates should be before making a commitment. In order to protect tourists from touts, the Ashok from time to time cordons off part of the beach, displaying 'residents only' signs. Take no notice, no-one in India is permitted to privatize the beaches, all of which are government property.

From the Ashok northward, there is little or no rubbish to be seen, buildings are well-maintained, and the standard of food is vastly superior to that generally found in the Lighthouse Beach region. This area will be preferred by those seeking a relaxed holiday in surroundings that approach European standards. Opposite the mosque is a small **Ganesh temple**, beside which a path leads to the **Dolphin Restaurant**, picturesquely laid out in tiers on a low hillock: food is excellent and service attentive. From a little further along the beach, another path leads up to the adjoining **Lobster Pot** and **New Seafood** restau-

rants. Just behind them is the long-established **Bright Resort**, a guest house surrounded by a wall and palm trees to ensure seclusion. The long-promised swimming pool, rather shallow and therefore excellent for children, was added in 1977.

A return to the beach path and a continuation northward leads to the **Samudra Hotel**. The approach to it is rather bizarre as the hotel's rocky grounds are usually draped with sheets and towels drying in the sun. It seems strange that KTDC, who operate the Samudra, cannot find a less public way of airing its laundry. The extremely popular hotel was upgraded in 1996 by the addition of a swimming pool and some refurbishment. At the time of writing, this was one of only four hotels in Kovalam to possess a liquor licence – but beer only! Guests speak highly of the Samudra's accommodation and service, but room rates now include Indian buffets, which are not to everyone's taste every day. Previously, the à la carte food had been overpriced for its quality, and few ate in the hotel's restaurant.

A major drawback for some residents is that the road linking the Samudra with Eve's and Lighthouse beaches curves inland through Kovalam village, a circuitous and surprisingly lengthy route, which brings a gleam of delight to the eyes of the auto-rickshaw drivers. However, a walk along the sands, followed by the road to the bus stand and a descent to Eve's Beach, will take no more than fifteen minutes as this route is much shorter and flatter. Many opt to walk one way and return by taxi or auto-rickshaw. The swimming pool is one of the best in Kovalam, and there seems little objection to non-residents using it; however, ask an attendant first and at least buy a drink.

The Indian Institute

Separated from the hotel by the **Sea Food Restaurant**, the main block of the **Indian Institute of Hotel Management** was rebuilt in 1997 and now provides accommodation for 180 students from all parts of India. Their cooking skills are exposed to tourists nightly between 6.30 and 8.30pm. Cuisines vary daily and include Indian, European (Continental), Chinese, Thai and Mexican. **An extremely reasonable inclusive price ensures the restaurant's popularity, and bookings should be made in advance (Tel 480283).**

On the opposite side of the newly-surfaced G.V. Raja Road, which joins the main Kovalam/ Trivandrum Road at Vellar Junction, **Hotel Green Park**, with a swimming pool, was opened in 1997; a small temple nestles beside the building. **Poem Number 1** restaurant, adjacent, occupies an open space beside the beach, which is unofficially known as Samudra Beach. Facing the sea are three

excellent restaurants in a row: **The Fat Fish, The Alices** and **Sands of Dee** – one of the smartest beach restaurants in Kovalam. Between the last two, a 50-bedroom hotel was under construction in 1997.

Further along the shore is the **Alitalia Beach House**, a hotel with a splendid roof terrace overlooking the sea. There are only five bedrooms, but the Alitalia's **Midway Restaurant** has built up a formidable reputation for its food. The unusual name of the hotel reflects that a former partner in the venture was an Italian. From here, the beach stretches in what appears to be an unbroken line as far as the eye can see; it is, however, a fishermen's beach, and therefore unfit for exploration by tourists.

Behind Alitalia, a lagoon is overlooked from its eastern edge by the **Kadaloram Beach Resort**, reached by a side road, which is linked with G.V. Raja Road. Although not strictly located on the beach, in spite of its name, this is one of Kovalam's most delightful hotels. Accommodation is in vernacular-style bungalows, which are comfortably furnished, most of them with air-conditioning. Residents, however, are advised against bringing many clothes as the wardrobes fitted are little larger than the average refrigerator. The cool, leafy grounds, which boast a spanking new swimming pool, are a delight, and the relaxed atmosphere is perhaps matched nowhere else in

Additional Information

The telephone code for Kovalam within India is 0471
Kovalam Tourist Information Office ☎: 480085 Open 10.00am - 5.00pm daily in season

Kovalam Police Station ☎ 480255
Indian Airlines ☎ 436870
Air Lanka ☎ 62309
Upasana Hospital ☎ 480632

Kovalam. When the excellence of the cuisine is also taken into account, it can be understood why so many of Kadaloram's guests return time and again to this splendid hotel.

A few other developments exist to the north of Kovalam in the direction of Trivandrum, and to the south past Vizhinjam, but these are dealt with in the following pages as excursions.

In conclusion

No other single beach resort in India offers as much variety as Kovalam, and few will get bored, even during a lengthy stay. So relaxed is the atmosphere, so reasonable the prices, so pleasant the climate, and so friendly the people that some find it very hard to move on. Nevertheless, many visitors to Kovalam, possibly still the majority of them in spite of the newly developed package holidays, simply regard the resort as a venue for a period of relaxation during a holiday that may also include other parts of Kerala, the southern states, and even north India. Due to its close proximity to Trivandrum, from where there are cheap direct flights to nearby Sri Lanka and the Maldives, Kovalam also serves as a resort at which many spend a few days either before departing to or after returning from these islands.

Unfortunately, Indian Airlines direct flights from Trivandrum to Goa ended in December 1995, when the Cochin to Trivandrum stage was terminated. This has meant that a tiresome five-hour journey by car, bus or train must now be made from Kovalam to Cochin before catching a plane to Goa. By 1998, however, the new Konkan railway is expected to be functioning, and fast trains between Trivandrum, Goa and Bombay will then cut the present rail journey time dramatically.

For those who will be based throughout their holiday at Kovalam, there are several enjoyable day or half-day excursions available, either directly from Kovalam or via Trivandrum. These excursions, and Trivandrum itself, are described in the next two chapters.

TRIVANDRUM (THIRUVANANTHAPURAM)

Trivandrum is one of India's most charming state capitals, and many will be tempted to make several visits to it from Kovalam. Lacking sea breezes, the city is most comfortably explored in the morning or late afternoon and evening.

As has been explained, there are direct buses from Trivandrum airport to the city centre, but most holiday-makers visiting the city will come from Kovalam. Buses leave at regular intervals from the bus station above Eve's Beach, and terminate in front of Trivandrum's Hotel Luciya Continental, a short walk from the Padmanabha Swami Temple.

An official reversion to Trivandrum's earlier name, Thiruvananthapuram, was made recently by the Kerala state government. Pronounced *Tiroovananta-poorum*, this has proved virtually impossible for most visitors, including north Indians, to read, pronounce or memorize; sensibly, therefore, the national government has not yet agreed to adopt this name for the airport, which is still called Trivandrum. A combination of Hindu religious enthusiasm and chauvinism led to the change of the city's simplified name, Trivandrum, which had been chosen by the British administrators to aid communication. A rough translation of Thiruvananthapuram is: place of the holy serpent: *thiru* – holy, *anantha* – serpent, and *puram* – place of; the v is inserted in Malayalam words simply to link two consecutive vowel sounds where they occur. It is not impossible to master the name – repeating it ten times daily before retiring is one suggestion – but everyone in Kerala knows what is meant by Trivandrum, which is the name that will be used in this book.

Most points of tourist interest in Trivandrum conveniently punctuate **Mahatma Gandhi (MG) Road**, the city's 2 mile (3.5 km) long north-south axial thoroughfare. Lying back from the west side of this road, just to the north of the City Bus Station, is Trivandrum's most important building, the **Padmanabha Swami Temple**, a unique blend of Dravidian and Keralan architecture. This cannot be entered by non-Hindus but the view of its monumental entrance tower (*gopuram*) from across the water tank should not be missed. The tank, in its present form, dates from the 18th century, when it was greatly expanded. Within,

Opposite: Padmanabha Swamy Temple

devout worshippers can usually be seen bathing from the enclosure's *ghats*. Low, white buildings and palm trees set around the tank are shimmeringly reflected in the water, but it is the seven-storey *gopuram* of the temple that commands the attention. Intricately carved, this towering structure is somewhat squatter in format than most south Indian examples. The temple's rectangular layout is rarely found elsewhere in Kerala.

Dedicated to Padmanabha, an aspect of Vishnu, the temple is said to have been founded to accommodate an idol discovered in a nearby forest. This depicts Vishnu as Padmanabha reclining on the serpent Anantha, from which the city's official name derived. The temple was entirely rebuilt during the reign of Raja Marthanda Varma (1729-58), who dedicated the state of Travancore to Vishnu, relegating his own position to that of the god's regent.

Trivandrum, built on seven wooded hills, has few high-rise buildings, and the city is still dominated by its temple's *gopuram*. The most picturesque views of this are obtained from the north-east corner of the tank, which is skirted on all four sides by a road, thereby allowing visitors to appreciate the *gopuram* from several angles.

As may be expected, the approach road to the temple's entrance is lined with stalls from which religious artefacts and souvenirs are sold; there must now be

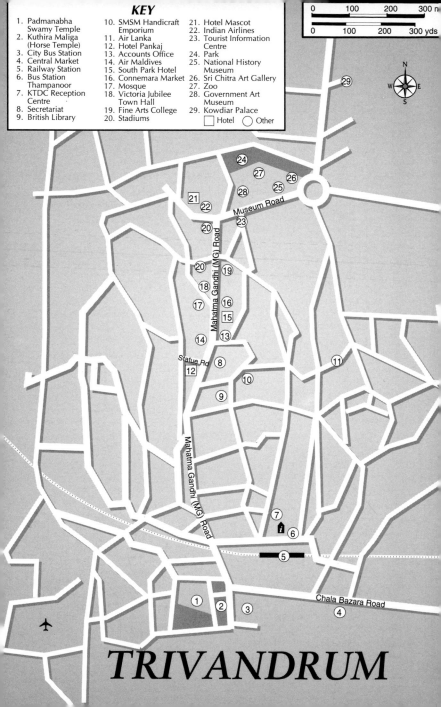

KEY

1. Padmanabha Swamy Temple
2. Kuthira Maliga (Horse Temple)
3. City Bus Station
4. Central Market
5. Railway Station
6. Bus Station Thampanoor
7. KTDC Reception Centre
8. Secretariat
9. British Library
10. SMSM Handicraft Emporium
11. Air Lanka
12. Hotel Pankaj
13. Accounts Office
14. Air Maldives
15. South Park Hotel
16. Connemara Market
17. Mosque
18. Victoria Jubilee Town Hall
19. Fine Arts College
20. Stadiums
21. Hotel Mascot
22. Indian Airlines
23. Tourist Information Centre
24. Park
25. National History Museum
26. Sri Chitra Art Gallery
27. Zoo
28. Government Art Museum
29. Kowdiar Palace

☐ Hotel ◯ Other

TRIVANDRUM

far more carved wooden elephants in India than real ones! Views of the *gopuram* do not improve with proximity, and it was at this point that, until recently, non-Hindu visitors, unable to enter the temple, felt a sense of deprivation. Now, however, splendid compensation has been provided.

Roughly halfway along the street, an insignificant archway on the south side denotes the entrance (not on Mondays) to Trivandrum's as yet little publicized **Kuthira Maliga (Horse Palace).** After a lengthy period of refurbishment, a significant part of the palace, which remains the property of the descendants of the maharajas of Travancore, was opened to the public in April 1995; restoration work continues. No photography is permitted, and shoes must be removed before entering the palace with the guide.

In 1812, the Maharaja of Travancore, Swathi Thirunal, a great lover of South Indian classical music, built this palace to provide accommodation for his court musician and composer. Constructed primarily of teak and rosewood, but with columns of granite, the building is reminiscent in style of the nearby Padmanabhapuram Palace, founded in the 16th century and described later.

Furnishings and various exhibits from the family collection are displayed in the rooms, which include a superb library. Look out for Venetian mirrors, Belgian chandeliers, a life-size figure of a Kathakali dancer, cots of ivory, *howdahs* and weapons – including a sword specifically designed for chopping off the heads of miscreants – 18th-century thrones of crystal and ivory, temple idols and an ambitious sundial, which announced the hour by firing a bullet as the sun's rays ignited carefully positioned gunpowder.

A particular delight of the palace is its carved lotus blossom ceilings to the principal rooms, and the upper floor's three linked music halls, in which concerts were given. From the windows of these halls can be seen the roof's teak frieze of 167 horses, which has given the palace its name.

In January 1996, a seven-day festival of south Indian classical music was first held in the grounds of the palace, and this has now become an annual event.

The long thoroughfare facing the approach to the Padmanabha Swami Temple, **Chala Bazaar Road,** is where Trivandrum's most important market is held. However, a lengthy walk is involved, and most tourists prefer the more conveniently located Connemara Market on MG (Mahatma Gandhi) Road.

Few will wish to walk the entire length of MG Road, particularly as there is little of interest at its south end; it is more comfortably traversed northward by an auto- rickshaw or taxi, ending at Trivandrum's delightful park, in which are housed botanical gardens, various museums and a zoo.

Almost half-way up MG Road, on the east side, is the **Secretariat**, a gleaming white colonial building, in which the most important administrative departments of the state are accommodated. The gardens are beautifully kept, but the building itself cannot be entered unless on official business; photography within the grounds is frowned on.

Kerala's first Secretariat was built at Quilon in 1830. It was then transferred to Trivandrum Fort for a short period; the present building, designed by W.C. Barton, was opened in 1869. As was usual in India, the Greek Doric style was adopted by the British, but with some quatrefoil windows to give a Gothic touch. From 1998, the Legislative Assembly will no longer convene in the Secretariat as its new building, to the north, will be ready for occupation.

To the rear of the Secretariat, on the south side and located within the YMCA complex, is the **British Library**, operated by the Indian Council for Cultural Relations. It is open Tuesday to Saturday, 11.00am to 7.00pm and only here can English newspapers be perused (usually up to 4 days old).

Behind the Secretariat, the **SMSM Handicraft Emporium** sells artefacts made in Kerala. Unfortunately, Kerala is not a 'crafts' state and there is little of great interest. Strangely, there are no Kathakali dolls.

Another delightful colonial building is the **Accounts Office**, which lies to the north; here again, photographs are not permitted in the grounds, and as only the dreary modern extension can be viewed from the road this rules out any photographs, which is a pity. Some may wish to walk from the Secretariat to the park (30 minutes) in order to gain more of a flavour of this, the most interesting section of MG Road. On the opposite side of the road to the Secretariat is the medium grade **Pankaj Hotel** (good lunchtime buffets), together with a handful of economical eating places, which although not for the gourmet are popular with youngsters on tight budgets.

The next landmark on the east side, is the multi-storey, luxury grade **South Park Hotel**, where some may wish to pause for refreshment, particularly at lunchtime, to sample its first-rate buffet.

A few minutes walk further on, and not to be missed, is the vibrant **Connemara Market**, an open fruit and vegetable market, featuring a cornucopia of pineapples, which will be peeled and sliced on request, at very modest prices – exceptionally modest when compared with the tariffs demanded by vendors at Kovalam Beach. An impressive feature of this market is the view from it of the mosque's lofty minarets rising picturesquely in the background.

Beyond the sports stadium, MG Road ends at its junction with Museum Road which, to the left, leads to the **Hotel**

Places to Visit

Kuthira Maliga (Horse Palace)
Open Tuesday to Sunday, 8.30am-12.30pm and 3.00-5.00pm

Trivandrum Park Museums
Natural History Museum
Government Art Museum (former Napier Museum)

Sri Chitra Enclave
KCS Paniker Gallery
Open Tuesday, and Thursday to Sunday, 10.00am-4.45pm
Wednesday, 1.00-4.45pm

Zoological Gardens
(within the park)
Open Tuesday to Saturday, 9.00am-5.15pm

The Government Art Museum in Trivandrum's Museum Park

Mascot, operated by the KTDC, and Trivandrum's oldest established. Built in colonial style, this is the only hotel in the city with a swimming pool. Food is available in the dining room or the coffee shop where, at lunchtime, a splendid buffet is served. There is a friendly bar, with drinks at reasonable prices. The rooms are air-conditioned, if somewhat old-fashioned. In the opposite direction, Museum Road leads to the **Tourist Information Centre,** which faces the main entrance to the park. Those who have visited the Tourist Centre at Kovalam are unlikely to obtain any additional information of importance here.

Trivandrum's park (no official name apart from the museums it accommodates), with its gentle slopes, is a delight, superb trees creating a botanical extravaganza. Buildings housing the museums are scattered along the south side, close to Museum Road. All may be entered daily (not Monday) but, rather inconveniently, the admission ticket, which is valid for all of them, can only be obtained from the most distant, the Natural History Museum, reached by following the main path to its end.

Few tourists will find the **Natural History Museum** of much interest, comprising, as it does, dusty, stuffed wildlife and dilapidated skeletons. Immediately to the south, the **K.C.S. Paniker Gallery** exhibits the work of this Indian painter (1911-77), who is little known to the world at large. Perhaps of greatest appeal are his earlier works in post-Impressionist style, particularly the refreshingly colourful watercolours. Paniker's later, abstract work makes much use of calligraphy and symbols.

The adjoining **Sri Chitra Enclave** houses part of the art collection of the maharajas of Travancore. There are paintings by Ravi Varma, Maharaja of Kilimanoor, who is best known for his rather academic portraits of Travancore maharajas and British residents of the late 19th and early 20th centuries. However, for many the highlight of the museum is the enormous chariot that belonged to the maharajas.

Standing proudly on its low hill is one of the most unusual buildings erected by the British during their long occupancy of India, the **Government Art Museum,** formerly known as the Napier Museum. It will already have been passed on route to obtain the entry ticket, and the structure's most impressive aspect is from the north path looking up to it. Completed in 1880, the building was designed as a museum by a British architect, Robert Fellowes Chisholm (1838-1915), and it warrants at least a quartet of 'e' adjectives: eclectic, egregious, engaging and endearing come readily to mind. A tiled, multi-gabled superstructure pays obvious homage to the traditional Kerala roof style, whilst the geometric-patterned brickwork, in delicate shades of pink and blue, might be described as vaguely

Saracenic. Cusping to the main windows owes much to the Hindu palaces of Rajasthan, although other fenestration has a varied provenance. In spirit, Chisholm's work evokes the somewhat later architecture of the Spanish Modernists. What a pity that the late 19th-century Gothic Revival in England took itself so seriously, few examples achieving Chisholm's lightness of touch or sense of fun – one must visit Barcelona for that.

Inside, the polychrome treatment is continued, and the skill of Chisholm's ventilation system, which provides natural air-conditioning, will be greatly appreciated. The collection is renowned for its bronzes, displayed in the main hall. Exceptional wood carvings occupy the wings, one of which also exhibits musical instruments and Javanese work, souvenirs of a visit by the Maharaja of Travancore to Indonesia in 1936. Not to be missed is a temple car (carriage), a model of the Guruvayoor temple in north Kerala (only by examining this model can the scale of that huge complex be appreciated by non-Hindus, who are not permitted to enter it) and a set of life-size carvings of Kathakali dancers.

Trivandrum's Zoo is entered from its south-west corner, not far from the main entrance to the park. Although the setting amongst trees and water is delightful, many will be shocked by the conditions in which most of the creatures are held captive. Why on earth the peacock, India's national bird, has to be caged when it roams free in Delhi's parks is a mystery; and when one reflects that relations of the miserable, imprisoned monkeys are scampering happily in the jungle not many miles distant, it is difficult to suppress anger. There are two tiger reserves, which are reasonably spacious, but these hardly compensate for the cramped cages in which the most dejected looking lions imaginable are squeezed. Plaques sternly instruct visitors not to tease the animals, but some take no notice, apparently finding great amusement in projecting missiles at the poor creatures. Bearing in mind the avowed Hindu respect for all forms of life, such behaviour is difficult to understand. Animal lovers, particularly those with a short fuse, might well be advised to give Trivandrum's zoo a miss.

Food and drink

The best food in Trivandrum is served in the above mentioned hotels, to which may be added the **Azad** at the south end of MG Road, locally renowned for its *birianis*, and the **Ruby Restaurant**, West Perumal Street. Bars in Trivandrum are few, but that of the **Safari Restaurant**, also in MG Road, is popular with locals.

3 DAY EXCURSIONS FROM KOVALAM AND TRIVANDRUM

Varkala may be reached easily on a day excursion by those staying at Kovalam, but as it is a resort in its own right the town is dealt with separately in chapter 5. If the overnight Trivandrum-Madurai train is taken in both directions, Madurai and its famous temple can be seen in one day, but most prefer to stay overnight, and the city is also described in the next chapter.

Bangaram Backwaters

Almost halfway between Kovalam and Trivandrum, the Bangaram backwaters meander to the sea at **Pozhikkara Beach**. Country boatmen offer two-hour, peaceful cruises – even at night during a full moon – through these backwaters, which encircle a small, tree-covered island on route to the sea.

The Kovalam/Trivandrum bus stops at Pachalloor L.P. School, from where auto-rickshaws must be taken to the boats, just one mile (1.5km) away. Usual backwater sights include the traditional making of coir, a temple, birdwatching and a visit to a fishing village. **Lagoona**, a small but exquisite hotel overlooking the backwaters, has been upgraded recently by its new German proprietor; there are only four rooms, and although the tariff is high, the hotel is fully booked by German holidaymakers for most of the season.

Those who have taken the lake boat tour operated by Hotel Blue Sea will find this a very different experience – it is certainly worth doing both, particularly if the much lengthier Quilon-Alleppey backwaters trip is not on the agenda. Two operators of tours are Bangaram Boat Service, and Golden Tours; several Kovalam tourist agents will make bookings.

Veli

Just 7 miles (11 km) north of Trivandrum, a freshwater lagoon has been made the centrepiece of a 'Tourist Village'. It is separated from the sea by a gleaming sand bar, and the effect is quite exotic. Few tourists make the trip, and it is primarily local families who are attracted to the lagoon for boating and picnicking on its shores. Low hills bristling with palm trees form a vivid green backdrop, and the grounds display huge

Opposite: Vizhinjam's Harbour is always packed with fishing boats

sculptures for the amusement of children.

The lagoon is approximately 10 feet (3m) deep, but no-one swims in it. A floating bridge crosses the western tip of the lagoon to the beach of sand, which at Veli is particularly golden in colour. Unfortunately, Big Wave is usually too much of a nuisance here to permit serious bathing in the sea. Apparently, it is possible to walk along the beach southward as far as Kovalam, a five-hour trek.

As may be imagined, Veli is packed on Sundays and holidays, which is a good time to observe Indian families enjoying themselves in their usual decorous fashion. Why the ever-polite children don't shout, scamper, cry or fight each other will mystify western visitors, most of whom will not be used to such restrained behaviour by youngsters in their own countries.

Veli has a 'floating' restaurant, which only seems to function at weekends, but the **KTDC Restaurant**, lying back from the lagoon, is first rate, and extremely good value (vegetarian and non-vegetarian). Buses run to Veli from Trivandrum but, as they are usually packed, an auto-rickshaw is recommended: the journey should not take more than 15 minutes.

Vizhinjam

It is when visiting the important fishing village of **Vizhinjam** that most holidaymakers who arrive in Kerala at Trivandrum will first come across the unpronounceable Malayalam vowel sound, mysteriously represented in Roman lettering by *zh*, but pronounced (very roughly) as *yluh*. Vizhinjam lies just one mile to the south of Kovalam, and it is possible to walk to it either along the main road or along the sands when the tide is out. Alternatively, there is a limited bus service from Kovalam, and there are always, of course, the dreaded auto-rickshaws. If you are hiring a car to visit Neyyar Dam (see below) you will pass the village on route. Nowhere else in Kerala are so many fishing boats to be seen on one beach, packed together like wooden sardines in a tin. Practically all fishing takes place at night, and it is an impressive sight to watch the armada of boats set out in the early evening. At dusk, their lights twinkle far out at sea even more spectacularly than at Kovalam.

Vizhinjam's harbour was artificially created when Kovalam's fishing community was forced to move to it. A new, much larger port is planned and this, it is expected, will greatly diminish the picturesque quality of the settlement. It is also feared that sand displacement may occur in the Kovalam region, to the detriment of the tourist beaches.

Villagers greet strangers with friendly waves and smiles, and a stroll around the narrow lanes, particularly in the Christian quarter, gives a good insight into the life of a south Indian fishing community that has been virtually unaffected by tourism.

Between the 6th and 11th centuries, Vizhinjam was a regional capital, but only a scattering of rock temples have survived from this period. The most impressive is a Shiva temple on the north side of the road that runs between the police station, 50 yards (50m) away, and the harbour; its gate is almost always locked, but it is easy to climb over the iron fence.

To the north of the port, a colourful mosque with towering minarets, and a gleaming, equally huge church to the south, denote the Muslim and the Christian sectors which, at Vizhinjam, are completely segregated. Unfortunately, the religious tolerance usually found in Kerala is only skin deep here, and clashes between followers of the rival faiths are all too frequent, on occasions even resulting in deaths.

The beaches immediately south of Vizhinjam, although scenically appealing, cannot be recommended, for hygiene reasons.

Pulinkudi, Chowara and Poovar

Behind Vizhinjam, the main road continues southward, eventually reaching Cape Comorin (Kanya-kumari), India's most southerly point; at

Mukkola Junction, a branch road follows the coastline, from which short side-roads lead to a group of resort hotels. Located from north to south, approximately 5 miles (8 km) from Kovalam, are Coconut Bay (4 rooms only), Surya Samudra, Bethsaida, Nikki's Nest, Somatheeram and Manaltheeram. It is certainly worth visiting the **Surya Samudra Beach Garden**, even if not staying at the hotel, which was opened by its German proprietor in 1986. Highlights of the development are the wooden Nallukettu houses, varying in age from 100-150 years. Originally the homes of the Nair caste, most were brought here in sections and re-erected. Traditional Kerala roofs and exquisite carving externally are notable features. Some who have visited Bali in Indonesia will recognize similarities with the vintage Hindu structures on that island. Although the Balinese were the first to convert the internal courtyards of their homes into bathrooms, the design of the buildings appears to have been brought to Bali by Hindu traders from Kerala, who also introduced their religion, which has survived there, in adapted form, to this day.

In 1996, accommodation was virtually doubled, and 60 guests can now be accommodated, some of them in luxuriously fitted tents erected on the beach below the hotel. The gardens are beautifully laid out, with paths leading to the main beach below, which is cleaned daily by hotel staff. A natural rock pool, for swimmers only due to its depth, is fed by a cascade of filtered seawater, which is constantly replenished. Although not the cheapest in south India, the Surya Samudra's cuisine is exceptional, much produce coming from the hotel's own grounds. Non-residents are welcomed in the dining room but advance booking is recommended throughout the season. Entertainment is provided in the restaurant every evening, ranging from south Indian classical music to Kathakali and other traditional dancing. Ayurvedic treatment is offered by the hotel. In 1997, the proprietor of the Surya Samudra was planning to sell to a large hotel group, but is expected to continue its operation for the 1997/98 season.

On the other side of the bay, the **Bethsaida Hotel**, which shares the same beach with the Surya Samudra, is a more basic establishment, but with very friendly staff providing excellent service to the bungalows in which guests are accommodated. A pool is said to be projected. Coconut Bay, Surya Samudra and Bethsaida are all located near the village of **Pulinkudi**, which can be reached by bus from Vizhinjam and Trivandrum.

About half a mile (1km) further south, two sister hotels specializing in yoga and ayurvedic

VARKALA
ANCHUTHENGU

VELI
TRIVANDRUM
(THIRUVANANTHAPURAM)

Arabian Sea

SOUTHERN
KERALA

To Quilon

Attingal River

PONMUDI

• Neyyar Dam

TAMIL
NADU

7

BANGARAM
KOVALAM
VIZHINJAM
PULINKUDI &
CHOWARA

POOVAR

47

PADMANABHAPURAM SUCHINDRAM NAGERCOIL

• Cape Comorin
  (Kanyakumari)

Bay
Ben

Indian Ocea

0	8	16	24	32		40 miles
0	8	16	24	32	40	48	56	64Km

Below: *The enormous gopuram of Suchindram Temple*

treatment are reached by short roads from the village of **Chowara**. Longest established, the **Somatheeram Beach Resort** offers 12 separate programmes, dependent on the ailments to be treated and the time available. Below is a beautiful beach, but access paths to it are rather steep and there is no swimming pool. Having said this, however, at certain tides, a natural swimming pool, in the form of a lagoon on the beach, is created by the sea. Guests of the **Manaltheeram Beach Resort**, a short distance to the south, stay in similar thatched accommodation, and most come for the yoga or ayurvedic treatments.

Southward from this hotel, the coastline becomes much flatter, rocky headlands disappear, and a broad fisherman's beach stretches southward as far as the eye can see. It is on this beach, 6 miles (10 km) further south, that the proprietor of Wilson's Guest House in Kovalam has built **Wilson's Beach Resort**, which is planned to open for the 1997/98 season. Located near the fishing village of **Poovar**, although the beach is less picturesque than further north, delightful backwaters immediately behind it provide compensation, particularly when Wilson's promised houseboat and water skiing facilities come to fruition. There is a rooftop restaurant and a swimming pool, but as Wilson's is the most remote of all the hotels in the area, Kovalam being 12 miles (20 km) away, those

seeking a lively 'international' ambience are likely to be disappointed – Poovar is very Indian.

Cape Comorin Tour

A visit to the south tip of India undoubtedly forms the most popular day excursion from Kovalam and Trivandrum. On the same trip, it is usual to take in the Amachai Plav temple at Neyyattinkara, the palace of Padmanabhapuram (not Mondays) and the Sthanumalayan 'Trinity' temple at Suchindram.

Kanyakumari was renamed **Cape Comorin** by the British, but has since officially reverted to its original name. Most will find it preferable to take a guided tour or taxi, even though there are buses and a train from Trivandrum and a direct bus from Kovalam. KTDC run excursions, and others are operated in conjunction with package tours, the latter being always more expensive. Be sure to ascertain what is included in the tour before booking. The disadvantages of public transport, in addition to standards of comfort, are that the bus station at Cape Comorin is 5 miles (8km) from the town centre, and schedules preclude seeing the palace and the temples mentioned above on the same day. However, some may prefer to take a bus or taxi on the outward journey, stay overnight at Cape Comorin, and return either by taxi or a series of buses. The advantage of an overnight stay is that the visitor can then observe sunset or sunrise over the three seas that meet at the cape: the Arabian Sea, the Bay of Bengal and the Indian Ocean; interestingly, this is the only point at which the Indian Ocean actually washes the shores of India. A special event occurs at Cape Comorin once a year only, during April's full moon, when sunset and moonrise occur in tandem on the same horizon; this day is known as Chaitrapurnima and, as can be imagined, many thousands arrive to witness the annual spectacle.

Neyyattinkara

Just over half way between Trivandrum and Padmanabhapuram is the small town of Neyyattinkara, where many excursions halt briefly to allow their passengers to visit the **Amachai Plav Temple**, dedicated to Krishna. Built in the 18th century, the chief interest of the temple is that in order to escape from his pursuers, the heroic Marthanda Varma hid in the hollow trunk of a jackfruit tree, which is preserved within the complex.

Padmanabhapuram

Padmanabhapuram lies a further 14 miles (23 km) to the south (34 miles - 55km from Trivandrum), and all the public buses to Cape Comorin stop here. For a brief period, Padmanabhapuram was the state capital of Travancore, but it is now little more than a village. The former **Summer Palace of the Travancore Maharajas** (closed Mondays) is the reason for making a visit. Originally, the south-west coastal strip of India formed part of Travancore but, unlike the rest of the state, due to language reasons it has been incorporated in Tamil Nadu rather than Kerala. Those on excursions will note that their coach driver will be required to halt for fairly lengthy formalities at the border between the states, almost as if another country had been entered. In spite of this, it is the state of Kerala rather than that of Tamil Nadu that has assumed responsibility for the building.

A reflection of the town's former importance is its imposing defensive wall of stone, which was built in the 18th century as a protective measure against Tipu Sultan's rebellious forces. The palace lies within the enclave, its oldest section, built in 1550, surviving as the core. Visitors must remove shoes and be accompanied by a guide, who will explain the various areas of the complex – at least, one assumes that he is explaining them, as the rolling accent of virtually all south Indian guides to public buildings is extremely difficult for many visitors to comprehend. Photography is permitted.

Although they appear to be constructed entirely of teak, most of the structures are supported by granite columns. Similarities throughout with Trivandrum's Horse Palace will be apparent, which is not surprising as most of the 18th century work here is contemporary with it. Particularly fine are the lotus flowers carved in the teak ceilings, none of which are identical. Displayed on the ground floor is a magnificent chair, the gift of Chinese traders to the maharaja.

On the upper floor, the **Council Chamber**'s timber floor has been coated with an extremely hard-wearing surface, which incorporates ground eggshells, coconut shells and charcoal. In the *puja* rooms are some of the finest murals in south India but, at the time of writing, they were hidden from view. The enormous dining-hall was built to accommodate 1,000 Brahmins at one sitting.

Set in its own courtyard, the **'Mother' Palace** of 1550 incorporates a pillared *mandapa* for Hindu worship; here, the floor also has a composite surface but as charcoal has been omitted the resulting colour is red.

Most will now continue to Cape Comorin, some tourist vehicles halting on the outskirts of the town for lunch.

Suchindram

On the return journey to Trivandrum, every attempt should be made to visit the **Trinity Temple of Sthanumalayan** at Suchindram, which is open from 4.00pm. Located 8 miles (13km) north-west of Cape Comorin, this immense temple boasts a towering *gopuram* and a labyrinthine interior of sombre power. An enormous leviathan stands near the entrance, and a great tank is located to one side. Non-Hindus are welcomed but, once again, all men must remove their shirts on entering. Unusually, the dedication of the temple is shared by the 'trinity' of Brahma, Vishnu and Shiva, each of whom are allotted their own shrines. As may be imagined, the iconography is overwhelming, and some visitors may find the primeval, pagan force of this temple somewhat disturbing. Not to be missed is an enormous statue of a towering Hanuman, the monkey god, who is frequently depicted in Vishnu temples. It is best to follow a circular route around the interior as far as possible.

Good viewpoints of the *gopuram* are provided by the balconies of the adjacent houses, and tourists are welcome to take photographs from some of them. A direct return is generally made by excursion buses to Trivandrum.

Neyyar Dam and Wildlife Sanctuary

Two annual monsoons and an abundance of mountain streams throughout much of south India encouraged the national government to put all its electricity supply eggs in one basket, and vast amounts of money have

Cape Comorin (Kanyakumari)

The British name for the town is not a direct translation from the Tamil as the word kanya means virgin not cape, and kumari means maiden. It is a reference to the tradition that Devi Karna, as an incarnation of the goddess Parvati, sought to become Lord Shiva's consort by serving penance at Cape Comorin. Rebuffed, Devi Karna proclaimed that she would remain a virgin.

At the very tip of the cape, the **Kumari Amman** (mother) **Shore Temple**, dedicated to Devi Karna, together with its adjacent ghats, is one of the three most sacred places in India. In order to attain salvation, Hindus must complete their pilgrimages to the country's holy waters by worshipping in this temple and bathing from its ghats. The building is closed from 11.45am until 5.30pm, and therefore most day visitors are restricted to admiring its exterior. Even when the temple is open, non-Hindus are only permitted to proceed as far as the sanctuary. On entering, all men (but not ladies fortunately!) are required to strip completely to the waist in addition to the usual removal of footwear.

An urn containing some of the ashes of Mahatma Gandhi was brought to Cape Comorin following his cremation in Delhi after his assassination in 1948, and displayed to the public beside the temple. The site is marked by the **Gandhi Mandapam**, a structure that resembles the distinctive style of temple architecture built in Kalinga (now the state of Orissa) between the 8th and 13th centuries. The statue of Gandhi within has been located so that on his birthday, 2 October, a shaft of sunlight passes through an aperture in the roof to illuminate his head: this is known as the 'light of freedom', representing Indian independence from Britain, the great aim of the 'father of the nation', which was achieved in 1947, the year before his death.

The road northward from the Kumari Amman Temple passes between the **Saravana** and **Samudra** hotels; a little further on, a right turn leads to the jetty from where ferries make the brief crossing to the **Vivekenanda Memorial**, picturesquely located just 200 yards (200m) off shore, like a lighthouse, on its rocky islet. If the sea is rough – and it frequently is, due to the confluence of the three seas – the ferries will not operate; between 11.00am and 2.00pm the service is always suspended, whatever the weather.

The temple-like mandapam was erected in 1970 to commemorate Swami Vivekananda, who came to the islet to meditate in 1892. He became one of India's best known philosophers, travelling to the west in order to promote the ideals of Hinduism (his work did not include conversion as all Hindus have to be born to the religion). A statue of the Swami has been erected inside.

Beach Road leads westward from the Kumari Amman Temple, skirting the less-than-exciting beach, where the only feature of interest is the multi-coloured sands. Much more picturesque is the fishermen's area further north, from where there are stunning views across the rocky bay to the magnificent **Church of Our Lady of Ransom**, a cathedral-like, cream-painted confection with a lofty Neo-Gothic spire, which completely dominates this part of the town. Those on a coach excursion will have to ask their guide to bring them here, as it is rarely included on schedules. 'Most tourists come to see the temples not the churches' is likely to be the bemused guide's initial response. However, only a very brief detour is involved, so persevere.

Although it is of no particular interest architecturally, before leaving Cape Comorin, those with time who are interested in the early Christian history of India may wish to seek out the **Church of Our Lady of Joy**, founded by St Francis Xavier in the mid-16th century.

The cathedral-like steeple of Our Lady of Ransom church gives a picturesque quality to Cape Comorin's fishing beach.

been spent in building dams that not only create reservoirs for the supply of water, but also hydro-electric power. For some reason, the fact that India's monsoons often fail, occasionally for several consecutive years, was disregarded. In consequence, south India usually lacks sufficient electricity, and power cuts regularly take place – inconvenient for tourists, but disastrous for industry.

However, the picturesque quality of the lakes formed, the usually abundant wildlife, and the cooler air of the mountainous regions in which the dams were located, combined to provide tourist attractions that have been admirably developed and maintained by the authorities. **Neyyar Dam**, the example closest to Kovalam, provides an easy opportunity for its visitors to sample the delights of the Southern Ghat mountains. KTDC daily coach excursions combine Neyyar Dam with Ponmudi; there is also a bus service, but this is too slow and uncomfortable for most. By hiring a car, visitors from Kovalam are able to approach the Neyyar dam via Vizhinjam, thus avoiding the traffic in Trivandrum.

Located approximately 20 miles (32km) from Trivandrum, the reservoir created when the dam was built in 1958, is 3.5 square miles (9sq km) in extent, and forms the centrepiece of the 49 square miles (128 sq km) wildlife sanctuary. Popular recreations include boating on the lake and a tour by park vehicle of a lion safari park; it is claimed that the animals are rare examples of Asian not African lions. Unfortunately, if the park's one vehicle has broken down, and it often does, no visit can be made, private vehicles not being permitted to enter: tours begin at the Information Centre. There is also a crocodile hatchery at Neyyar, but this is in a decrepit state and hardly worth bothering with.

Gardens around the dam (from which photography is not permitted) are rather garishly embellished with giant figures. Mountains rise up to a maximum height of 6,203 feet (1,908m) from the water's edge, rather in the manner of a Scottish loch, and the scenery and pure quality of the air are really the greatest attractions of Neyyar. Although wild animals are abundant they will rarely make an appearance during the hours of daylight.

Ponmudi

Ponmudi is a hill station situated 38 miles (61km) north east of Trivandrum, at a height of 2000 feet (615m). It lies within the Golden Valley, close to the Tamil Nadu state border, and is surrounded by the undulating Cardamom Hills. Ponmudi is a favoured destination for several tour organizers, who include it in day trips from Trivandrum. Indians are par-

Places of Interest

Neyyattinkara
Amachai Plave Temple (closed 12.00-4.00pm)

Padmanabhapuram
Summer Palace of the Travancore Maharajas (open Tuesday to Sunday 10.00am-5.00pm)

Cape Comorin
Kumari Amman Shore Temple (closed 11.45am – 5.30pm)

Suchindram
Trinity Temple of Sthanumalayan (closed 12.00-4.00pm)

Tours
Bangaram Boat Service ☎ 481729
Golden Tours ☎ 481647

ticularly attracted to Ponmudi in the March-May period in order to gain respite from the intense heat at lower levels. Foreign tourists are, of course, more interested in the scenery, which is extremely beautiful, although frequently shrouded in mist.

Tea estates will be passed, but they are not as extensive here as further north. Ponmudi has a **Government Guest House**, but there is little else of interest at the resort, and few will wish to stay here unless planning treks through the forests. A wildlife sanctuary was established in 1983 just 6 miles (10km) south of Ponmudi, at Peppara, covering 20 square miles (53 sq.km). It is reached from Vithurai on the Trivandrum-Ponmudi road.

4 MADURAI

For those who decide to make one major excursion inland from the beaches of Kerala, Madurai (frequently pronounced Madoora) is the most frequently chosen destination. Devotees claim that Madurai's enormous Meenakshi Temple is the most extensive in India, and few will not already have seen photographs of its lofty *gopura* rising majestically above the palm trees. Apart from the two sanctuaries, non-Hindus are permitted to enter all parts of the complex, and many regard this as the most interesting Hindu temple in the country. The city of 1.2 million inhabitants is located 190 miles (305km) from Trivandrum and 347 miles (556km) from Madras, and there are air, bus and overnight train services between the three cities; many who arrive in southern India by scheduled flights to Madras proceed to Kerala via Madurai. An alternative and much shorter journey to Madurai can be made by those who visit Kerala's most popular wildlife sanctuary, at Periyar.

Above: The central pavilion in the Mariamman Teppakkulam Temple's tank.

It is known that Madurai was the capital of the Pandya empire from 1100 BC until 900 AD, when the city fell to the Cholas. The settlement is referred to in Ancient Greek documents of the 3rd century BC, indicating its early importance as a trading centre. The Pandyas regained Madurai in the 12th century, but were to lose it finally to the Muslim Delhi sultanate, when Alu-ud-din Khalji's troops, led by Malik Kafur, took the city in the 14th century. Because of its distance from his master in Delhi, Malik Kafur was able to establish his own independent dynasty, which ruled Madurai until c1560, when the Vijayanagar emperors regained the city for Hinduism. Their appointed governors, the Nayaks, who became rulers after the fall of the Vijayanagars in 1565, designed and built most of the temple in its present form, and Madurai became a centre of Tamil culture. In 1781, the East India Company took over control of the city, demilitarizing it, laying out new roads, and constructing the usual British Cantonment on the periphery.

Meenakshi Sundereshwar Temple

The temple takes several hours to explore, and a return in the evening is recommended, when the lamplit halls and corridors acquire a heavily-charged atmosphere.

The East India Company demolished Madurai's fortress in 1840, levelling its walls and filling its moat, over which Veli Street (North, East, South and West) was built. This thoroughfare still delineates what is known as Old Town, and the temple stands roughly in its centre, an easy walk from the station and most bus stands.

Work on the present temple began in about 1560, early in the governorship of Vishvanat, founder of the Nayak dynasty, but most of the temple was commissioned in 1623-55 by Tirumalai Nayak. Rectangular in shape and orientated north-east to south-west, an outer wall protects what are, in essence, the adjoining temples of Meenakshi and Sundereshwar, each of them similarly walled. Lofty *gopura* rise above the gateways in both the inner and the outer walls, providing one of India's most spectacular sights.

Admission to the complex can be gained from gateways in any of the wall's four sides, beside which shoes must be deposited; it is then suggested that visitors proceed to the east entrance, and penetrate the inner core westward from there.

Immediately ahead is a short, painted hall, the **Ashta Shakti Mandapa**, named from the eight (*ashta*) figures of the goddess Shakti, which support the roof. At the end, flanking the gate, are figures of Ganesh and Kartikaya, the two sons of Shiva. A selection from the 64 miracles enacted by Shiva in Madurai is represented.

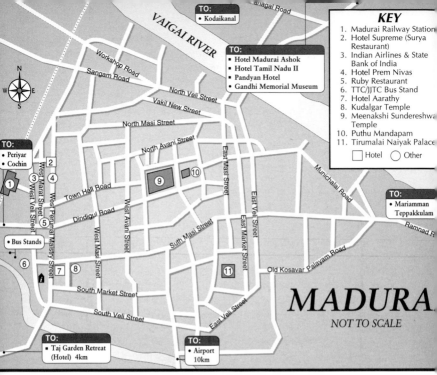

TO:
• Kodaikanal

TO:
■ Hotel Madurai Ashok
■ Hotel Tamil Nadu II
■ Pandyan Hotel
• Gandhi Memorial Museum

TO:
• Periyar
• Cochin

TO:
• Mariamman
Teppakkulam

TO:
■ Taj Garden Retreat
(Hotel) 4km

TO:
• Airport
10km

KEY

1. Madurai Railway Station
2. Hotel Supreme (Surya Restaurant)
3. Indian Airlines & State Bank of India
4. Hotel Prem Nivas
5. Ruby Restaurant
6. TTC/JJTC Bus Stand
7. Hotel Aarathy
8. Kudalgar Temple
9. Meenakshi Sundereshwa Temple
10. Puthu Mandapam
11. Tirumalai Naiyak Palace

□ Hotel   ○ Other

VAIGAI RIVER

Workshop Road
Sangam Road
North Veli Street
Vakil New Street
North Masi Street
North Avani Street
Town Hall Road
West Perumal Maistry Street
West Marat Street
West Veli Street
Dindigul Road
West Avani Street
West Masi Street
Suth Masi Street
East Masi Street
East Veli Street
East Market Street
Munichalai Road
Ramnad R
Old Kosavar Palayam Road
• Bus Stands
South Market Street
South Veli Street
East Veli Street

MADURA

NOT TO SCALE

The **Meenakshi Nayak** (or **Yali**) **Mandapam** follows; its first name commemorates the hall's builder, who was the predecessor of Tirumalai Nayak. *Yalis* are meant to represent southern Indian lions, although their long snouts give them more the appearance of mythical dragons; here they surround the entablatures of the columns, hence the alternative name of the hall. Swaying from side to side, the decorated temple elephant receives offerings from the faithful; he passes the coins to his attendant and then lightly taps the donor's forehead in thanks with the tip of his trunk.

Ahead, a narrow corridor broadens out via the **Mudali Pillai Mandapa**, to an open quadrangle, most of which accommodates the **Potamarai Kulam** (Tank of the Golden Lotuses). Steps in the manner of *ghats* are descended by worshippers who immerse themselves in the tank's holy water where once, by tradition, the goddess Indra bathed. This is the **Temple of Meenakshi's Shrine**, and it is noticeable that the commercial vendors' stalls are no longer to be seen. Strangely, the tank itself is set at an angle to the rest of the complex, more accurately lining up with the cardinal points of the compass. One suspects therefore that the tank may predate the present temple.

Behind the tank rises the south

gopuram, at 155ft (48m) the temple's highest. Until quite recently, visitors were permitted to ascend to the top, but maintenance of the staircase has been neglected and this is no longer permitted for safety reasons. Unfortunately, therefore, the famous view of the temple over the palm trees from this *gopuram* can no longer be gained; for the nearest equivalent, visitors must now seek alternative vantage points from high buildings outside the temple. In 1996, a five-year-long redecoration of Madurai's *gopura* was completed, and the formerly dignified grey stonework has once more become a gaudy riot of colour. Although perhaps not to the taste of most westerners, this is how the *gopura* originally looked: each detailed carving gleaming with shiny, polychrome paintwork. It should perhaps be remembered that not until the Renaissance did Europeans prefer their own statuary undecorated.

The west arcade of the tank widens into a hall that skirts the Meenakshi shrine. It is known as the **Panja Pandava** or **Kilikoondu** (Parrot-cage) **Mandapam**. Cages with parrots were once kept in this hall, but all have been removed in recent years. Columns are carved on either side to depict *yali* interspersed with the five legendary Pandava brothers.

Non-Hindus are forbidden to enter the Meenakshi shrine but can observe the parrot decoration around its entrance. By local tradi-tion, Meenakshi, the daughter of a Pandya king, was born with three breasts, but her father was told she would lose one of them as soon as she met her husband-to-be. Lord Shiva, in his incarnation as Sundareshwar, appeared before the girl, and the third breast instantly disappeared; their marriage took place at Madurai a few days later.

A continuation northwards leads to the gateway of the **Sundareshwar Temple**. This may be entered by all, and the visitor is immediately struck by the huge figure ahead of Ganesh, Shiva's elephant-headed son; it is said that this monolithic carving was found during excavation for the Tank of the Mariamman Teppakkulam to the east.

Those who make a late evening visit to the temple may be interested to observe the nightly ceremony, at 9.30pm, when a figure of Shiva is taken from his shrine to that of Meenakshi, thus signifying the closure of the complex for the day. By tradition, an early Pandya king built the first temple here, which was dedicated to Shiva. The god himself attended the opening ceremony and blessed the worshippers; nectar (*madhura*) fell from his hair and the city that had evolved around the temple was named Madhurapuri - the city of nectar.

A right turn leads to the **Kambatadi Mandapam**, one of the finest halls to be found in any Hindu temple. The hall fronts the

Places of Interest

Meenakshi Temple Open daily 5.30am - 12.30pm and 4.00 - 9.30pm	Palace of the Tirumala Nayak Open daily 9.00am - 1.00pm and 2.00 - 5.00pm
The Temple Art Museum Open 7.30 -10.30am and 6.00-7.30pm	Gandhi Museum Open daily 10.00am - 1.00pm and 2.00 - 5.30pm

entrance to the shrine of Sundareshwar, and its monolithic pillars have been carved to depict events connected with Shiva. They include Shiva's chief consort Parvati as the demonic Kali, and Shiva himself performing exuberant aerobatics. Most interesting of all, Lord Vishnu is shown presenting his sister, Meenakshi, to Sundareshwar in marriage; although this does not accord with the local belief that Meenakshi was the daughter of a Pandya king, it has a much wider following amongst Hindus in general.

Non-Hindus, who are not permitted to enter the Sundareshwar shrine, may proceed directly eastward, through the **Nandi Mandapam**, to the **Temple Art Museum**, which now occupies part of the **Ayirakal** or **Sahasrastamba** ('thousand-pillared') **Mandapam**. The hall is, in fact, supported by 985 pillars, each carved to represent various historic and mythological events. This is one of the oldest sections of

the temple, being constructed around 1560 during the reign of Vishvanat Nayak, founder of the Nayak dynasty, who is depicted on horseback left of the entrance.

Exhibits displayed in the museum section of the hall, most of which relate to Tamil culture, feature outstanding bronzes; unfortunately, as with so many Indian museums, their presentation, in particular the captioning, leaves much to be desired.

Inset in the angle between the museum and the Nandi Mandapam is the **Raya Gopuram** of the outer hall. This formerly provided the main entrance to the temple, but it is said that someone committed suicide by jumping from it, and the *gopuram* has been closed ever since. Its only partly used foundations measure 174ft (53m) by 107ft (33m), indicating that a far larger structure was originally intended; if built as planned, it has been deduced that this *gopuram* would have been the highest in India.

Outside the temple area, directly facing the Raya Gopuram, is the **Pudhu** (New) **Mandapam**,

Opposite: The world famous views of the Meenakshi Temple's gopura at Madurai

built 1623-45 by Tirumalai Nayak, and also known as Tirumalai's Choultry. Built for Sundareshwar, it is said that the god appeared in the hall ten days each year, seated on the pedestal installed for him. His sojourn took place in the spring, which explains the hall's third name, the **Vasanta** (spring) **Mandapam**. Ten of the hall's columns are carved to represent life-size members of the Nayak dynasty; the canopied figure denotes Tirumalai. Behind him to the left is his consort, the Princess of Tanjore; there has been no attempt to disguise the stab wound inflicted on the Princess's thigh by her husband during a dispute.

Visitors wishing to take photographs that approximate to those that could once be obtained from the south *gopuram* of the temple are advised to proceed to the south-west corner of the outer wall. Here, there are several high buildings with good viewpoints. Touts will invite visitors to enter some of them, although generally, a souvenir shop occupies one of the floors! However there is, of course, no compulsion to buy or even inspect the merchandise on offer.

Kudalgar Temple

Those with time available may now wish to visit the **Kudalgar Temple**, which is believed to be contemporary with the Meenakshi Temple. Located on South Masi Road, this can be reached by foot in less than 20 minutes; to gain entry, visitors must arrive, as usual, before midday or after 4.00pm. Dedicated to Vishnu, a particular interest here is the delicate lattice work that screens the apertures.

Palace of Tirumalai Nayak

Roughly the same distance away from the Meenakshi Temple as the Kudalgar Temple, although lying south-east of it, is the **Palace of Tirumalai Nayak**, which closes only between 1 and 2pm. Built circa 1636 for the most important Nayak king, the palace was originally four times its present size. Entered from the east side, the granite portico was erected in honour of Lord Napier, Governor of Madras 1866-72, who was responsible for restoring what survives of the building. This gives access to the courtyard in which Son et Lumière performances in English are given each evening at 6.45pm. Arcades on three sides are Saracenic in style with ornately decorated, cusped arches.

Facing the entrance, the west side is occupied by a domed, octagonal audience hall, the 'Celestial Pavilion' in which the original throne of Tirumalai Nayak stands. A further hall, to the north, now accommodates the museum. Columns are of granite encased with highly polished plaster, known as chuman, which in its pristine state resembles marble.

Mariamman Teppakkulam Tank

Located about 3 miles (5 km) east of the palace and reached by the number 4 bus from the state bus stand, via Ramnad Road, is the enormous **Mariamman** (or **Vandiyur**) **Teppakkulam Tank** and its adjacent temple. It should be noted that the tank, which is artificially fed by water from the nearby River Vaigai, will not be filled until the 12 day **Tepam (Float) Festival** takes place in late January or early February; for much of the rest of the dry season it is likely to be empty and have little appeal. On an island in the centre is a romantic pavilion, to which boatmen will row visitors. Idols of Meenakshi and Sundareshwar are taken on highly decorated floats to and from this pavilion during the Tepam Festival.

Apparently the tank, enclosed by a balustrade, occupies a pit that was excavated by Tirumala Nayak in 1646 for building materials used in the construction of his palace and parts of the Meenakshi Temple. By tradition, it was here that the huge figure of Ganesh in the Meenakshi Temple was discovered. There is little of interest to be seen in the small temple that faces the tank on the west side.

Gandhi Memorial Museum

Many that have seen either of the two museums in Delhi commemorating Mahatma Gandhi will probably not find Madurai's **Gandhi Memorial Museum** of particular interest, situated as it is on the north side of the River Vaigai, some distance from the city centre. However, it is only a short distance away from the **Ashok, Tamil Nadu II** and **Pandyan** hotels, and can be reached by buses 1 and 2.

The museum occupies the **Tumkum Palace**, a serene building with a cupola, constructed in the late 17th century for Rani Mangama, a renowned Nayak queen. During British rule, the palace was called the Tumkum Bungalow, and served as the official residence of the local administrator, the Collector of Madurai.

Exhibits comprise photographs, paintings and memorabilia connected with Gandhi's life. Of greatest, albeit rather macabre, interest is the dhoti cloth worn by Gandhi on the morning of his assassination; it is said that the marks on the cloth are his bloodstains.

In the **Memorial Gardens** outside stands a reproduction of the hut in which Gandhi lived at Sevagram, 1936-46. Adjacent, housed in a separate building, is the **Local Government Museum**.

Madurai's three top hotels are situated $2^1/_2$ miles (4 km) south of the city centre (**Taj Garden Retreat**) or 4 miles (6 km) north (**Madurai Ashok** and **Pandyan**). Most of the other hotels in Madurai are much more centrally located, within easy walking distance of the railway and bus stations and the Meenakshi Temple;

the accommodation selected is therefore dependent on one's preference for either luxury or convenience. Recommended air-conditioned, central hotels include: **Hotel Aarathy** with wonderful views of the temple, **Hotel Prem Nivas** and **Hotel Supreme**.

Undoubtedly Madurai's finest hotel is the **Taj Garden Retreat**, which lies to the south of the town centre, on Pasumalai Hill, from where there are great views over Madurai. Set in terraced grounds with, at lower level, a swimming pool, the hotel's bedrooms consist of 50 luxurious bungalows. The main building's rather small restaurant is to be enlarged; currently, at peak times, it is not only pleasant, but virtually essential that some guests dine al fresco on the lawn. If staying at the Taj, it is best to book a taxi from the hotel's reception to the town centre, rather than do battle with the rapacious auto-rickshaw drivers who believe that guests of the Taj can be conned into paying any ridiculous sum that they can dream up. An alternative is to take the footpath down through the grounds (not the drive) to the main road. From outside the hotel's main entrance, many buses go to the central bus station, a short distance from the temple. Also with a swimming pool, the **Madurai Ashok** has the expected facilities, but its rooms are in urgent need of upgrading, as are those of the **Pandyan** (no pool) located slightly to the south. Both hotels are 4 miles (6 km) from the town centre, and auto-rickshaw drivers believe their guests to be only slightly less well-heeled than those of the Taj; thwart them by catching any bus, e.g. 2, 16, 20 to the Racecourse Road/Alagarkoil Road junction, which lies just short of the hotels.

One will naturally dine well at all three of the top hotels, particularly the Taj on weekend evenings, when a sumptuous buffet is served on the lawn for a ridiculously cheap price. In the town centre, most restaurants are vegetarian, including those run by the hotels; however, the **Ruby Restaurant** serves first-rate non-vegetarian food in its garden, as does the **Surya Restaurant** on the roof of the **Hotel Supreme** (evenings only).

Depending on the itinerary preferred, visitors may proceed directly from Madurai to Munnar, Thekkady (for Lake Periyar) or Trivandrum, all in Kerala; even closer is the hill station of Kodaikanal, whilst other parts of Tamil Nadu, particularly the great Chola temples located in the central delta, Trichy, Kumbakonam and Chidambaram, will attract some, especially if a leisurely journey northward to Madras is planned. It should be borne in mind that although the route from Madurai to Kodaikanal is relatively straightforward, it takes a great deal of time to reach any part of Kerala from Kodaikanal, due to the disintegration of the west and southbound roads from the town.

VARKALA, THE QUILON/ ALLEPPEY BACKWATERS AND PERIYAR WILDLIFE SANCTUARY

Varkala

Although Kerala's long coastline is studded with attractive sandy beaches, most of them are the preserve of fishermen. Apart from the Kovalam region, Varkala is the only place where a beach resort has been developed. Varkala is very different from Kovalam, much more compact and quieter; in addition, prices are significantly lower, and in consequence youngsters predominate. Package tourists and those seeking luxury facilities in the resort are limited to the superb Taj Garden Retreat, which opened in 1995.

Varkala lies just 34 miles (54 km) north of Trivandrum, and

Above: Patchwork sails add variety to the backwater's craft.

therefore may be visited on a day trip from Kovalam, either direct by taxi or by bus or train (faster), from Trivandrum. However, it is generally regarded as a beach resort in which to stay as an alternative to Kovalam.

The small town of Varkala, where the railway station is situated, lies 1 mile (2 km) from the beach, and auto-rickshaws or taxis are plentiful. Most accommodation is located either on Beach Road, which runs from the Janardana Temple to the sea, or along the north cliff after the restaurants have been passed. The Taj Garden Retreat and the Government Guest House behind it are built on rising ground to the north of Beach Road. There are good reports of the medium price range **Sea Pearl Chalets**, which are located on the cliff top to the south of Beach Road. These are reached from a path at the sea end of Beach Road, and the proprietor is extremely helpful.

Varkala's beach, although also of golden sand, is very different in appearance from those at Kovalam, steep cliffs of red laterite rock rising from immediately behind it rather than palm trees. Due to the configuration of the cliffs, a welcoming updraught refreshes patrons of the open-air restaurants that line the clifftops. Every establishment has a thatched roof, and these are the only buildings that can be seen from the beach itself, where no construction work has been permitted. A road ending at a helipad winds up to the clifftops from the direction of Varkala town, but the most popular approach is via an ill-defined path beside the **Beach Palace Restaurant**, just past the rice paddies. It seems strange that the owners of the clifftop establishments have not got together to improve the approach which, at night, is far from straightforward. Precipitous paths from the beach up the cliff face are even worse, and best left to youngsters with mountaineering aspirations, but even they will find them too dangerous to use at night.

Varkala beach offers little protection from Big Wave: children must be watched carefully, and poor swimmers should not become too ambitious. The cliffs, all of which are virtually identical in height, form a partly tree-lined plateau above the beach; unlike Kovalam, there are no palm trees on the beach itself. Although laterite rock, of which the cliffs are formed, is always described as red, it is, in reality, more a rusty orange colour, a hue that pleasingly complements the bright green vegetation that has somehow managed to gain a foothold on much of the cliff face. Laterite is extremely soft, and large slabs of grey granite have been scattered at the base of the cliffs to protect them during the monsoon period; unfortunately, they give a somewhat fortified appearance to the beach.

Varkala has developed a reputation as a health resort, partly due to its fresh breeze which, it is claimed, provides relief to sufferers from asthma, but also because of the healing properties of the three mineral water springs that gush through conduits from the cliffs in the centre of the beach. These may be sampled free of charge, but strangers are advised to avoid the one on the left as, apparently, the spring is not protected by a conduit throughout its entire course, and there are fears that pollution could occur. The other two both taste fine; they are not as cold as most springs, but the flavour is very sweet.

In addition to the usual luxuriously appointed rooms expected of the Taj Group, the **Taj Garden Retreat Hotel** features the only swimming pool at the resort; it is large and overlooks the beautifully maintained garden towards the sea. The Taj offers the finest cuisine in Varkala: guests may dine either in the restaurant or by the poolside. The relatively small size of the Taj combined with its compactness seems to encourage a particularly friendly atmosphere that is not always found at luxury hotels.

Varkala's restaurants, like those at Kovalam, currently find it difficult to maintain standards. Of the clifftop establishments, **Oceanus** would appear to be one of the most reliable, and the service is particularly attentive. Beside the Janardana Temple's tank, the **Sree Padman Restaurant** is highly regarded for its fish and 'continental' food. **Sea View**, which lies below Beach Palace, should most

definitely be avoided. Again as at Kovalam, service in Varkala's restaurants is generally slow and specialities, particularly fish, tend to disappear quickly from the menu: patrons are recommended, therefore, to take both lunch and dinner reasonably early.

It is believed that Varkala's **Janardana Temple** was founded 2000 years ago, and many Hindus make a pilgrimage to it, particularly during major festivals. The temple's bell is said to have been presented by the Dutch captain of a sailing ship in the 17th century. After cremation, ashes of the departed are brought to the temple by devotees who, once prayers have been said, scatter them on the sea from Pabanasham (Sin Destroyer) Beach.

There is not a great deal to see in Varkala town, although the daily food market is always colourful. Bottles of alcoholic drinks can be purchased to take away from either of the two hotel bars (there are no such establishments near Varkala Beach). Day trips to Trivandrum and Kovalam are easily arranged.

As the road from Varkala to Quilon (National Highway 47) curves inland, it is quicker to make the journey by express train, which takes only 45 minutes.

Quilon (Kollam)

Quilon is the most usual point from which those travelling

Kerala Backwaters

Although the majority of tourists confine their backwaters experience to the Quilon/Alleppey sector, the waterways stretch for almost 2000 kilometers along Kerala's coastline; all were formed by the interaction between the sea and 40 rivers, together with their tributaries. Alluvial deposits and sand encroachment during the monsoon storms have combined to form strips of land running parallel with the mainland from which they are separated by canals, estuaries, lakes and lagoons. Most of these are linked naturally, but a little help from man has been necessary in straightening out the canals and dredging blocked stretches from time to time.

For centuries, long before road or rail links existed, the backwaters provided storm-free routes for transporting merchandise to Kerala's trading posts. However, the journeys were still dangerous as pirates and brigands preyed on the small country vessels.

Numerous tiny villages and hamlets evolved on the banks of these waterways, which still provide many of them with their sole access to the outside world and their only supply of drinking water.

Most of the craft are long and narrow, and designed so that even the shallowest waterway can be navigated. Some will be provided with thatched covers, primarily to protect their cargoes, a legacy from the same Chinese fishermen who introduced their picturesque fishing nets which can be seen overhanging the banks of the lakes in addition to Cochin's waterfront. Until recently, these thatched vessels became virtually extinct, but tourism has led to their revival – now fitted out as houseboats with all mod cons for luxury cruising.

Enjoyable though the Quilon/Alleppey excursion certainly is, every effort as well should be made to cruise the more intimate backwaters on a non-motorized craft, from which one is in much greater proximity to the activities of the villagers, and the overhanging branches of the palm trees create an unforgettable symphony of greens.

Boats operated for tourists will stop at villages to visit a market, watch coir-making the traditional way and observe the growing and harvesting of crops, primarily rice, and the farming of prawns. 'School pen' requests by local younsters will certainly be made, however remote the region. Children scamper along the narrowest tow paths, following the craft until the required pen is thrown to them or exhaustion sets in. What they seek is a ballpoint pen – quality irrelevent – which has been made outside India: all children are given pens in class, but to own a foreign pen bestows great prestige. A few Mrs Grundies deprecate this craze, claiming that it encourages venality at an early age, but the entertainment provided by the youngsters undoubtedly outweighs the cost of an average pen. Don't worry if a child falls into the water in his or her enthusiasm; it will certainly be shallow, and, in any case, all can swim.

Half-day waterway excursions arranged in Cochin are particularly delightful examples of this type of cruise. One word of warning, the sun is very strong and many boats will proved no cover: long sleeves, cotton trousers, headwear – a baseball cap is ideal – and high-factor sun protection cream are strongly recommended.

northward embark to explore the famous **Kerala Backwaters**. As long as an early departure is made, it is possible to reach Quilon's jetty from Varkala or Trivandrum in time to catch the tourist boats to Alleppey, which leave at 10.30am and take eight hours to complete the excursion. In 1997, silting-up necessitated a new departure point for the boats, but transport to it was provided from the jetty; it is expected that dredging will be completed by 1998. As there is little of tourist interest to see in Quilon, and accommodation leaves much to be desired, many prefer to avoid an overnight stay.

The town, located at the southern extremity of **Ashtamudi Lake**, is Kerala's most important cashew nut production centre. Founded in 825 by Persian immigrants as a trading port in the medieval period, ivory, spices, timber and textiles were exported from Quilon. Marco Polo (1254-1324) knew the town, which he referred to as Koilum, still the correct pronunciation of the name. The development of Malayalam culture in the 9th century is associated closely with Quilon. In the 13th century, Chinese traders settled here during the reign of Kubla Khan, with whom envoys were exchanged. Many examples of chinaware have been discovered in the area, and the distinctive 'Chinese' fishing nets (*cheena vala*), together with thatched cargo

boats, were introduced to India by the immigrants. The Portuguese built a trading post in 1502, which was acquired by the Dutch in 1661 and the British in 1795. In 1530, Friar Jordanus was ordained in Quilon Cathedral as India's first Roman Catholic bishop.

Quilon railway station is located almost 2 miles (3 km) from the town centre, the most convenient lodging area for those staying overnight. The **Sudarsan** is probably the best hotel, but as it faces the busy main road insist on a rear room; the hotel has a non-vegetarian as well as a vegetarian restaurant. If rooms are available, some may alternatively opt to stay at the picturesque **Government Guest House**, roughly 3 miles (5 km) from the station, with the usual enormous rooms and slightly faded atmosphere. *Honi Soit Qui Mal Y Pense*, still displayed above the entrance, is a reminder that the building was once the British Residency, and it is said that Lord Curzon slept here whilst Viceroy of India. Behind the Guest House, a short path leads to a small jetty on the lake, from where small boats may be hired; a floating restaurant opened in 1996. Those staying at the Guest House should be sure to make advance arrangements for transport to the main jetty in the town centre if proceeding by boat to Alleppey the following morning.

Quilon is compact, and

judged to be the quintessential Kerala market town. The name of its **Chinakada Bazaar** reflects Quilon's Chinese past. Main Road runs northward from Chinakada at the clock tower, and it is here that most restaurants and commercial hotels are situated; the **Azad Hotel** offers non-vegetarian food. Those seeking European fast food will find **Chef King** clean and efficient; it is located in the **Bishop Jerome Nagar Shopping Centre**, a modern development over-looking the national highway, about 500yds (450m) south of Hotel Sudarsan.

Between the Sudarsan and the boat jetty, but on the opposite side of the highway, stands the **Shrine of Our Lady of Velamkani**, a vivacious example of the Catholic shrines venerating saints that are to be found in most of Kerala's coastal towns. It is the only structure of any real interest in Quilon, as the fragments of the town's fort, built by the Portuguese and remodelled by the Dutch, are really not worth making the effort to see.

A right turn, well indicated, leads to the boat jetty, close to which stands the **Tourist Information Office** and the **Bus Station**. Quilon has a beach, separated from the town by a canal, but there are no facilities. Those travelling directly between Quilon and Trivandrum might care to note that Super Express buses, preferably booked in advance, make the 44 mile (70km) journey in 90 minutes.

Most of those who travel from Quilon to Alleppey via the backwaters (or vice versa) will take a KTDC excursion boat departing at 10.30am, but it is also possible to hire vessels privately, including house boats (see the Kerala Backwaters feature box). All excursion boats carry supplies of iced drinks, and stops are made for lunch and tea at small villages. For those who wilt under a baking sun, there is an enclosed area, but most passengers will be Europeans who prefer to sit on deck; photographers will find the prow end of the vessel preferable as for most of the journey the sun will be shining on what they wish to photograph rather than into their lenses.

Almost one third of the 8-hour cruise, the central part, is spent traversing **Kayamkulam Lake,** where all motorized vehicles, including tourist boats, are required to keep to the centre; the lake is quite broad, and little of interest apart from passing craft will be seen. The first and last parts of the voyage are therefore of greatest appeal, as then the varied activities on the banks of the waterways may be more closely observed.

Ashtamudi, the first lake crossed, means 'eight creeks'; these are well defined, although passengers will not see them all, as a turn northward along the canals is made before the entire lake has come into view. Promontories of red laterite and

The Alleppey Snakeboat Race

Until recently, the famous Alleppey snakeboat race took place only at the height of the monsoon, so few tourists ever witnessed the town's most popular event. Now, a re-enactment takes place on 19 January as part of what is called 'The Great Elephant March'. This strange name refers to the admirable three-stage event arranged by KTDC, which also includes, at Trichur and Kovalam, a parade of caparisoned elephants: the elephants do not march, nor are they, understandably, squeezed into the narrow snakeboats – in fact they make no appearance here at all. Tourists can obtain complimentary tickets from their hotels or at KTDC Information Offices, which provide them with boat transport from the jetty to free covered stands overlooking the canal to the east, where the event takes place. All, however, have to make their own way to Alleppey unless they have booked a Great Elephant March luxury package, which includes all transport and top grade hotels, and in consequence is certainly not cheap. Bookings can be made in Kerala from agents and tourist offices, also in the United Kingdom before departure for India.

Races begin mid-afternoon, and the regatta lasts for around two hours. An apprentice race ends the day's events, after which tourists are invited to join the ever-smiling lads in their boats for a short cruise (take plenty of school pens). Snakeboats (chundan valloms), up to 130ft (40m) long, are thus named from their serpentine prows; around 100 oarsmen propel each craft, furiously churning up the water with their oars. It is believed that the first snakeboat was built for the Chempakassery king in the 9th century as a speedboat for his private navy in times of war. Around 40 craft exist, but only 16 of these take part in the races. Cool drinks and snacks are available from vendors. Those who are able to attend the real thing on the second Saturday in August, as part of the harvest festival of Onam, will experience a somewhat longer and more colourful event, the highlight of which is the Nehru Trophy Boat Race, inaugurated by Prime Minister Jawarharlal Nehru in 1952. An umbrella will almost certainly be essential.

Opposite: Snakeboats are manned by crews of 100 or more.

china clay jut into the water, providing good vantage points for amateur fishermen. After the stop for tea, excursion boats leave the north end of Kayamkulam Lake in the late afternoon, just when the children come out of school, and great amusement is caused by cheeky youngsters beseeching a 'school pen' from western tourists who pass by in their boats.

Alleppey (Alappuzha)

Boats from Quilon reach Alleppey just before sunset. In addition to its situation on **Vembanad Lake** as the point of arrival or departure for backwater cruises, the city's greatest tourist attractions are the famous snakeboat races which take place twice a year.

Alleppey, founded as recently as 1762, is built over two canals, which hardly seems to warrant its grandiose sobriquet, 'Venice of The East'. The town is the centre of the coir manufacturing industry, the first factory being built in 1859. Black peppers are produced in abundance: before the Portuguese introduced chillies to India from South America in the 16th century, black peppers were all that there was to supply 'heat' to Indian food.

Boats from Quilon approach Alleppey from the North Canal which, it will be noted, is crossed by several bridges. The Boat Jetty faces the Bus Stand, but the railway station is 2.5 miles (4km) from the town centre, and from here trains follow the coast. Top class accommodation is very limited in Alleppey; popularly considered the best place to stay is the **Prince Hotel**, on the north side of the town, approximately 1 mile (2km) from the jetty. It is the only hotel in town with a swimming pool but, strangely, not all rooms are supplied with hot water – ensure there are two taps on the shower before taking the room offered. Dinner is served by the poolside, and the food is good.

Even better food, however, is provided in the **Komala Hotel's Arun Restaurant**, which faces the Boat Jetty from the opposite side of the canal. This is, in fact, a gourmet's delight, and nowhere else in south India will the local cuisine be bettered. Not only is the food superb, but the service is also attentive and knowledgeable: apparently the Arun Restaurant has maintained its high standards for many years. Try the pickled beetroot, a house speciality, and the light-as-air pappadums. Some may also wish to stay above the restaurant, at the Komala Hotel, which is very reasonably priced; some rooms are air-conditioned and there is a popular bar. Whichever hotel or restaurant is chosen in Alleppey, never, never, risk the drinking water, possibly the most dangerous in India. An added hazard in Alleppey is that the region has the unenviable reputation of being south India's centre of the mosquito-transmitted disease, Japanese encephalitis.

In the mid-19th century, the sea receded one mile from the town, where the long beach is now to be found; unfortunately, as the sand slopes steeply and fishermen abound, it is not possible to bathe there. Like Quilon, Alleppey has no major sights of great interest, however, on Mulakal Road, a short walk from the Boat Jetty, stands the small **Mulakal Temple**, dedicated to Rajarajeshwari Bhadraka, an incarnation of Vishnu's consort Lakshmi. Built of wood, the temple is carved and decorated: with some reason, it has been likened to Nepalese temples. A short distance away is the **Kidangampararambu Temple**, dedicated to Devi; its vibrant *gopuram* was added in 1978.

Few make the Quilon-Alleppey journey by boat in both directions, however, little of interest is passed on the highway that links them; surprisingly, not even a great deal of water is seen. The town of **Kayamkulam** lies almost halfway between Quilon and Alleppey, on National Highway 47, and those with time at their disposal may wish to visit its **Krishnapuram Palace**, by tradition built for Maharaja Marthanda Varma. It is a typical example of a Kerala mansions with tiled, gabled roofs and dormer windows. Inside there is a 53ft (16m) long mural, one of the most impressive in Kerala, which depicts the story of Gajendra Moksha from the Dhasavathara epic relating ten of Vishnu's incarnations. A small museum displays sculptures, paintings and bronzes.

At **Haripad**, 20 miles (32km) short of Alleppey, the **Manarasala Temple** (off the main road) is noted for serpent worship. The pathway to the temple is lined with numerous small idols of serpent gods. Two miles (3km) away, **Payipad** celebrates a three-day Onam festival in August, with its own snakeboat race held on the third day. Payipad's **Subramaniya Temple** is famed throughout Kerala.

Further east, on the Trivandrum – Kottayam road, **Aranmula's** Onam Snakeboat Race rivals Alleppey's in colour and activities, with decorated floats and caparisoned elephants taking part. Here, the event assumes more of a religious significance, being allied to the ritual of the local temple, which is dedicated to Parthasarathy (Krishna as Arjuna's charioteer). Onam is celebrated for seven days at Aranmula and, on the last day, the installation of the Parthasarathy idol in the temple is commemorated. The town is a centre for bell-metal mirror craft.

Alleppey offers an even greater choice of boat excursions than Quilon, both public and private, and several organizations have their offices adjacent to the jetty, including

Above: Boats originally covered to protect cargoes now provide houseboats for tourists. *Below*: The red laterite cliffs of Varkala beach contrast with Kovalam's palm trees.

the District Tourist Promotion Council, located at the Tourist Information Office. Apart from Quilon, the most popular boat trips from Alleppey are to Kottayam and Changannassery, taking around $2^1/_2$ and 3 hours respectively. Both combine attractive canals with stretches of Vembanad Lake, and some visitors may prefer to take either of these shorter trips rather than spend a whole day on the Quilon journey. **Vembanad Lake**, the longest in India, is navigable as far as Cranganore, and many of its islands are favoured by migratory birds.

Those travelling by road from Alleppey to Kottayam will drive alongside part of the **Changanassery Canal**, one of the prettiest in Kerala. The town of Changanassery, 18 miles (30km) from Alleppey, is connected with Kottayam by main road and rail routes.

Kottayam

This lively, prosperous city was India's first to achieve 100 per cent literacy, and it has become a centre for education and book publishing. For those who prefer a speedier journey than the boat provides, there are frequent buses from Alleppey. From Trivandrum, the 90 miles (144km) can be covered by bus or train in around two and a half hours. Kottayam is located close to the foothills of the Southern Ghat mountains, and tea, coffee, pepper and cardamom are grown locally. The most important industry of Kottayam, however, is rubber, and it is this that has earned the city its wealth. It cannot be said that Kottayam centre is of outstanding tourist interest, but the market area is lively, and there are picturesque examples of Kerala tiled roofs, many of which can be viewed from above, due to the undulating ground. Kottayam – the name means 'inside the fort' – is the headquarters of Kerala's Syrian Christians.

Whether arriving by boat, bus or train, an auto-rickshaw will be needed to reach the town centre, where most hotels are located. Pre-eminent is the **Anjali**, on KK Road, a member of the Casino Group which is a guarantee of high standards. Excellent meals are served in its western-style coffee shop, a popular venue for members of the local business community. Those who prefer a quieter location might like to try the **Vembanad Lake Resort**, a mile (2km) to the south, with its cottages, some of them air-conditioned, set beside the lake. The hotel specializes in barbecues by the water's edge, and meals are also served in a floating restaurant converted from a traditional Kerala boat.

Kottayam possesses two of Kerala's most interesting and ancient churches, both dedicated to St. Mary, and located close to each other, $1^1/_2$ miles (2.5km) west of the city centre; many tourists stop at them on route to or from Kumarakom. They were founded by Nestorian Syrians who, as refugees, colonized the area following their condemnation by the Council of Ephesus in 431. First seen is the **Cheriapally** (Small Church), built in 1579, but allegedly founded in the 13th century. An open, covered passageway leads to the west door, from where the church is entered and where shoes must be removed as is usual in south Indian churches. The facades of the passageway and the west front of the church are extravagantly Baroque, indicating later rebuilding.

The beamed roof of the nave is embellished with pendants and brackets. Vegetable-pigment frescoes around the sanctuary are reputedly 16th-century work, although those behind the altar are much brighter in colour, suggesting later retouching. Depicted left are the Garden of Gethsemane and the Last Supper; to the right is a Crucifixion scene.

Just 100 yards (90m) away, set on a hillock with good views over a cocoa plantation, is **Valiapally** (Big Church), which is now smaller than Cheriapally due to the latter's rebuilding. It is said to have been founded in the 9th century, but the present structure dates from 1550. The west facade is extremely plain, even though there is an adjacent bell tower. However the stone entrance arch is of interest as its spandrels are carved with birds and elephants.

Twin altars in the chancel are brightly decorated, and a stone Persian cross has been inserted in the face of the north altar on the left (the cross in the south altar is a copy of it). By tradition, it was carved by St. Thomas ('Doubting Thomas'), and presented by the Saint to the first church that he founded in Kerala (at Cranganore); however, scientists who recently examined the cross date it as 7th-century work, somewhat too recent to have had any connection with St. Thomas. The white inscription around it is in the Persian Pahlavi language.

Bosses are suspended from the coffered timber roof of the sanctuary. Below, the high altar is gilded and decorated with paintings in western style.

In the possession of the church is a visitor's book with entries dating back to 1899, including a visit from Emperor Haile Selassie of Ethiopia in 1956.

Kumarakom

Kumarakom is a village on the east shore of Vembanad Lake, 6 miles (9km) west of Kottayam. There is nothing particularly special about the village itself, but its tranquil location and bird sanctuary (best for bird-watching during the monsoon) has attracted developments of tourist importance around it. Of particular appeal is **Coconut Lagoon**, developed and operated by the Casino Group to provide a unique Kerala experience. There are regular buses between Kottayam and Kumarakom, but a taxi is advantageous as the distance is so short, and the two churches just described may then be seen on route. The last part of the journey will be made by Coconut Lagoon's private boat, which collects all patrons from beside a small bridge in response to a telephone call; the local taxi drivers know where the special phone box is located. Those travelling to or from the Casino Hotel on Cochin's Willingdon Island can now make the 3$\frac{1}{2}$ hour journey direct by morning boat *Grey Heron*; breakfast is served on board. The hotel will also provide transport by boat to or from Alleppey by arrangement.

Coconut Lagoon comprises 37 vintage Kerala cottages and mansions, brought in sections from various locations in the state and reassembled on the east shore of Vembanad Lake. Most overlook canals, which were originally excavated to irrigate the coconut plantation that previously occupied the site. Wisely, no attempt has been made to air-condition the accommodation, large, silently efficient fans enhancing the vintage atmosphere. Venetian-style bridges span the canals, providing access to the restaurant, where enormous buffet meals are served, and the large swimming pool, which acts as a focal point for the development.

If possible, stay in one of the mansions, which have been subdivided vertically to provide two separate units. Bedrooms in these are located on the first floor, all of them having delightful views. Much of the carved woodwork is antique, helping to evoke an Indian version of Snow White's cottage. The buildings certainly seem to have been designed with dwarfs in mind, as extreme care must be taken to avoid a painful bang on the head from the low lintels of the doorways.

Moored on the lake are the hotel's houseboats, luxuriously converted from rice boats to provide alternative accommodation. They are not motorized, and leisurely journeys, propelled by boatmen with poles, may be made on Lake Vembanad and along the more intimate backwaters; staff are provided to cook meals on board as required. Houseboats can be hired for 24 hours or longer, and as the serenity can become addictive, some book them for quite lengthy periods.

Serenity, in fact, is the hallmark of Coconut Lagoon where, unlike so many ambitious schemes of this type, there is no disquieting sense of staying in a theme park. Bookings can be made in the UK through several tour operators.

An alternative luxury development at Kumarakom is the **Taj Garden Retreat**, where all accommodation is air-conditioned. The usual high standards of the Taj Group are

Above: *Tourists are invited to join apprentices for short cruises on their snakeboats at Alleppey, when the races have ended.* **Below left**:*Tourists help fishermen inspect their cat* **Below right**: *This former British Residency at Quilon is now a Government Guest House*

maintained, even though the development is quite small. A swimming pool was added to the amenities in 1996. Those on a lower budget might like to spend a night or so on a house-boat at the **Kumarakom Tourist Village**, operated by KTDC.

Many proceed inland from Coconut Lagoon directly to **Spice Village**, another Casino Group development, this time situated beside the famous **Periyar Wildlife Sanctuary**, Kerala's most popular spot for wild elephant spotting. A direct link by hotel transport is projected. Alternatively, some will prefer to continue northward, hugging the coast, towards Cochin. A taxi will take around 3 hours to the Periyar area; frequent buses from Kottayam take around 4 hours: their route will have begun at Ernakulam and ends at Thekkady.

Some may have heard of **Sabarimala** and its nearby pilgrimage temple of Ayapa, set on a hilltop. Devotees live a life of austerity for 40 days before making their visit, the men's self-denial being demonstrated by their long beards and the black or saffron robes that they wear. The most popular time to worship at the temple is late December/early January, when several festivals take place. Surprisingly, non-Hindus are permitted to visit the temple, but a 3 mile (5 km) trek through jungle is involved from the Pambayar River. It is not possible to reach the temple from the

Kottayam to Thekkady road; a roughly parallel route must be taken, via Rani, and a knowledgeable taxi driver employed.

From Kumarakom, on route to Periyar, the two Syrian churches already described are passed shortly before Kottayam and those that have not seen them already will have an opportunity to do so. Inland from Kottayam, the delightfully scenic foothills of the Southern Ghats are soon reached. In spite of its great length, because of the mountainous terrain fewer than 20 roads, some of them little more than tracks, cross Kerala in an east-west direction. The heights of the main peaks do not vary dramatically, and trees are rarely absent, so that pastoral rather than dramatic scenery predominates. Around the town of **Peermade**, the peaks average 7,000ft (2150m) in height, but tea plantations at lower level soon take the eye. Those who have not seen tea growing before are always impressed by the vivid green of its leaves and the neatness of its bushes – as though a topiary expert had been at work.

Periyar

The Periyar Wildlife Sanctuary, established in 1934, was extended to its present area of 300 square miles (767 sq km) in 1950. Its centrepiece, the man-made **Periyar Lake**, at a height of 2,000ft (615m), covers 10

square miles (26 sq km), and was formed by the British, who dammed the Periyar River in 1895. Water that had flowed southward to the Indian Ocean was thereby redirected eastward to flow, via a 6,000 ft (1,850 m) long conduit, as the River Vaigai, supplying water to Madurai and irrigating much of south Tamil Nadu before flowing into the Bay of Bengal.

The lake is an important source of water not only for man but for the many wild animals that inhabit the sanctuary, which is why the area has become so popular with tourists; however, although there is a greater likelihood of spotting big game here than anywhere else in Kerala, good fortune will still be needed. The best chance of sightings occurs during the hot months of March, April and May, when smaller watering holes have dried up and the animals are forced to visit the lake. As the tourist boats on Periyar Lake are motorized, and their passengers not always as silent as they might be, the resultant noise disturbs many of the beasts. Sundays and public holidays, when Indian families come on outings to Periyar, are best avoided as the additional boats and people cause more noise than at other times.

Fortunately, everyone will always see monkeys, which gather around the boat jetty cadging titbits, and stealing from unwary visitors – take care. Deer of some sort are also usually in evidence, particularly the spotted deer and larger sambar, the favourite meal of tigers and leopards which are rarely sighted as there are no more than 35 big cats in the entire sanctuary. Bison, boar and the great squirrel may also be seen, but it is the 800 elephants, in herds of up to 30, that are Periyar's greatest attraction, although even these, in spite of their numbers, cannot be guaranteed to make an appearance.

Boat cruises on the lake last 2 hours and depart from the jetty between 7am and 4pm, the earliest and last trips usually providing the best chance of viewing animals before they retreat into the jungle. During much of the dry season, the dead trunks of trees that stood here before the lake was created protrude starkly above the water level; they provide a surreal landscape – and good perches for birds. Exotic examples of birdlife such as the Malabar Hornbill, Grey Jungle Fowl and the Jungle Mynah live in the sanctuary but are rarely seen. Those with accommodation overlooking the lake, of course, have an additional chance of seeing the wildlife, particularly around dawn, dusk or on moonlit nights. Care, however, must be taken anywhere within the park at night as some animals, particularly elephants, can be dangerous. Near-escapes and accidents have been reported but, fortunately, no fatalities.

The further into the sanctuary the accommodation is sited, the greater the likelihood of seeing big game. Best of all is the 6-roomed **Lake Palace**, a former summer retreat of the maharajas of Travancore. In recent years, unfortunately, the laws of supply and demand have been strictly followed by the KTDC who operate the hotel, and only the wealthy can now afford its tariff, which is outrageous for India, even though food and the use of a boat are included. For those on a somewhat lower budget, **Forest Lodge** is adjacent, but as there are only two rather basic rooms it is extremely difficult to make a reservation. Nearby stands a watchtower, which is possibly the best place of all from where to observe the wildlife, however, its bedroom is not provided with a mattress or linen, and only well-equipped backpackers will find it suitable. The Lake Palace, Forest Lodge and the watchtower are located on the west bank of Periyar Lake, and can only be reached by boat. Residents, who must have booked accommodation in advance, are obliged to be at the Boat Jetty no later than 4pm, otherwise they will not be taken to their accommodation that night.

Also within the area of the sanctuary, but located on the Thekkady peninsula, is the **Aranya Nivas** (this means Forest Lodge in the Malayalam language and should not be confused with the small Forest Lodge already referred to). The hotel possesses 30 rooms, some with views across the lake, and the food is excellent. Further back, on the same peninsula, is **Periyar House**, with 44 rooms, which is cheaper but not of quite such a high standard. Like the Lake Palace, both Thekkady hotels are operated by KTDC. Towards Kumily Village is the Casino Group's **Spice Village**. Luxuriously-appointed thatched cottages are set in undulating grounds. Enormous buffet meals are served in the restaurant or on its verandah, and the hotel's swimming pool, the only one in the Periyar vicinity, is a boon in the hot season. The popularity of Spice Village is reflected by the addition of 15 de-luxe cottages in 1997.

KODAIKANAL, MID-KERALA, COCHIN AND LAKSHADWEEP ISLANDS

Several places of interest are easily reached from Periyar, and there are direct buses to Cochin (Ernakulam), Trivandrum, Kovalam and Munnar in Kerala, and to Kodaikanal and Madurai in Tamil Nadu; the most important of these, Madurai, has already been described. Those wishing to visit the hill station of Kodaikanal are advised to go there first from Periyar if continuing onward to Madurai, as to return westward directly from Kodaikanal (to Munnar, for example) is extremely difficult. It takes many hours to reach the town from other points of tourist interest, even by private transport.

Kodaikanal

This hill station, generally regarded as south India's most attractively sited, spreads over a 7,400ft (2,277m) high crest on the steep eastern edge of the Southern Ghats. Like all the hill stations, Kodaikanal is popular amongst Indians mainly because of the relief it provides from the intense heat of the plains during the spring and early summer. Foreign tourists will delight in the mountainous scenery and, though perhaps to a lesser degree than Indians, the lower temperatures. Much of the town itself is scruffy, and only those with plenty of time to undertake the picturesque but exhausting walks around it will find a visit really worthwhile in view of its difficult access. At Kodaikanal, reasonably warm clothing will be needed, particularly in December and January, and the sky, normally clear blue at lower altitudes in southern India during the dry season, will often become overcast.

To get to Kodaikanal from Periyar, first take the Madurai road. Much of the early part of the route follows a flat, not particularly interesting terrain, even though the mountains are always visible to the west. Maps show a road from Periyakalam to Kodaikanal, which is just over 2 miles (4km) away, but this is now impassable, and an additional 7 miles (12km) must be added to the journey as it is necessary to continue eastward to join the Madurai/Kodaikanal road (known as Laws Ghat Road on approaching Kodaikanal).

Five miles (8km) before reaching Kodaikanal, look out on the right hand side for **Silver Cascade**, the most impressive of several waterfalls in the region. Just over a mile (2km) further

on, the **Flora and Fauna Museum** is accommodated in the Sacred Heart College. As background information for their walks, hikers will find much of interest in the museum, including a description of the Kurinji, a shrub with pale blue blossom, which spectacularly carpets the surrounding hillsides – but only once every 12 years: its next appearance is scheduled for 2004. The road soon winds steeply upwards to the town, and temperatures fall appreciably.

Kodaikanal, generally known as Kodai, really begins at the picturesque, although not very conveniently located, **Hotel Kodai International**. A little further on, a short road connects Laws Ghat Road with **Ana Salai** (or Bazaar Road), where many shops and economically-priced restaurants and hotels are to be found. It is also in this road that the spartan Bus Stand is located.

Before Bazaar Road is reached, all hikers should visit the **District Forest Office** in Laws Ghat Road, where they can obtain an invaluable booklet detailing walks of various extent in the area. The most popular of them, known as **Coaker's Walk**, begins on Noyce Road, east of the lake, near the Kodai Resort Hotel. Although short, the views obtained on the walk are rated amongst the finest in south India. Coaker's Walk ends at Telescope House, where there is a viewing telescope.

Just below this, St. Mary's Road may be followed westward to **Pillar Rocks**, 4 miles (6km) distant, for a lengthier hike. There are several guides who will accompany visitors on the more ambitious journeys for a reasonable fee. Whichever walk is taken, bear in mind that skies tend to be clearer in the mornings, and an early start will usually result in better views.

The most popular feature of Kodai is its boating lake, encircled by a 3 mile (5 km) long road. Rowing boats and pedalos may be hired from the boathouse on the lake's east shore. Behind this rises the town's most luxurious hotel, the **Carlton**, greatly favoured by Indian honeymooners. A stylish modern building, the Carlton's beautifully appointed bedrooms overlook the lake and the hotel's terrace. Regrettably, it is the hotel's policy that all residents must take (or at least pay for) the Carlton's three buffet meals. There ought to be no great objection to this, but at the time of writing the food fell well below the standard of this hotel's accommodation. Until something is done about the cuisine, visitors to Kodai are advised to give the Carlton a miss, in spite of its well appointed rooms.

A short distance back from the Carlton is the **Kodaikanal International School**, founded by American missionaries circa 1845 to provide education (Christian-based, of course) for European children, most of whom were British; there is still a surprising number of American Christians doing charitable work. However, Kodai first became famous when the British Governor, Sir Charles Trevelyan, made a visit in 1860, inaugurating the town's development as a hill station.

Bryant Park, laid out by an eponymous British officer, is reached from Club Road, and lies immediately south-east of the lake and to the west of Coaker's Walk. It is a delightful spot for relaxation, and the grounds are well maintained. In May, when the park is at its most colourful, an annual floral and horticultural show is held.

At 7,700ft (2,369m), the highest point in the area, stands the **Astrophysical Laboratory**. This was transferred here from Madras in 1889, when its present building was constructed. Useful research work is still carried out and the laboratory incorporates a small public museum, reached from Observatory Road, which begins at the end of Law's Ghat Road. Although the distance involved is only 7 miles (4.5km), most of the journey comprises a tiring uphill slog.

It is still possible to stay in the **Kodaikanal Club**, for a touch of the old colonial atmosphere, but there are only 16 rooms, which are in essence suites, and a reservation confirmed well in advance is essential, particularly in the high season. Also on Club Road, **Hilltop Towers** is extremely well run. There are already good reports of the recently opened **Valley View Hotel** in Post Office Road, some of its rooms, but not all, having splendid views over the valley, hence of course its name; dishes from north India and Gujarat are served in the hotel's restaurant. Opened in 1996, the **Sivapriya** is a three-star hotel of stark, 'office block' modernity but with comfortable, well-appointed rooms; there is also a bar, quite a rarity in the town.

As none of the restaurants in Hospital Road is particularly outstanding, most visitors will opt to eat in hotel restaurants. Presumably due to the steep gradients, there are no autorickshaws in Kodai, only taxis.

Kodaikanal to Madurai via Munnar

Buses from Kodaikanal to Madurai are reasonably frequent, covering the 75 miles (121km) in $3\frac{1}{2}$ hours. Those who have developed a taste for south Indian hill stations can alternatively travel by bus from Kodaikanal direct to Ooty (in the high season only), but it will take all day to get there and the opportunity of experiencing the famous miniature train will be lost. It is possible to proceed westward from Kodai to the tea plantation centre of **Munnar**, but cars and buses must follow a circuitous route, and a change of bus must be made – allow almost 8 hours!

A direct route to Munnar necessitates a 4-wheel-drive vehicle (which can be hired in Kodai) and consists of a series of jolts along a road which deteriorates in stages to a track and then a dusty, boulder-strewn indentation, which seems completely impassable. Almost two hours are saved on the bus journey – taxis, understandably, will not attempt the drive. Much of the route passes through the mountainous **Eravikulam Wildlife Sanctuary**, and there are brief glimpses of lakes and wonderful scenery – but only glimpses, as the 'road' cuts through impenetrable jungle for mile after mile. As may be expected, the area teems with wild animals, but the chance of seeing any, apart from monkeys, is remote. Towards the end of the long journey, the route passes the **Mattupatty** and **Kundaly Lakes**, both created by dams; they may also be visited easily from Munnar itself. To summarize, the journey is expensive, uncomfortable and best avoided; it is more advisable, as already indicated, to approach Munnar direct from Madurai.

Those who are not visiting either Madurai or Kodaikanal can proceed directly to Munnar from Periyar (one bus daily) via **Udumbanshola** and **Devikulam**, a most attractive route, which is just 27 miles (44km) in length but takes almost 3 hours to complete owing to its mountainous nature. Some motorists may wish to lengthen the journey

further by taking a diversion, via a branch road, to **Idukki**. The name of this town means narrow gorge, a reference to the Periyar River, here squeezed between the Kuravan and Kurathi hills. By tradition, Kuravan and Kurathi, gypsy lovers, were turned to granite by a curse. The gorge is bridged by the Idukki dam, which forms a lake and creates Kerala's most extensive hydro-electric scheme. A wildlife sanctuary of 27 square miles (69 square km) was established around the lake in 1976.

Munnar

Munnar, at 6,000ft (1,846m) the highest town in Kerala, is surrounded by peaks of up to 8,000ft (2,461m), which have earned it the description of 'The Scotland of India'. Commercially, it is completely dominated by the Tata Tea Company, who now own all the plantations in the area. Together with Darjeeling and Assam, in north India, Munnar is responsible for producing most of the country's tea. Unlike Kodaikanal, the views are tranquil rather than dramatic, but the town is infinitely more attractive. Surprisingly few tourists include Munnar in their itineraries, and the region therefore retains an 'undiscovered' quality.

The three rivers that meet at Munnar and which give the town its name, are crossed by a series of quaint pedestrian bridges evoking Japanese prints. Perched on separate hillocks, set in a straight line as if competing for attention, are Anglican and Catholic churches and a mosque. The main bus station is located in the town centre, but all Munnar's better hotels are found on the periphery.

A new (1995) and much needed arrival on the hotel scene is the delightful **Dassery East End**, its de-luxe bungalows arranged in a garden setting with good views over the town centre, from which the hotel is just a 5 minute walk away. Almost opposite rises **Isaac's The Residency**, acceptable but in need of some upgrading; here can be found the only bar near the town centre. Those on a tight budget may be tempted to join young Indian students and stay at the **Government Guest House** nearby. Ensure, however, that the promised refurbishing has been completed.

Two almost adjacent hotels, **Royal Retreat** and **Hill View**, are both excellent, but lie over half a mile (1km) from the town centre, and are not, therefore, particularly convenient. There are no outstanding restaurants in Munnar, though all the hotels mentioned serve acceptable food.

It is sometimes possible to stay at the vencrable **High Range Club**, set in 20 acres of grounds. This is now the social

Opposite: The great cascade of Athirampalli Falls.

centre of Tata's managers, but was founded by tea producers James Finlay and Co in the 1890s. The present clubhouse was built in 1910, and old photographs prove that its appearance has changed little, in particular the 'Men's Bar', where stuffed animal heads still decorate the walls. Golf and tennis are played, but rugby football has recently been abandoned. Sunday is the most popular day for members, who congregate in the bar early in the afternoon following a round of golf. Only 17 bedrooms are available, and lodging priority is given to members of affiliated clubs and guests of members – in that order; the only affiliated club outside India is London's Overseas Club. Unless a member of that club, those wishing to reserve a room must convince the club's secretary that their credentials are unimpeachable – quote schools, profession, qualifications and clubs – and apply at least one month in advance. It is well worth the effort, as guests may use all the club's facilities. Non-residents who are not members are not permitted to dine at the club.

The High Range Club is near **Old Munnar**, which was all there was of the town before Indian independence: only a fruit and vegetable market stood where the present town centre has been developed. Old Munnar's **Church of South India** survives a short walk away from the club, near the

town's second bus station.

Those who have made the difficult approach to Munnar through jungle from Kodaikanal will have already passed Kundaly, where its serene lake has been created, as usual, by a dam. The famous **Kundaly Golf Club**, reputedly the largest in Asia, takes up much of the area; its members are all connected with the local tea plantation, but visitors are welcome to join them for Sunday lunch. Kundaly is 17 miles (28km) from Munnar. A similar lake at **Mattupatty**, only 9 miles (15km) from the town, is a favourite picnic spot for locals.

For overseas visitors, the most popular short excursion from Munnar is northward to **Rajamalai**, hopefully to spot Nilgiri *tahr*, the only wild goat found in India south of the Himalayas. Recently saved from imminent extinction, these rare animals congregate in a very small section of the 37 square mile (94 sq km) **Eravikulam Park**, which was created to protect them in 1978. It is said that everyone has a 90 per cent chance of seeing a herd, but they are fairly nervous creatures and often appear as little more than specks in the distance – those with binoculars should certainly take them. The scenery on route to Rajamalai is quite magnificent, and tea picking can be observed. Those wishing to see the tea production process can make arrangements at Tata's administration office in the town – note its superb garden before leaving.

As at Kodaikanal, *karinji* blossom carpets the hillsides of Munnar every 12 years.

Anamudi, at 8,841ft (2,695m) the highest mountain in south India, rises 15 miles (25km) north of Munnar, within the Eravikulam Sanctuary. Tata Tea have assumed responsibility for protecting the sanctuary, and at its entrances an official will sometimes and, rarely, sometimes not, demand money to proceed past his barrier; he will, of course, pocket the rupees. At the Rajamalai road entrance, however, all is much more organized, and official tickets are issued. There is one ticket for a car and its occupants, but a separate ticket (50 rupees) must be purchased by all foreigners before proceeding to the car park. Overseas visitors who are not mad about wild goats may, understandably, prefer not to accept this prejudice and return instead to Munnar.

Cochin, together with its 'twin town', Ernakulam, is a 4 hour drive from Munnar. There is much of interest to see in the area to it's northeast, which is more easily explored from **Alwaye**. An added advantage in stopping off at Alwaye is that tourists heading northward after seeing Cochin are able to keep to the coastal road without being tempted to make deviations inland. There are regular buses from Munnar to Ernakulam; one of them leaves the central bus station mid afternoon, thus avoiding peak travel times – and for this reason it usually will be the most comfortable. Allow three hours to Alwaye (Ernakulam takes an hour extra).

Just over halfway between Munnar and Alwaye, ornithologists may wish to alight at Kothamangalam, 12 miles (20km) from Kerala's only major bird sanctuary, at Tattekkady. This occupies a 25 square mile (64 sq km) peninsula between two arms of the Periyar River; species include hornbills, parrots, woodpeckers, the rare Ceylon frogmouths and rose-billed rollers. There is one forest bungalow in which it is possible to stay the night.

Alwaye (Aluva)

Alwaye is sited beside an inlet where the Periyar River (also known hereabouts as the Alwaye or the Purna) flows into the Arabian Sea. On the north bank of the river is a **Shiva temple** and, in front of this, on a sandbank, a Shiva *lingam* is venerated by pilgrims. A ferry crosses the river at this point to a jetty beside the former maharaja's summer palace, now a **Government Guest House**. In February 1996, the President of India passed through Alwaye on route to open the splendid new sports stadium at Ernakulam, and just in case he dropped in for a 'pit stop', the entire facade of the building was repainted, and an immaculately tiled bathroom created on the ground floor. Externally, therefore, this guest house is in unusually good condition, and as its rear rooms have curved balconies with delightful views across the river, it can be recommended to budget travellers.

Those seeking higher quality accommodation are restricted to the modern **Hotel Periyar**, located a short walk away beside the bridge. The hotel's restaurant is excellent, two of its most popular tables being squeezed on to balconies overlooking the river. Nowhere else in central Alwaye can be recommended for food, apart from a reasonable KTDC restaurant at Thaikattukara, on its outskirts.

It will be appreciated that Alwaye, an industrial town, is neither a gourmet centre nor a tourist mecca. However, it does provide a convenient base from which to spend one day exploring by car a beautiful part of Kerala that most tourists neglect.

Kaladi

Alwaye's coastal inlet is crossed by a long bridge, and the road then continues north-eastward, via Angamali, before branching south-eastward to Kaladi. A short distance from Kaladi centre rises a 150 ft (46 m) high octagonal tower, the '**Pagoda of Kaladi**'. This commemorates a local philosopher and religious reformer, Sri Adi Shankaracharya, who lived in the 8th century. It is possible to enter the tower (closed 12.00-

4.00pm) and ascend its gentle ramp. Murals throughout the nine levels depict the life and works of Shankaracharya and his disciples; surprisingly, the captions are in English only.

The road continues ahead to the **Shankara Janmabumi Temple**, built beside the river, traditionally on the site of the philosopher's birthplace. Pleasingly, no restrictions are placed on non-Hindus, who are permitted to approach the shrines closely. Those venerated include Sharadadevi, a philosopher; Aryamba, the mother of Shankara; Ganesh and Shankara himself. The idols are clothed in silk, evoking statues of Roman Catholic saints in Spanish and Portuguese churches.

Immediately behind the shrine of Sharadadevi, a black stone lamp-post is claimed to mark 'the very birth-place of Shankaracharya'.

The adjacent **Krishna temple**, accredited with great age, was allegedly the temple where the family of Shankara worshipped, and the philosopher is believed to have installed the idol of Krishna himself.

By tradition, St. Thomas meditated on the 2,000ft (615m) hill which rises outside the nearby town of Malayatur, and on its summit built a shrine in which he prayed. Indentations in the rock are said to be the footprints of the Saint. Beginning on the Sunday after Easter, the Feast of St. Thomas is celebrated for a week by thousands of pilgrims. Those who are tempted to visit the shrine should remember that there is no substantiated evidence that St. Thomas ever visited India – and the climb will exhaust all but the fittest.

Metala

The Kalil (Rock) Temple of Metala has been created within a monolithic slab of rock perched on the summit of a low hill, 6 miles (10km) outside the small town of Perumbavoor, south-west of Kaladi. It can be visited immediately after the Kaladi temples before continuing to the Athirampalli Waterfalls or, preferably in the evening, on returning southward from the falls. This rare example in Kerala of a temple built by Jains is believed to be around 2,000 years old. Later, it was taken over by Hindus, and is now dedicated to Shiva.

A steep slope with broken steps must first be climbed, followed by a flight of 66 steps leading to the small entrance to the temple, above which is a small figure of Shiva. Few tourists will enter the cave-like shrine, as it is open 6am-10am only. A great joy of visiting this temple is the sylvan countryside around it, with extensive views of shimmering paddyfields backed by tiers of palm trees.

Athirampalli Waterfalls

The route to the falls from Metala returns northward through Kaladi to the main Alwaye/Trichur road, which it leaves at Chalakudi. From here, another road branches eastward, gradually climbing the northern foothills of the Southern Ghats; below can be seen the beautiful valley of the River Chalakudi. Eventually, the **Athirampalli Falls** are reached, and the road and river then run in parallel at the same level. There are no more dramatic waterfalls than those at Athirampalli to be seen in south India; even in the dry season, when most tourists visit them, the volume of water is guaranteed to be impressive.

The falls can be seen from the road, but may be approached more closely on foot from the car park. As the river bed is extremely slippery, great care should be taken by would-be bathers, as several have been swept to their deaths in recent years. A short distance further on is another, much gentler cascade, the **Vazhachal Waterfalls**. Paddling is safer here, and Indian families like to picnic beside it; cold drinks and ice creams are sold at an adjacent snack bar.

A return direct to Alwaye can now be made; alternatively, as already mentioned, some may now prefer to visit the rock temple at Metala. Cochin lies 49 miles (78km) to the south and can be reached in less than 2 hours by car, thus avoiding having to spend the night at Alwaye.

Cochin (Kochi) and Ernakulam

Cochin is best known from a tourist viewpoint for its picturesque Chinese fishing nets which line the north shore of Fort Cochin. Facing the waters of Vembanad Lake, Fort Cochin, together with the adjoining district of Mattancherry, to the south, is undoubtedly the most interesting part of the Cochin/Ernakulam conurbation for sightseeing. Both occupy the narrow spit of land sheltering Lake Vembanad from the open sea, whilst Ernakulam stretches along the east bank of the lake, on the mainland proper.

Between them, from west to east, are the inhabited islands of Vypeen, Gundu, Vallarpadam, Willingdon and Bolgatty, by far the most important of these being Willingdon Island, which accommodates two major hotels, harbour buildings and Cochin Airport. Cochin's new international airport is under construction at Nedumbassery, 19 miles (30kms) east of Ernakulam.

A bridge connects the Fort Cochin/Mattancherry peninsula with Willingdon Island, which itself is linked by road and railway bridges with Ernakulam. However, these bridges are situated some way south of Cochin's main points of interest, and tourists will usually find it more convenient, as well as more appealing, to use the ferries. There are ten separate ferry terminals involved, so be sure to note their names and always check carefully that the appropriate ferry is boarded.

For tourists, the best time to visit the region is during the last week of December, when Carnival is celebrated at Fort Cochin. At that time, the town is illuminated, the Indira Gandhi Snakeboat Race is held and, on New Year's Day, a colourful procession, the highlight of Carnival, winds its way through the streets. This is not a Hindu religious event, its origin being the New Year celebrations of Cochin's Portuguese colonizers.

Although almost everything of greatest tourist interest in Cochin is to be found on the narrow Fort Cochin/Mattancherry peninsula, at the time of writing there is very little accommodation, none of it top class, and most of its visitors will be lodged either at Willingdon Island or Ernakulam. The situation will soon change, however, as the Casino and Hilton groups are building luxury grade waterfront hotels with swimming pools, both designed to complement Fort Cochin's architectural heritage of colonial buildings.

Half-day excursion boats are a good way of visiting the most important sights in a relatively short space of time. These depart from the **Sealord Boat Jetty** at Ernakulam, calling at Willingdon Island to pick up more passengers, and thence

Mattancherry to visit, on foot, its palace (not Friday) and synagogue; the ferry then continues northward to Fort Cochin, where tourists are taken to see St Francis Church and the Chinese fishing nets. Some may wish to forego the boat's continuation to Bolgatty Island and spend more time at Fort Cochin; Bolgatty can be visited easily on another occasion as it only lies a short distance offshore from Ernakulam from where there is a direct ferry.

Mattancherry Palace

In 1557, Portuguese built this palace, which stands adjacent to the **Mattancherry Boat Jetty**, as a gift for the Maharaja of Cochin, Virakerala Varna, to compensate him for recent damage they had caused to a nearby temple: if good relationships with the ruler of Cochin were not maintained the Portuguese risked losing their trading rights. In 1663, the Portuguese surrendered these rights to the Dutch who, similarly wishing to please the Cochin Raja, remodelled the building for him; it was their work that gained the palace its nickname 'The Dutch Palace' though no Dutch ever lived there.

As may be expected from its history, the two-storey building, constructed around a courtyard, is eclectic in style, with an oriental emphasis. For some unfathomable reason photography within the palace is not permitted. Facing the entrance is the building's most important chamber – its **Durbar Hall**, in which maharajas of Cochin were crowned; their portraits are now displayed on the walls.

Coffered ceiling panels of teak are a feature of the interior, similar in appearance to those already described in other Kerala palaces. Even more important, however, are the outstanding murals, which depict traditional Hindu themes, in particular, episodes from the Mahabharata and the Ramayana epics.

Another room of great interest is the **Private Audience Chamber**, where maharajas received their guests whilst reclining on the swing that remains in situ. Seen throughout the palaces are royal palanquins, turbans and coronation robes. Ceremonial swords are displayed in the **Armaments Room**, from where steps descend to the **Ladies' Bedchamber**. Here, the murals depict a mischievous Krishna, all six of his hands, plus both feet, working overtime to physically excite eight milkmaids simultaneously. Presumably, this decor was intended to prepare the court ladies for their master's exercise of his conjugal rights.

Within the courtyard, the circular **Krishna Temple** has a tapering tower evoking the stupas of Buddhist temples, common in Kerala until Hinduism ousted Buddhism in the 8th century. One of the temple's walls is shared with the adjoining Mattancherry synagogue.

Mattancherry Pardesi Jewish Synagogue

Jews had long traded with the Malabar coast, possibly from the time of King Solomon, and many settled in India soon after the 2nd temple in Jerusalem had been destroyed by the Romans in 70AD. Initially they selected Cranganore as their base, and by 370 it is known that 10,000 of them were living there. Referred to as Black Jews, they were supplemented by Sephardic Jews fleeing from the early 16th-century Inquisition in Spain and Portugal; the new, paler-skinned arrivals were soon to be referred to as White Jews. Later, Ashkenazy Jews from central Europe, escaping the pogroms, came to join the Sephardic Jews, and the two groups of White Jews banded together to form a separate community, from which the Black Jews were excluded. When, in the mid-16th century, the Portuguese took over Cranganore, they persecuted the Jews who fled en masse to Cochin, establishing a residential area still known as Jew Town, and building synagogues.

In 1997, only seven Jewish families still remained in Jew Town, virtually all the others having migrated to Israel, but their historic **Pardesi Synagogue** at Mattancherry survives as the most impressive Jewish place of worship in India. The walled

Below. Evoking modern sculpture, the delicate Chinese Fishing Nets are Cochin's greatest tourist attraction.

Chinese Fishing Nets

By tradition, Chinese fishing nets were introduced to Kerala by immigrants during the reign of Kubla Khan, but they eventually fell into disuse. After many centuries the nets were reintroduced by the Portuguese, following their acquisition of the Chinese port of Macao.

The supporting platforms, protruding above high-water level, are constructed of coconut tree trunks, which stand on thick stanchions of teak. For obvious reasons, the nets can only function at high tide, and then a team of four fishermen swing into action. The complicated operation of each net involves the skilful adjustment of pulleys and counterweights (slabs of rock). After approximately 15 minutes under water the net (nowadays nylon) will be raised, and a fisherman must climb one of the four supporting poles from which it is supported, transfering the catch into a bucket. The net is then lowered once more and the procedure recommenses.

Graceful curving poles combined with the swaggered netting, particularly when viewed in a group from the sides, evoke a giant piece of abstract sculpture, which never fails to impress. This is not, as might be imagined, a particularly cost-effective way of fishing, and some fear that it will come to an end before long. However, tradition dies hard in Kerala, moreover, it is fully appreciated that the Chinese fishing nets are a major tourist attraction, and steps will surely be taken to ensure their continued operation, perhaps through state subsidies.

synagogue, founded in 1568 by Black Jews, suffered from Portuguese shelling in 1662 and was rebuilt two years later. To mark the centenary of this building in 1764, renovation, which included the construction of the clock tower, took place under the guidance of Ezekial Rahabi. Before entering the synagogue, note the stone with Hebrew lettering set in the enclosing wall, all that survives of the Kochangadi synagogue, built nearby in 1344.

Cool but vibrant, the interior is one of the finest of any synagogue in the world. The crystal chandeliers were made in Belgium in the 19th century, and the mid 18th-century floor tiles brought from Canton by Ezekial Rahabi as part of his reconstruction work. Each of the 1,100 hand-painted blue and white tiles differs slightly in design. Suspended from the ladies' gallery are silver lamps, a gift to the synagogue from Cochin's first British Resident.

King Ravi Varma I (962-1020) presented the village of Anjuvanam, near Cranganore, to Joseph Rabban, a Jewish trader, confirming the grant by inscribed copper plates, which are retained in the synagogue and may be viewed on request if convenient. Also in the possession of the synagogue are 200-year-old scrolls of Mosaic Law (kept within the tabernacle) and crowns of gold, gifts from the maharajas of Cochin and Travancore.

Passengers on the boat excursion will return to the jetty, continuing by water to Fort Cochin. As the jetty is approached, the long frontage of the former Aspinwall spice warehouse can be seen; this is to be converted by Hilton to a luxury hotel. Adjacent to it, the open site is where the Casino Group are constructing a 35-suite hotel, with garden and swimming pool overlooking the water.

Those not on the guided tour, however, may prefer to further explore Mattancherry before continuing to Fort Cochin by road.

Jew Town is now mainly given over to spice merchants, many of whom occupy buildings dating from the 17th century. Just over half a mile (1km) from the synagogue is an ancient stone cross known as the **Coonen (Leaning) Cross**. In 1653, Christian followers of the Patriarch of Antioch bound themselves to this in protest against the Latinisation of their church by the Portuguese, whose religious intolerance seems to have brought them into conflict with just about everybody in Kerala.

Fort Cochin

It is pleasanter to follow the lake by road from Mattancherry on route northward to Fort Cochin, at the tip of the peninsula. About half way, on Calvetty Road, the lakeside **Hotel Seagull** is the only hotel of note in the area. As this hotel is extremely good value and has only nine rooms, reservations should be made well in advance. Buffet meals can be taken on the terrace overlooking the water, and there is a bar. Located west of the hotel, where the Chinese fishing nets begin, is the boat jetty for the Vypeen Island ferry. At last, the architectural importance of Fort Cochin's ancient buildings is appreciated by the authorities, and venerable buildings may no longer be demolished; the spur to this regulation was the erection of an unsuitable multi-storey block of flats near the waterfront. In 1997, a great deal of maintenance and repainting of properties took place, and the town probably looks better than at any time since the British left.

Chinese fishing nets

Whether arriving at Fort Cochin by road or water, most will make immediately for the famous Chinese fishing nets, which hang in a straight line westward from the Bus Stand at the end of Calvatty Road. Many tourists will already have seen examples on the backwaters trip from Quilon to Alleppey, but those will almost certainly have been less picturesque as the nets themselves are usually taken down between dawn and evening, leaving just the stark superstructures of framework and poles. In contrast, apart from monsoon time or when repair work is necessary, the nets at Fort Cochin are generally left suspended from their poles throughout the day. They prove a delight for photographers in all lights but particularly at sunset, when it is well worthwhile returning (but check the time of the last departing ferry).

St. Francis Church

Cemetery Road leads southwestward from the fishing nets to the **Church of St. Francis**, the first church built by Europeans in India. It is believed to have been founded by Franciscan friars in 1503 as a small wooden chapel dedicated to St. Bartholomew. When built, it formed part of **Manuel Kolati** (Fort St. Emmanuel), erected by Admiral Albuquerque, the Portuguese conqueror of Goa. The fort was needed to protect Portugal's trading rights on the Malabar coast, which had been granted on Christmas Day 1500 to Cabral, a Portuguese adventurer. Albuquerque, on his arrival, assisted the Cochin ruler in dispelling the Zamorin of Calicut, who was besieging the city. As a reward, three years later the Portuguese were granted more permanent trading rights, and it then became worthwhile for them to reconstruct the temporary wooden structures within Fort St. Emmanuel in more solid form. By 1516, the original simple chapel had been replaced by the present stone church with a tiled roof – this time dedicated to St. Anthony, although remaining Franciscan. The Dutch took Cochin from the Portuguese in 1663, restoring the church and remodelling it for Protestant worship. By 1795, the British were in control of Cochin and, in 1804, the Dutch who had remained voluntarily presented them with the church for Anglican services; rededication to St. Francis probably occurred in the mid-19th century.

The interior is surprisingly plain, much more Dutch Lutheran than Baroque in appearance – but without the superb woodwork that is the great joy of many contemporary churches in Holland. Dutch tombstones are displayed on the walls of the vestibule and the nave, but of greater interest is the original tombstone of the explorer Vasco da Gama, who died in Cochin on Christmas Eve 1524. Brass rails have been erected on the south side of the nave to protect the stone,

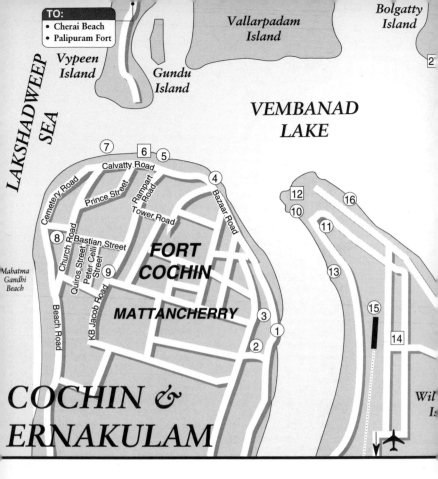

Bolgatty
Island

Vallarpadam
Island

Vypeen
Island

Gundu
Island

LAKSHADWEEP SEA

VEMBANAD
LAKE

⑦ ⑥ ⑤

Calvatty Road

Cemetery Road

Prince Street

Rampart Road

Tower Road

Bazaar Road

④

⑫
⑩

⑯

⑧

Church Road

Bastian Street

Quiros Street

Peter Celli Street

FORT
COCHIN

⑪

⑨

⑬

Mahatma
Gandhi
Beach

KB Jacob Road

MATTANCHERRY

③

⑮

Beach Road

①

⑭

②

COCHIN &
ERNAKULAM

Wil
Is

which is simply identified 'VASCO GAMA': the body of the navigator only rested here for 14 years before being transferred to its splendid tomb in Belem monastery outside Lisbon.

Remaining in the possession of the church is the deed inscribed on a palm leaf, by which the Cochin ruler gave the Portuguese their trading rights. A Dutch register of baptisms in the church, the *Doop Boek*, is also retained by the Church of South India, to which St. Francis now belongs.

Santa Cruz Basilica

A much larger church, the Roman Catholic **Basilica of Santa Cruz**, lies south-east of St. Francis, in KB Jacob Road. It occupies the site of an early 16th- century Portuguese church, similarly dedicated, which was consecrated as a

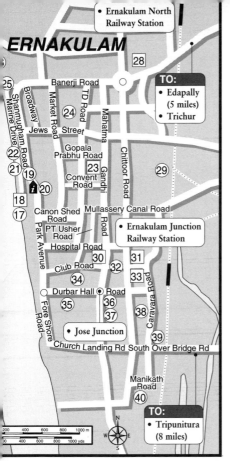

ERNAKULAM

Ernakulam North Railway Station

28

Banerji Road

TO:
• Edapally (5 miles)
• Trichur

25

Broadway
Shanmugham Road
Marine Drive

Market Road

TD Road

Mahatma

Jews Street

24

Gopala Prabhu Road

Chittoor Road

23

Gandhi

Convent Road

29

22
21 **19**
20

18

i

17

Canon Shed Road

Mullassery Canal Road

PT Usher Road

Road

• Ernakulam Junction Railway Station

Park Avenue

Hospital Road

Club Road

30

32

31

34

33

Durbar Hall ⊙ Road

Fore Shore Road

35

36

37

38

Caravara Road

• Jose Junction

39

Church Landing Rd South Over Bridge Rd

Manikath Road

40

TO:
• Tripunitura (8 miles)

N
W — E
S

200   400   600   800   1000 m
0   400   800   1000 yds

KEY

1. Mattancherry Jetty
2. Jewish Synagogue
3. Dutch Palace
4. Customs Jetty (ferries to Ernakulam and Willingdon Island)
5. Jetty for Vypeen Island
6. Hotel Seagull
7. Chinese Fishing Nets
8. St Francis Church
9. Santa Cruz Basilica (RC)
10. North Jetty
11. Government of India Tourist Office
12. Taj Malabar Hotel
13. Harbour Terminus Jetty
14. Casino Hotel
15. Cochin Harbour Station
16. Embarkation Jetty
17. Main Jetty
18. Taj Residency Hotel
19. GCDA Shopping Centre & Indian Perfrming Arts Centre
20. Tourist Information Centre / KTDC
21. Sealord Boat Jetty
22. Ancient Mariner Restaurant
23. Abad Plaza Hotel
24. Market
25. Jetty for Vypeen Island
26. High Court Jetty
27. Bolgatty Palace Hotel
28. Presidency Hotel
29. KSRTC Central Bus Stand
30. Grand Hotel
31. Metropolitan Hotel
32. Pandhal Restaurant
33. Paulson Park Hotel
34. Parishath Thanipuram Museum
35. Indian Airlines
36. Bimbi/Khyber Restaurants & Joyland Hotel
37. Bus Stand for Fort Cochin
38. South Bus Stand
39. See India Foundation
40. Cochin Cultural Centre

☐ Hotel   ○ Other

cathedral in 1557. The present building, dating from 1902, possesses little of architectural interest, but the paintings inside are impressive.

Most, however, will prefer to follow Church Road from St. Francis to the cricket ground ahead where, with luck, a match might be in progress. Delightful colonial houses, venerable trees, and of course the church, impart the atmosphere of an English village green – if only there were a pub to complete the scene!

Cemetery Road, as may be expected, leads to the **Dutch Cemetery** which, although rarely open, can be observed from a gateway. Its restoration, sponsored by KLM, is imminent.

Immediately to the west in front of Beach Road, a splendid stretch of sand, **Mahatma Gandhi Beach**, faces the open sea. Locals enjoy promenading here in the evening and at weekends, but would not dream of bathing in the sea; any foreign tourist who dips just one toe in the water will cause amazement. In Princes Street, the Casino Group are converting an ancient house allegedly occupied by Vasco da Gama into a museum and speciality restaurant: telephone the Casino Hotel for up- to-date information.

Willingdon Island

Ferries depart from Fort Cochin's Customs Jetty either to Willingdon Island's North Jetty or to its Harbour Terminus Jetty further south. There is also a less frequent service from Mattancherry Jetty to Harbour Terminus Jetty. Those staying at Willingdon Island will, of course, make the journeys in reverse order.

A freak storm opened up Cochin harbour to the sea in 1341 and, at the same time, blocked the inlet to Cranganore, which stands at the north end of Vembanad Lake. In consequence, Chinese settlers eventually migrated from Cranganore to Cochin, introducing their fishing nets, wide-brimmed hats, and roofs that curve upward at the gable ends – now a common architectural feature throughout Kerala. Whilst crossing the harbour, some may fear that *India*, an immense tanker-like ship, is polluting it by spewing out black liquid into the water; there is no need for alarm, the vessel is a dredger, its only task being to transfer black silt from the centre of the waterway to the edges. This work has to proceed continuously as alluvial deposits from rivers, particularly during the monsoons, are constantly threatening to block the harbour.

Most of Kerala's backwater islands have been formed by such natural deposits, but not so Willingdon Island, which was created by the British in the 1930's by depositing silt between Fort Cochin and Ernakulam when the harbour was deepened. Its name commemorates Lord Willingdon, Viceroy of India 1931-36.

Unless visiting either of its splendid hotels, there is absolutely no reason why any tourist should wish to spend time on Willingdon Island. Two-thirds of the area is taken up by the airport, whilst structures connected with harbour activities account for most of the remainder; there are no shops, and only a handful of restaurants. Few will need to use its railway station (Cochin Harbour Station) situated opposite the Casino Hotel, as none of Kerala's most popular tourist routes are served from here. Having said this, the northern point of the island does offer splendid views across the water: of Fort Cochin to the west, palm-clad islands ahead, and Ernakulam to the east. It is here that a boat jetty, the **Taj Malabar Hotel** and the **Government of India Tourist Office** are located.

The Taj Malabar Hotel is undoubtedly one of the finest hotels in India, skilfully catering for businessmen as well as tourists. Located at the very tip of the island, with water on three sides, the Malabar was for many years the only hotel of consequence to be found in Cochin. Originally it comprised merely the two-storey block that still survives, which has been completely remodelled to provide the hotel's public and administration areas. The eight-storey tower block, added in 1986, accommodates the hotel's 100 bedrooms, nine of them suites, and all with lake views. Only the seven executive suites have been given balconies, but the corner 'Superior' rooms boast the most stunning views (particularly those on the upper floors), thanks to their large windows on two sides; these can be opened wide, but take care as there is no protective rail. Few

more entrancing views exist in Kerala than those of Fort Cochin's picturesque waterfront from the upper bedrooms of the Malabar Hotel. Far below, looking like toy boats and sometimes accompanied by schools of dolphins, vessels of all types constantly ply to and fro.

The hotel possesses three restaurants, all on the ground floor: **Rice Boats** for seafood, the **Jade Pavilion** for Chinese cuisine and the **Waterfront Café**, a 24 hour restaurant serving Indian and continental dishes; food and drink can also be ordered beside the hotel swimming pool. Unfortunately, the pool has not been given a lakeside setting, which would have made it quite sensational; instead, the waterfront of the Malabar is reserved for private functions held on the lawns. The hotel's **Sao Gabriel Bar** is one of the best appointed in Kerala, albeit one of the most expensive. It is expected that a boat service for guests will soon be in operation between the Malabar's private jetty and that of its sister hotel, the Taj Residency, across the lake in Ernakulam.

Owing to its desirability, the Malabar is often fully booked and, in any case, not all can afford its tariff; however, just half a mile (1km) to the south is the **Casino Hotel**, with 70 luxuriously fitted, air-conditioned rooms and two excellent restaurants, its thatched sea-

Kodaikanal
Astrophysical Laboratory,
Observatory Road
Open Friday 10.00am - 12noon and
3.00 - 5.00pm

Flora and Fauna Museum (Sacred
Heart College), Law's Ghat Road
Open Monday to Saturday,
10.00am - 12noon
and 3.00 - 5.00pm

Cochin
Hill Palace Museum (Tripunithura)
Open: Tuesday to Sunday 9.00am -
12.30pm and 2.00-4.30pm.
Mattancherry Palace
Open: Saturday to Thursday
10am - 5pm.

Mattancherry Synagogue
Open: Sunday to Friday
10am - 12pm and 3 - 5pm.

Ernakulam
Parishath Thampuram Museum
(Durbar Hall), Durbar Hall Road.
Open: Tuesday to Sunday
10am - 12.30pm and 2.00 - 4.30pm

Museum of Kerala History (Edapally)
Open: Tuesday to Sunday
10.00am - 12noon and
2.00 - 4.00pm.

Hill Palace Museum (Tripunitura)
Open: Tuesday to Sunday
10.00am - 4.30pm

*Making of coir rope from coconut fibre in the old-fashioned way is
demonstrated to tourists in the backwater villages.*

food restaurant, set beside the swimming pool, having built up quite a reputation in South India. The Casino Group attaches great importance to all its swimming pools, and the Casino's at Cochin is one of the finest in the region. Visits to the Lakshadweep Islands can be arranged at the Casino, which is a sister hotel of the Bangaram Island Resort, the only location on the islands where foreigners are permitted to stay. The hotel's boat leaves from the nearby Casino Jetty to transport guests to another of its sister hotels Coconut Lagoon, at Kumarakom.

Unfortunately, due to lack of demand, flights between Trivandrum and Cochin were terminated in 1996, and appear unlikely to be resumed. This is particularly inconvenient for tourists wishing to travel between India's most popular beach resorts, at Kovalam and Goa, as they must now make their way overland from Kovalam to Cochin airport, a 5-hour journey by road or train.

Ernakulam

Ferries cross the lake regularly to Ernakulam's **Main Jetty** from Fort Cochin's **Customs Jetty** and Willingdon Island's **Embarkation Jetty**. Although short, both journeys are a constant delight, particularly as Fort Cochin is approached. In the opposite direction, the modernity of Ernakulam is immediately apparent as multi-storey blocks gradually dominate its skyline.

Ernakulam is Cochin's commercial centre, and here will be found hotels and restaurants in all grades, together with the usual Indian shops and bazaars – however, not much is likely to be of great interest to tourists. On the waterfront, just north of the jetty, rises the **Taj Residency**, matching the usual Taj standards of luxury and service, and providing the best food in Ernakulam. However, as the hotel is primarily intended for Indian businessmen, no swimming pool was incorporated, a disadvantage that, because of the growth of tourism, it is planned to overcome shortly – check the up to date situation.

Two hotels that do have pools are the **Presidency**, to the north, near Ernakulam Town Railway Station on Parvamara Road, and the **Abad Plaza**, located half way down the main shopping street, M.G. Road. The Abad Plaza has a rooftop pool, rare in India, from which there are great views over the town. However, a hotel swimming club has been formed and no males, even those accompanied by their wives, are allowed anywhere near the pool between 6pm and 7pm – even though some of the ladies apparently swim at that time in wet suits just in case the regulation is accidentally breached! As male as well as female tourists frequently like to cool off in the early evening after a hard day's sightseeing, and have almost certainly not been told about this rule when checking in, it is hardly surprising that some disappointment is created.

Apart from restaurants located within the hotels, the most popular in Ernakulam is the **Pandhal**, in M.G. Road, almost facing the Grand Hotel. Operated by the Casino Group, the restaurant is very western in appearance, serving fast food (but not breakfasts) as well as north Indian specialities; its dessert menu is unusually imaginative.

The **KTDC Tourist Information Centre** stands beside a children's park, close to the Taj Residency: from here, tours can be booked and information obtained about the locality. Marine Drive leads northward from the Taj Residency, providing the town's most popular lakeside promenade. Ahead, the **Sealord Boat Jetty** is the boarding point for the half-day city tours already referred to. Beside it, the floating **Ancient Mariner Restaurant** is a delightful venue for al fresco refreshment. It seems, however, that few clients are expected at lunchtime, as then most dishes on the menu are 'off', and really exotic items such as cold mineral water have to be obtained from elsewhere – but only after an un-Indian fuss has been made.

Behind the jetty, the **GCDA Shopping Centre**, a modern development, incorporates the **Indian Performing Arts Centre**, one of three important venues in Ernakulam for Kathakali dancing. Marine Drive ends at the jetty for ferries to Vypeen Island, and further along, to Bolgatty Island (High Court Jetty). Four blocks inland from the Vypeen Island jetty, Banerji Road skirts Ernakulam's **market**, the most vivacious sector of the town.

A large roundabout, Jose Junction, where Durbar Hall Road crosses MG Road, serves as a landmark at the south end of Ernakulam. Immediately west of the roundabout, on Durbar Hall Road, the **Parishath Thanipuram Museum** (closed Monday) occupies the former Durbar Hall. Exhibits include models of Hindu temples, sculptures, coins, Mogul paintings, copies of murals and memorabilia of Cochin's maharajas.

Those who wish to take a bus from this part of Ernakulam to Fort Cochin (particularly after the ferries have stopped running) will find the appropriate Bus Stand on MG Road, just south of Jose Junction. Occupying the same building, which overlooks the roundabout on its south-east curve, are the **Bimbi** fast food and **Khyber** restaurants, the latter, on the first floor, offering Mogul, Chinese and Continental cuisines. A short distance to the east is the highly recommended, medium price range **Hotel Joyland**, with a rooftop restaurant.

From Jose Junction, follow Durbar Hall Road eastward to

Chittoor Road, which runs southward, parallel with MG Road. Soon reached is the Ernakulam South Bus Stand (the KSRTC Central Bus Station is a mile (1.5 km) distant, to the north). **The See India Foundation**, at Kalathil Parambil Lane, lies to the south, and performances of Kathakali 'with clear explanations' are given here every evening on the building's rooftop. Around 500 yards (450m) to the south, just past the MG Road / Sahodaran Ayapan Road junction, the **Cochin Cultural Centre** also gives Kathakali performances, but in a theatre designed as a temple courtyard; although not open air, the building is air-conditioned.

Returning northward, Durbar Hall Road ends at Ernakulam Junction Railway Station. Caravara Road, which fronts the station, has several hotels in the medium and lower price ranges, including the modern, fully air-conditioned **Metropolitan** and the **Paulson Park**, both of which can be recommended.

At Edapally, 5 miles (8 km) north of Ernakulam, the **Museum of Kerala History and its Makers** portrays, by the use of models, the history of the area covered by the present state. A 60 minute recorded commentary in English is given.

Of greater interest to most, however, will be the **Hill Palace Museum**, at Tripunitura, 8 miles (13 km) to the south-east. This is the palace of the maharajas of the former Cochin state. Long flights of steps lead up to the building through its rather unkempt, terraced grounds. Inside there are splendid examples of wood carving, paintings, photographs and the maharajas' throne.

Absolutely not to be missed are the half-day backwater excursions from Ernakulam in small 'dugout' vessels, powered by a bamboo pole, which are able to penetrate the narrowest of canals. Those who make the long backwater journey on motorized vessels from Quilon to Alleppey usually find that the more intimate nature of these trips gives even greater pleasure. Stops are made to observe village life which includes a market, coir rope-making, prawn farming and toddy tapping. Shimmering blue skies, parrot-green palm trees and the multi-coloured silk saris always worn by the women, combine to produce a blinding kaleidoscope of colour. Once again, however, it will probably be the huge eyes and welcoming smiles of the children that will linger longest in the memory. Both KTDC and Visit India operate these tours, the latter picking up clients from any hotel in the area.

Vypeen Island

Approximately 16 miles (25km) long, **Vypeen Island** is most easily reached by ferry from the boat jetty beside the Chinese fishing nets at Fort Cochin, a

Above: Once the palace of Cochin's rajas, the Hill Palace Museum, just outside Cochin, displays royal treasures. *Below*: Bolgatty Palace, on Bolgatty Island, just off Ernakulam's waterfront, is now operated as a hotel.

10 minute cruise; it can also be approached from Ernakulam's jetty at the end of Marine Drive, as already mentioned, and from Willingdon Island's Embarkation Jetty, by the ferry that continues to Fort Cochin. The straight road from south to north provides the island's main route for buses; however, these stop just about everywhere and take an hour to reach **Cherai** where the best beach in the Cochin region is to be found. Only a few buses continue from Cherai to the beach, and it is much more convenient to travel there by auto-rickshaw from the jetty; ensure that arrangements are made to be collected for the return journey as few auto-rickshaws ply along the beachside road. There is talk of developing Cherai Beach, but as yet only an ice cream parlour has been built. As with most Indian beaches, Big Wave is usually in evidence so care must be taken.

At the northern tip of Vypeen Island, **Palipuram's Fort**, built by the Portuguese in the 16th century, may be visited on Thursdays. Together with Cranganore's now ruined fort across the water on the mainland, this guarded the narrow inlet against enemy vessels, notably pirates.

Bolgatty Island

As well as being part of half-day excursions from Cochin, **Bolgatty Island** may also be reached easily by ferry from Ernakulam's **High Court Jetty.**

The excursion boats tie up at the **Bolgatty Palace Hotel**, but ferries dock a short walking distance away. Ensure that 'Bolgatty Island' is displayed on the vessel as there are occasional services to other islands, their destinations usually identified by signs in Malayalam only.

Built by the Dutch in 1744, the palace later became the British Residency to the Cochin court, and remained so until 1947. The building's architecture in Dutch Kerala style is impressive, as are its six hectares of grounds studded with huge trees. Now an 11-bedroomed hotel operated by KTDC, the former palace is being upgraded. At present, non-residents are welcome to dine in the restaurant and there is a separate refreshment kiosk.

Lakshadweep Islands

Apart from the Andaman and Nicobar Islands, which lie close to Burma, the only coral beaches on Indian territory are to be found in the Lakshadweep Islands located approximately 200 miles (320km) offshore from Cochin. At present foreigners are permitted to visit only **Bangaram**, just one of the 36 islands that make up the archipelago.

Ten of the Lakshadweep Islands are inhabited, the other 26, including Bangaram, do not have sufficient fresh water to support an indigenous population. Together they form the smallest of India's Union Territories, but surprisingly, in spite of their diminutive size, the islands' population totals around 50,000. The islands are not administered by Kerala, though there is no apparent difference between Keralans and the islanders who also (apart from those living in Minicoy) speak the Malayalam language. Minicoy is the most southerly of the islands and its inhabitants, like those of the Maldive Islands to which it is nearest, speak Mahli.

Tradition has it that the first inhabitants of the Lakshadweep Islands were shipwrecked sailors from the Kerala port of Cranganore who decided to settle; all were Hindus but, in the 7th century, Hazrat Abaidullah from Mecca was shipwrecked on the island of Amini, and eventually converted the islanders to Islam.

Although practically all now follow the Muslim religion, the Hindu traditions of caste according to trade, and inheritance down the female line, have been maintained. It was not until the 16th century that the Laccadive Islands, as the Lakshadweep were then known, came under Muslim rule – from Cranganore. In 1783, Tipu Sultan controlled the islands but, following his defeat in 1799, the East India Company took over in the administration.

There are four prime reasons for visiting the islands: the powdery coral beaches of white sand protected from waves by reefs; the clear-as-gin water; the opportunity to observe the vibrantly colourful underwater marine life; and the tranquillity of the unspoilt scenery. Foreign tourists are only permitted to arrive at the islands by air from Cochin airport. It takes a maximum of three days for official clearance to be arranged at Cochin, but most foreigners will have booked the trip before arriving in India, and this clearance procedure will have been completed.

A small plane with a capacity of 35 occupants takes 1 hour 20 minutes to fly to Agatti Airport (3 times a week); from there, a boat docked nearby will arrive at Bangaram Island 1 hour 45 minutes later – a delightful cruise through calm, clear waters of turquoise blue. During the monsoon season, 15 May to 15 September, a helicopter service from Agatti replaces the boat. Unlike most of Kerala's resort hotels, the Bangaram Island Resort does not close during the monsoons, as the rainfall in the Lakshadweep Islands is almost half that of the mainland, usually comprising no more than short-lived, tropical showers.

Tear-shaped Bangaram Island is 128 acres in extent, and it takes little more than one hour to walk around the coastline; nowhere does its height above sea level exceed 3 feet (1m). Apart from the **Bangaram Island Resort**, the only buildings to be seen are the handful of thatched huts that are used for overnight stays by the 50 or so locals who regularly visit Bangaram from the other islands in their fishing boats. As with most coral islands, a palm-fringed lagoon occupies the centre of Bangaram. The Casino Hotel Group operates the Bangaram Island Resort, where the accommodation consists of 30 spacious thatched huts, all comfortably fitted though, as might be expected, there is no television, air-conditioning or running hot water: it is surprising how quickly the lack of those amenities is perceived as an advantage, contributing as it does to the 'Robinson Crusoe in comfort' nature of the holiday. Indian and continental buffets are served in the enormous thatched restaurant – the hotel's 'swimming pool' can be either the lagoon or the calm Lakshadweep Sea, whichever is preferred.

Bangaram Island is ideal for all who seek tranquillity, but for underwater sport enthusiasts it is a paradise, with facilities for scuba diving, snorkelling and deep sea fishing – marlin, barracuda, tuna – laid on by the hotel. Also provided is a glass-bottomed boat, instruction in scuba diving at the **Poseidon Neptune School**, and boats that visit one of the three even smaller islands that share the atoll with Bangaram (Tirmakara, Parali 1 and Parali 2). Lying within the same atoll are a wrecked ship and a submerged former British vessel, the *Princess Royal* with five cannon, that went down in 1795 whilst under French ownership. Its bell has been recovered and is displayed in the hotel's bar; the ship's logbook is in the possession of the Royal Naval Museum at Greenwich. Both wrecks may be visited.

Note that it is a punishable offence to break off pieces of coral, protection of the Lakshadweep environment being rigorously enforced; this is one of the reasons why foreign tourists are not permitted to visit other islands in the group, nor may they join the luxury cruises run from Cochin as these are restricted to Indians only.

NORTH KERALA AND TAMIL NADU HILL STATIONS

Although only one third of Kerala's area has yet been described, relatively few tourists visit much of the remainder of the state. This is undoubtedly because the beach resorts of Kovalam and Varkala, the Periyar Wildlife Sanctuary, Munnar and Cochin – Kerala's touristic highlights – lie in the south, relatively close to each other and to the international airport of Trivandrum. However, those with time available, particularly if travelling between Kerala and Karnataka, will find that there is still much of interest to be seen, and if the massive beach resort development planned for Bakel goes ahead the whole picture is likely to change dramatically.

Cranganore (Kodungalloor)

Shortly after leaving Ernakulam, National Highway 17 branches westward and follows the coastline. Standing at the northern point of Vembanad Lake, **Cranganore**, known to the Ancient

Greeks as Muziris, was once a trading port of significance, but this ended in 1341 when the town's deep water entrance to the sea was blocked during the great storm that opened up Cochin harbour. Although Cranganore centre has little of tourist appeal, its surroundings are well worth exploring; an overnight stay, however, is not recommended, due to the town's lack of suitable accommodation. If a taxi is hired, ensure that the driver knows the area and comprehends which locations are sought as this is not 'tourist territory'.

On the way to Cranganore, the 600 year-old Shiva **Temple of Tiruvanchikulam** merits a visit, primarily for its ancient *padipuram*, an impressive form of carved entranceway that preceded the *gopuram* in Hindu temple architecture. Probably because so few non-Hindu tourists come to the Cranganore region, those that do are not prevented from entering this temple – a welcome novelty in Kerala which, one hopes, will eventually become the norm elsewhere in the state.

An important dynasty, the Cheramans, ruled from Cranganore until the 7th century, and what is believed to be the site of their palace, passed en route to the Portuguese Fort, is commemorated by a small white pyramid erected on open land.

Opposite: Bakel Beach is earmarked for Kerala's number one tourist development.

Standing on Cranganore's headland which juts into the Arabian Sea are vestiges of **Kottapuram Fort**, erected by the Portuguese in 1523 to guard the narrow inlet (together with the fort on Vypeen Island, which it faces). Only a stretch of wall and a small gunpowder store have survived, but the location is extremely beautiful and well worth a visit. It was here that the Periyar River flooded in 1341, its alluvial deposits blocking up the inlet and making it impossible for large ships to enter and berth. Until this natural phenomenon occurred, Cranganore had been the busiest port on the west coast of India. Legend has it that St. Thomas landed nearby in AD 52 to begin his missionary work in India.

Until 1980, it was worth making a detour to see the **Cheraman Mosque**, founded in AD 629 by a disciple of Prophet Muhamad, Malik-bin-Dinar, whilst en route to Sri Lanka. Allegedly, this was the first mosque to be built in India; however, its ancient facade, which was more Hindu than Muslim architecturally, has recently been replaced by a sugary confection flanked by minarets. Apparently some earlier work survives within, but this cannot be seen by non-Muslims and a visit for them is no longer worthwhile. It seems strange that unlike the Muslims in north India, who protect their ancient architectural heritage with loving care, those who live in the south appear to have little interest in the past, iconoclastically tearing down practically all their ancient mosques and replacing them with new work for the sake of expansion and modernity. Regrettably, it is now too late to save most of the country's earliest Islamic buildings, all of which had been built on the Malabar coast.

Half way between Cranganore and Trichur, the small town of **Irinjalakuda** possesses what is believed to be the only temple in India dedicated to Bharata, brother of Rama. Approximately 2000 years old, the temple is entered from a splendid *padipuram*. Immediately ahead is the *mandapam* hall, its columns unusually decorated with frescoes.

Trichur (Thrissur)

The route now approaches the great central plain of Kerala. Inland there are no cooling heights, hazy, far-distant mountains delineating the south and north ends respectively of the Western Ghats and the Southern Ghats. As may be guessed, the build-up of heat between the two mountain ranges is intense, and the temperatures reached on an annual basis are the highest in India – there is no cool season here. In consequence, those considering a journey inland are advised either to pay the 100 per cent supplement for hiring an air-conditioned car – or to give the region a miss. It

must be said that for most, a brief overnight stop at Trichur before continuing northward to Calicut will prove a better option.

Trichur is located on the west coast railway line which passes through Irinjalakuda but not Cranganore, from where direct buses must be taken. It is the main centre of Kerala's cultural activities, and three state academies are based in the town. Unless visiting Trichur during the April/May Pooram Festival, or in mid-January when the first stage of the 'Great Elephant March' takes place, for non-Hindus a stay of one night will suffice, as there is little of interest to be seen in the town for them. Once the capital city of Cochin state, Trichur was taken by the Zamorin and later Tipu Sultan before falling to the British, who anglicized its original name Trissivaperur (Town named after Shiva).

Trichur's famous **Vadakunathan Temple**, dedicated to Shiva, stands on the brow of a hillock around which streets have been laid out for trade. According to tradition, the temple was founded by Parasurama, who is also credited with creating the entire state of Kerala. There is exquisite carving in Keralan style inside, where non-Hindus are not permitted to enter. During the Pooram Festival, more than 100 caparisoned elephants are paraded outside the temple, and in the evening, what has been described as the most elaborate firework display in Asia takes place – lasting until dawn! A version of the elephant parade is now held annually for tourists on 9 January, as few come to face Trichur's debilitating heat in late April. The barren hillock on which the temple stands is known as 'The Round'; it was formerly covered with trees, and an attempt is being made to reintroduce a few. Surprisingly, in view of the fame of its temple, Trichur also has two splendid churches: **Rutanpali**, the most central, and **Our Lady of Lourdes Cathedral**, on St Thomas College Road. **St Thomas College**, a rare example in India of the European Baroque style, has an impressive dome.

To the north, Museum Road starts at the **Town Hall**, a delightful neo-classical building, typical of British colonial architecture at its restrained best. Immediately opposite, the **Government Guest House** is one of Kerala's most comfortable. Further east are grouped together the **State Museum**, the **Zoo** and the **Archaeological Museum** (closed Mondays), though none of them of much interest to foreign visitors.

South of the town, in the vicinity of the railway station and the KSRTC Bus Stand will be found the **Casino Hotel** (no connection with Cochin's Casino Group), rated the best in Trichur. A new 60-bedroom block has been built, and the management gives assurance that the long-projected swimming pool will soon be constructed.

Although the food is acceptable, the hotel's restaurant itself is depressing, mainly because, as with so many Indian hotel restaurants, the curtains are kept drawn throughout the day.

A short distance from Trichur is **Elephant Lodge** (Punatoor Kota). Here, 40 temple elephants are watered and fed. However, this does not provide the impressive spectacle that might be expected; each beast is tethered separately, and swings constantly from side to side – apparently the sign of a bored elephant. There is a bathing pool for the tuskers, but bathing times are variable.

Easily reached by train or bus from Trichur, **Guruvayoor** lies 18 miles (28kms) away to the north west. Its **Krishna Temple** is one of the most sacred Hindu centres in India but, as at Trichur, non-Hindus may not enter. Similarly, and once again like Trichur, nothing of architectural interest can be seen of the temple from its exterior. In view of this, many non-Hindu foreign visitors will only find it worthwhile to visit the town during its 10 day Ulsavom Festival (February/March), when there are elephant processions and an elephant race to mark the beginning of the celebrations.

Enthusiasts of Kathakali dancing may like to visit the town of **Cheruthuruthi**, which lies approximately 20 miles (32km) due north of Trichur, from which it can be reached by train or bus. Here is based

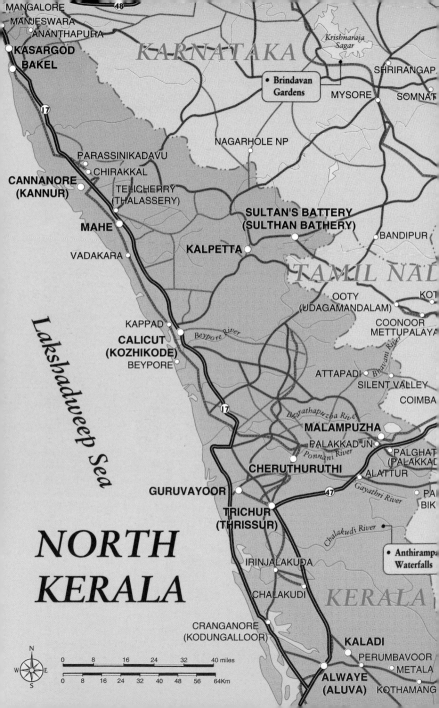

Kerala Kalamandalam, a dance training centre where, following its establishment in 1927 by the Keralan poet Sri Vallathol, the rebirth of Kathakali dancing took place. Visitors are admitted to watch and photograph training sessions Monday-Friday, but not 12.00- 3.30pm, a rest period. The centre also closes on all public holidays, in addition to 31 March and 15 June and it is worth checking the current situation locally before making the journey. Occasional performances are also given in the evening; one of these, on 26 January, is particulartly convenient for many tourists.

Trichur to Malampuzha

As has already been said, there is no great reason why foreign tourists should proceed eastward into the burning hot, flat interior of central Kerala, but those who wish to, or need to, can reach Malampuzha and Coimbatore direct from Cheruthuruthi without returning to Trichur, thereby shortening the journey considerably; however, the more usual approach is via National Highway 47 direct from Trichur. Alternatively, if Malampuzha is not on the itinerary and the destination is Coimbatore, a much more attractive route, albeit slower, is to follow the Calicut to Palghat road, and branch north eastward from it at Mannarkkad, proceeding through the Western Ghats and the beautiful Silent Valley Wildlife Sanctuary. From both Trichur and Cheruthuruthi, Mannarkkad can be reached via Shoranur, Pattambi and Perintalmanna.

Palghat (Palakkad) is reputedly the hotspot of this torrid region, and few will wish to explore it on foot outside the cooler early morning/early evening periods. Around Palghat, an abundance of flat land, irrigated by rivers to the north and south, has resulted in an extensive area of paddyfields that form the 'rice bowl' of Kerala. A centrally located fort, built by Hyder Ali in 1766, is the town's only point of tourist interest. It has been well cared for, and although partly converted to administrative offices the remainder can be explored by visitors.

Malampuzha lies off National Highway 47, 9 miles (14km) north of Palghat. It is picturesquely surrounded by the foothills of the Western Ghats, and spreads along the south shore of a large lake formed by damming the Bharathappuzha River. As will have been seen, it is common in Kerala for the tourist potential of dams to be developed, and Malampuzha is one of the most popular examples. Indian families come from far and wide to boat on the lake, picnic on its shores, stroll through the terraced gardens and gasp at the illuminations. The greatest attraction at Malampuzha, however, is its **cable car**, the only example in south India; this can transport 400 passengers per hour between a point known as Hermits End, just below the Government Guest House, and the Garden House Hotel, on the opposite side of the dam.

All this is heady stuff for the locals, and understandably so, but it will not greatly impress foreign tourists. However, those who find it convenient to spend a night at the town are advised to stay at the **Hotel Govardhana**, which also serves the best food in Malampuzha, usually al fresco on the delightful lawns. There is no swimming pool as few foreigners stay in the town. The **Garden House Hotel**, run by KTDC, is rather dilapidated, but there is a friendly bar, and the receptionist (in 1996) was far more knowledgeable and helpful than the staff at the official Tourist Office in the town centre – this had many staff but few of them spoke English and none could provide useful information about the region or answer queries.

Buses run from Malampuzha to the Tamil Nadu hill resort of Ooty, but it is a tiring 8 hour journey, and the visitor is thereby deprived of a trip on the famous 'toy train', which chugs slowly up the mountains to south India's highest resort. This leaves Mettupalayam, its starting point, at 7.40am, enabling visitors to arrive at Ooty by mid-day, allowing 3 hours in the town if a return has to be made on the same day. From April to mid-June, the high season for Indian tourists, there is an additional train, which leaves Mettupalayam for Ooty at 9.10am, returning from Ooty at 2.00pm. Check that all the train times quoted are current. Alternatively a connecting train, *The Nilgiri Express*, leaves Coimbatore for Mettupalayam at an unsociable 6.30am; tourists can decide, therefore, whether to stay at Mettupalayam (more convenient) or Coimbatore.

Coimbatore is reached from Malampuzha either directly by car, or by train via Palakkad Junction, or by bus via Palghat. Frequent trains and buses connect Coimbatore with Mettupalayam.

Coimbatore

This cotton-manufacturing town lies in the plains, but bus journeys from here to the hill stations of Tamil Nadu soon begin their ascent. There is absolutely nothing of tourist interest in **Coimbatore** unless the visitor is in urgent need of a cotton shirt, the town speciality. Conveniently located near the station in Davey & Co. Lane are a group of hotels in the economy class; recommended are the **Anaud Vikar** and the **Sivakami**. Not too far away, on Racecourse Road, is the **Surya International Hotel**, Coimbatore's most luxurious.

Near both the Gandhipuram Bus Stand and the State Bus Stand, north of the town centre, is the **Hotel City Tower**, slightly cheaper than the Surya International, but also air-conditioned; it has two very good restaurants, vegetarian and non-vegetarian. Due to its situation opposite the station, many will prefer the **Hotel Thaai** where the food is excellent, particularly the tandooris.

Coimbatore is an important rail junction, with services not only to Mettupalayam but also to Calicut, Madras, Bangalore, Cochin and Cape Comorin. Buses also serve the first three of these destinations, in addition to Mysore and Trichy; it is best, whenever possible, to reserve a seat in advance. Those proceeding by train from Coimbatore to Cochin may find the midnight *Tea Garden Express* convenient – but book a sleeper in advance if possible; there is no night train in the reverse direction.

Mettupalayam is an equally uninteresting town but, as has been said, more conveniently located for reaching Ooty. The **Surya International Hotel**, near the station, can be recommended; **Jenny's Residency** is another tourist class establishment.

Ooty (Udagamandalam or Ootacamund)

Ooty, created by the British early in the 19th century as a hot season retreat for their Madras administrators, soon became the most popular of Tamil Nadu's hill resorts, as well as its highest, at 7,280ft (2,240m). Because of the altitude, temperatures can fall to minus 2 ° C in the cool season, and warm clothing should be taken. Frost often occurs at night in mid-winter, but it never snows.

Although Ooty is higher than Kodaikanal it is generally much sunnier, as well as being far more appealing.

Those who knew Ooty some years ago bemoan the spread of bungalows over the green swards of the uplands; however, the mountain peaks are still dramatic. The highest, **Mount Dodabetta** is also, at 8,640ft (2,623m), the highest point in Tamil Nadu. Fortunately for tourists, a road now climbs up to its summit, which is known as The Peak. From Ooty, the journey takes no more than 20 minutes by car, passing through a forest of tall eucalyptus trees as the summit is approached. Magnificent views on all sides are usually at their clearest in the morning; a telescope house may be visited for a small fee.

In spring, a gigantic species of gorse covers the mountain top with its yellow blossom. Many will note that almost all the open land around Ooty has been terraced; this is so that as much space as possible can be made available for growing vegetables, which thrive in the cool climate. It is amusing to be offered a 'bouquet' of splendid

The 'Toy Train' to Ooty

For most overseas tourists, the spectacular train journey to the resort from Mettupalayam frequently proves as great an attraction as the town itself. An unbelievably small steam locomotive climbs ever upward, pushing the cream and blue carriages forward, often at walking pace, across ravines, through tunnels and along switchback track, hugging the steep mountain slopes, and passing rushing streams and waterfalls.

Train enthusiasts will note that the central cog is dog-toothed to serve as a brake where the gradient is particularly steep. Between the carriages (usually a maximum of five) are external platforms on which sit brakemen, each of whom can operate the brakes, and also act as the 'eyes' of the driver; they pass instructions to proceed ahead or stop down the line by displaying either a green or a red flag. The engine pushes uphill but pulls downhill.

Passengers might like to bear in mind that the most spectacular views are to the west. Those on route to Ooty should therefore take a seat on the left-hand side and from Ooty the right-hand side. Each train has one first class carriage: in the front for the up journey, at the rear for the down. Seven vintage steam engines are maintained, all of them built in Switzerland in the 1920s. The line was completed in 1887, and without it Ooty could never have been developed as the only alternative method of supplying the town with goods before the motor car age was by ox cart, a slow business at such a height. There are no toilets on the train, but several lengthy stops are made at stations, many of which have comforting English names such as Wellington and Runnymede. On Saturdays and Sundays, a sightseers' 'Heritage' diesel train with large viewing windows, leaves Ooty at 10.00am to Coonoor, arriving back at Ooty at 4pm.

The journey from Mettupalayam to Ooty takes about 4 hours 30 minutes – an hour less for the return. Just after the half way point between Mettupalayam and Ooty has been reached a stop is made at Coonoor where since 1966, the steam engine has been replaced by a diesel for the remainder of the journey. From Coonoor, the scenery gradually become less spectacular.

carrots by street vendors, rather than the usual tropical fruits. Also terraced, immediately below Dodabetta, is Ooty's famous **Botanical Garden**, laid out in 1840; its May flower show is an important local event. Government House was added at its far end 40 years later, and serves as the governor's residence when he is staying in the town.

To the south west, **Reflections Lake** is skirted at its east end by the 'toy train' railway track, giving passengers a pleasant introduction to the town. The narrow lake is 2 miles (3km) long, and boats may be hired from the Tourist Café.

Below the Railway Station is the Bus Stand, from where services follow many routes through the **Nilgiri Hills**. Adjacent to this is the track where horse racing takes place in April and June. The commercial centre of Ooty, created by the junction of three roads, is still known, surprisingly, as Charing Cross. It is only a 10 minute walk from the railway station to Commercial Road, the main shopping street, which ends at Charing Cross. Here the not particularly useful Tourist Office and several medium-grade hotels are located: **Hotel Nahar**, with its two restaurants, is good value, as is the more up-market **Hotel Khems** nearby on Shoreham Palace Road. Recently opened are the **Holiday Inn** and **Gem Park**, both of which can be recommended.

South of the lake, the **Fernhill Palace**, a former summer palace of the maharajas of Mysore has been operated as a hotel by the Taj Group since 1990. In south India, unlike the north, only a handful of royal palaces have been remodelled as hotels and, until recently, the Fernhill offered a rare opportunity to sample the exquisite luxury once enjoyed by India's princes. However, in 1997 the hotel was closed pending much-needed refurbishment, and its reopening date is uncertain. Most of the building dates from reconstruction by the maharaja in 1884, its pride being the galleried ballroom, with a barrel vault ceiling and exquisite papier maché decoration. Also operated by the Taj Group is the **Hotel Savoy**, west of the Charing Cross area, on Sylks Road; this is Ooty's most atmospheric hotel, accommodation being in separate bungalows, some of them 1920s vintage, with period fittings to match. In winter, wood fires are lit in the bedrooms at sundown when temperatures fall dramatically. The hotel's bar, Logan's Lounge, is named to honour a popular British administrator (collector), who did much to help the local people. Logan apparently spoke and wrote Tamil perfectly, a rare achievement for a foreigner.

Close to the Savoy is the **Ooty Club**, occupying premises built in 1832 for Sir William Rumbold.

Many snooker enthusiasts would like to pay homage to the club's billiard room, where a plaque on the wall records that the game of snooker was first played on its tables; however, it is necessary to be invited by a club member in order to gain admission.

Buses leave Ooty for various destinations including Coonoor, Coimbatore, Palghat, Hassan, Mysore, Bangalore, Madras, Cape Comorin, Kodaikanal and Sultan's Battery.

Coonoor

Situated at 6,000ft (1,850m), about 1,300ft (400m) lower than Ooty, **Coonoor** is also designated a hill station resort. It can be reached by bus from Ooty or Coimbatore in addition to the 'toy train'. Although not as large as Ooty, its town centre is similarly commercial, but the more sedate Upper Coonoor, where the better hotels are sited, is easily reached. It may have been noted that the Taj Group seems to prefer elevated positions for their resort hotels wherever possible, and Coonoor's **Taj Garden Retreat** is no exception. As may be expected, this hotel offers by far the best accommodation and cuisine in the town, and its guests can appreciate much of the former charm of a south Indian hill resort. An alternative recommended location in Coonoor for dining is the **Blue Hill Restaurant**.

Kotagiri

Regular buses link Coonoor with the village of **Kotagiri**, located 17 miles (28km) to the east, at approximately the same altitude. This is now tea plantation land, and the region offers splendid walks. In spite of being the smallest of this group of hill resorts, Kotagiri is, in fact, the oldest of them, having been founded in 1819. Highly recommended for its relaxation is the **Queenshill Christian Guesthouse** which, although not a luxury hotel, has comfortable rooms and excellent home cooking. Frequent buses link the village with Ooty and Mettupalayam as well as Coonoor.

Sultan's Battery (Sulthan Bathery), Wynad

A scenic, although fairly straight road heads north west from Ooty to the small town of **Sultan's Battery**, 62 miles (100km) distant and located just within Kerala. The name of Sultan's Battery commemorates Tipu Sultan, who erected a fort here in the 18th century. It lies in the Wynad district of Kerala, where India's second most extensive wildlife sanctuary (132 square miles – 337 sq.km)) was established in 1973. Wynad has an extensive tribal population and a Jain community, now rare in India, which has nine temples. Much of the area is a plateau, averaging 2,000ft (615m) in height. In addition to possessing extensive wildlife, Wynad is important agriculturally, its crops including cardamom, coffee, pepper, rubber and tea. Rice, however, is the most important crop: the name Wynad means 'land of paddy fields'. Accommodation is available in Sultan's Battery at the **Government Guest House**. Good roads link Sultan's Battery north-westward with Cannanore and south-westward with Calicut. As the Calicut road descends to the plain, signs request visitors 'not to disturb the monkeys', but it is more likely to be the monkeys who do the disturbing, by cadging food from any motorist stopping to take their photograph.

An alternative route from Ooty to Kerala's west coast may be taken by returning to Coimbatore and then following the fast road via Palghat, or the slightly longer, but magnificent road through **Silent Valley**, which is the last remaining area of primeval rain forest of any size to survive in India. There are idyllic views of the valley from the road, which is kept open 24 hours a day, in spite of the abundance of elephants and big cats. As usual, the only realistic chance of seeing them is around dawn or late in the evening; great care should be taken after nightfall in case a wild elephant wanders on to the road – such an event is best avoided.

Situated at the end of Silent Valley is the tribal centre of Attapadi, on the Bhavani River. Only tribal peoples are permitted to live in the reserve; most are very dark-skinned, wear bright-coloured clothing and can be immediately identified by other Keralans, although most tourists will be hard put to distinguish them. The road is quite high, and the delightful views continue across the valley to the mountainous peaks opposite. At Mannarkkad, the main road from Palghat is joined, and the scenery gradually becomes less dramatic as the coastal plain is reached.

Those who have not made the inland excursions detailed here can proceed directly northward from Trichur to Calicut by rail or road. Nothing of great interest is passed on route, although Kottakkal is renowned for ayurvedic treatments.

Calicut (Kozhikode)

Calicut is a pleasant enough town, but considering the important role it has played in Kerala's history, surprisingly little of tourist interest remains. Portuguese bombardment in 1510, followed by Tipu Sultan's assault in 1789, ensured that nothing of architectural importance prior to British rule in 1791 survived. The airport is at Karipur, 14 miles (23km) from the town centre. It should be noted that Calicut marks the point at which Kerala's auto-rickshaw drives become completely honest, a great point

Above: Working elephants are a common sight throughout Kerala. *Below*: Painted coffered ceilings are a feature of Kerala's ancient buildings. This example is within the gateway to the Chirakkal Temple.

of local pride. Miraculously, meters work – even for tourists – throughout virtually all of north Kerala, and no visitors need think twice about using auto-rickshaws.

In ancient times, Calicut was the busiest port on the Malabar coast, the Phoenicians and Greeks dealing there in spices and the coarse, hand-woven cloth known as calico. Arabs trading with Calicut in the 7th century are believed to have been responsible for the introduction of Islam to the sub-continent, many of them settling on the Malabar coast, intermarrying with the locals and becoming known as Mappilas. Their skill in seamanship was instrumental in successfully defending Calicut's Zamorin Rajas against invaders. Allegedly Cheraman Perumal, the last ruler of united Kerala, sailed to Jeddah to meet the Prophet Muhamad, who converted him to Islam. He then married the sister of Malik bin Dinar, founder of the mosque at Cranganore, and changed his name to Tajud-din. It is said that the Cranganore sailors who were shipwrecked on the Lakshadweep Islands, staying to become their first inhabitants, were seeking Cheraman Perumal, ignorant of his pilgrimage to Jeddah.

From the 13th century, Calicut was the headquarters of the Samoothiri (Lords of the Sea) Rajas. When Vasco da Gama landed at nearby Kappad Beach in 1498, the Raja first treated him with hospitality, envisaging a new trading partner, but the Portuguese had ambitions of conquest, and their fleet attacked the city in 1509 and 1510, being repulsed on both occasions. The Portuguese called the Samoothiri Rajas the Zamorin, and the dynasty is generally referred to as such.

Calicut's Malayalam name, Kozhikode, is believed to have derived from the Zamorin's palace of **Koyil Kotta**. The building has survived, 4 miles (6km) north of the city centre, but is now dilapidated and accommodates the Meenchanda English Medium High School: only historical enthusiasts will find a visit worthwhile. The Dutch, as usual, came after the Portuguese, and a brief period of French occupation followed before the British took over.

Cotton is still an important industry in Calicut, but most is now printed, and spices, coconuts and timber are the main exports. The city centre, **Mananchira Square**, comprises a large park, formerly Ansari Park, with its rectangular tank (*chira*) fed by a spring which still provides much of Calicut's water supply. The square is overlooked by the town hall, the library, the CSI Church and two hotels, KTDC's **Malabar Mansion** and the **Malabar Palace**. Behind the Malabar Mansion is the **Paramount Tower Hotel**; its rooftop restaurant specializes in barbecues, and the view towards the Arabian Sea is splendid, especially at sunset – which is no doubt why this restaurant is called Sunset Point. Strangely, Calicut's three museums are located at **Seat Hill**, 3 miles (5km) from Mananchira Square; none, however, is worth a special trip, except perhaps by those older visitors who recall the 'neutral' posing of white-haired Krishna Menon, India's former representative at the United Nations: the **Krishna Menon Museum** exhibits memorabilia of the statesman. Adjacent are the **Pazhassirajah Museum** of archaeological finds, and the **Art Gallery**, with western-style paintings by Raja Ravi Varma and Raja Raja Varma.

Calicut's beach, one mile (2 km) west of the town, has been provided with a children's park by the local Lions Club, but in spite of a lighthouse and two piers it is not particularly inviting. On occasions, early risers can see dolphins at play from **Dolphin's Point. The Seaqueen Hotel**, which faces the sea, serves good sea-food, albeit in a depressingly darkened restaurant: avoid its lunchtime gloom. Seaqueen is a medium-price range hotel with some of its rooms air-conditioned.

Mention should be made of Calicut's **Government Guest House**, by far the best in Kerala – perhaps because (a rarity in India) it is managed by a woman! Since 1997, Calicut's hotel and dining scene has been transformed by the arrival of the brand new **Taj Residency Hotel**, built around a swimming pool –

the only hotel pool in the city – and with extensive gardens. It is located a short distance from the lighthouse end of the beach, and is far and away Calicut's most luxurious venue.

Almost 10 miles (16km) north of Calicut is the small fishing beach of **Kappad**, where Vasco da Gama landed in 1498. No doubt there will be some local commemoration in 1998, the 500th anniversary of the event. Buses from Calicut to Kappad are numerous, but as few of them continue to the beach, an auto-rickshaw will usually be required. A small white obelisk erected at the beginning of the beach is inscribed 'Vasco da Gama landed here, Kappakadavu (Kappad's original name) in the year 1498'. Obviously, this is not the precise spot, which can no longer be identified. Apparently, when the Portuguese navigator landed, the beach was significantly wider and the trees stood much further back.

A rocky promontory divides the beach into two sections, which initially appear to be great for bathing – not only is there no Big Wave, there are hardly any ripples. All, however, is deceptive: after a few steps have been taken into the calm water, the reason for their calmness is discovered – squelchy black mud. It would appear that the River Bharatappuzha, to the south, deposits alluvial soil at this point, thereby taming the waves but making bathing an unpleasant experience.

A better option for would-be bathers is to make for the town of **Beypore**, situated 7 miles (11 km) south of Calicut on the north bank of the Beypore River, and proceed to the beach immediately beside its creek. Casuarina trees and the river outlet's stone wall, combined with the golden sand, form an attractive vista. It is also possible to swim here in comfort, as the river wall snakes out to sea past the beach, thereby breaking up Big Wave. Further back along the creek is a large boat yard of little interest to most, but which can be visited for a small fee.

An appealing trading town situated on another wide creek 31 miles (50km) north of Calicut, is **Vadakara**. The best part is its Muslim quarter, situated between the railway line and the beach, where lively streets are overlooked by the unusual pointed roofs of the mosque, once, a common feature in north Kerala. The beach would be attractive, but is marred by the higgledy-piggledy blocks of granite which protect the shoreline (as at Varkala) from monsoons.

Mahe, just over 6 miles (10 km) north of Vadakara, has no intrinsic interest except to those in search of cheap beer, due to its historic situation as one of a group of small French enclaves in India – but the only one on the west coast – Mahe is Union Territory. It therefore avoids Kerala's draconian alcohol restrictions. Originally called Mayazhi, the town, with an area of only 2.5 square miles (6 sq. km), was captured in 1725 by the French commander, Mahe de Labourdonnais, and renamed to commemorate him.

The British took Mahe in 1761, but it was returned to the French in 1817 following Napoleon's defeat at Waterloo. Buses stop by the bridge across the creek just before leaving Mahe. A pleasant view is obtained from the hill that overlooks the creek and on which is located a **Government Guest House** with a most helpful manager; this is acceptable for an overnight stay, but as no accommodation in the medium or upper range exists in Mahe, most tourists continue to Telicherry unless bent on a long, cheap binge. Apparently, only one reminder of Mahe's colonial past has survived – its police continue to wear pillbox caps that are indistinguishable from those of French gendarmes.

Telicherry (Thalassery), a fishing town less than 6 miles (10 km) to the north, can hardly be called a tourist centre, but it has a much wider choice of accommodation than Mahe. A few picturesque Mappila houses have survived near the beach, but the town's only building of importance is its **fort**, built by the East India Company in 1708. Unusually for Kerala the beach is protected by a low reef, and swimming is possible as long as the fishing fleet is not in evidence, which it does seem to

Above: The beach at Beypore, outside Calicut, is sheltered by the enclosing wall of the Beypore River. *Below*: Neat tea plantations appear to have been tended by a topiary expert.

be for much of the day, resulting in an overpowering stench of fish, which will appeal to few. **Hotel Pranam**, in the Navangapuram quarter, and the **Paris Presidency** opened in 1994, are considered to be the best hotels in the town.

Those wishing to visit **Mysore** without continuing along Kerala's coastline into Karnataka may follow good roads that lead directly inland to the city. Much time is thus saved, particularly if the temples of Belur and Halebid are not on the schedule.

Cannanore (Kannur)

Apart from a few streets in Fort Cochin and Trivandrum, no urban quarter in Kerala matches the charm of **Cannanore**'s Muslim sector which, combined with the town's clean beach at Payyambalam and the splendid mosques and important temples in the vicinity, make Cannanore and its district one of the most exciting tourist prospects in Kerala. Strangely, it currently receives little promotion from KTDC, which means that those in the know will find the area virtually untouched by tourism.

Many buses and trains connect the town with Telicherry, but private transport, in addition to being more convenient, will enable tourists to make detours to the beaches on route. From Darmadam Railway Station, 3 miles (5km) north of Telicherry, a branch road leads westward to the coast where rocks of varying size protrude from the sea, culminating in **Darmadam Island,** just 100 yards (100m) from the shore. Thick with coconut palms and a mere 5 acres in extent, the island is privately owned but can on occasions be reached on foot when the tide is out. In spite of its great length, Kerala's coastline, apart from the Cochin and Ezhimala regions, is studded with surprisingly few islands. Two miles (3 km) further north, on the opposite side of the Darmadam River's estuary, stretches **Muzhapilangad Beach,** much of its 4 miles (6km) of golden sand protected by a semi-circle of rocks, beside which the water is shallow and ideal for bathing. It seems likely that alluvial deposits from the river have much to do with the calmness of the sea in this region but, unlike Kappad, there is no mud within wading distance.

Cannanore's wealth once depended almost entirely on its port, but textiles are now the major industry. On arrival at the station or bus stand, tourists might wonder what on earth they are doing in Cannanore but, as has already been indicated, Cannanore's attractions are to be found around its periphery rather than in its town centre. For many centuries, Cannanore was ruled by the Mushaka dynasty, known from the 14th century as the Kolathiri Rajas, and from here they opposed their chief rival on the

Malabar coast, the Zamorin of Calicut. The familiar Portuguese, Dutch and British occupations followed, but an unusual interim period began in 1772, when the Dutch sold Cannanore and the Lakshadweep Islands to a local Muslim family, the leader of which, the Ali Raja (Lord of the Sea), could be succeeded by a female (the Bibi). Known as the Arakkal Rajas, these were the only Muslim rulers in Kerala. After giving support to Hyder Ali and later his son Tipu Sultan, the rajas were ousted by the British.

In the town centre, on SM Road, is the town's highest graded hotel, **Hotel Kamala International**. At the time of writing, however, this hotel was building an extension at the rear, leading to some disruption of services; the food is acceptable although room service is not very efficient. Alcohol is not available at any of Cannanore's hotels or restaurants: those in dire need will find a bar close to the bus station.

A new hotel, **The Mascot**, opened in 1997, completely air-conditioned and overlooking the sea. This is situated in Cannanore's highly desirable residential area, a short distance from the owner of the Leela Hotel Group's private mansion. Adjacent is the **Government Guest House**, where tourists can usually find accommodation in the 1986 vintage block. Rooms all face the sea and have private balconies. Plumbing and electricity is as eccentric as usual, but this is a small price to pay for the incredibly cheap tariff. Another option, in the same peaceful area, is the **Palm Grove Tourist Home**: family run, with charming, old-fashioned rooms – some air-conditioned – meals provided as required, and a delightful lawn on which to relax.

A good way to begin exploring Cannanore is to take an auto-rickshaw to **Fort St Angelo**, a landmark built on a headland by the first Portuguese viceroy, Francisco de Almeida, in 1505. After the British took over the fort in 1792, following the Mysore Wars, it became one of their most important military installations on the Malabar coast. Although the fortification, of red laterite, is in reasonable condition, and some mounted cannon are on display, the views from it are the fort's greatest appeal, encompassing as they do the picturesque fishing harbour of Mappila Bay, dominated by its mosque and with the distant Darmadam Island visible to the south.

It is a deceptively lengthy walk from the fort to the harbour, and most will prefer to continue by auto-rickshaw to the sea-facing mosque, particularly in the afternoon heat. Apart from visiting what remains of the late 18th century **Palace of the Muslim Arakkal Rajas** and its adjacent mosque, the Mappila quarter imposes no strict itineraries on the visitor, and is best explored by wandering haphazardly through its intimate lanes and streets, acknowledging the surprised smiles of friendly locals who rarely see a foreign tourist. Houses are notable for their tiled roofs and shuttered windows, a few of which are pointed, in Islamic style. Happily, the streets never descend to the squalor so often found in India, and given a lick of paint this could become one of Kerala's, if not the country's, showplaces. For some reason, goats and cows are permitted to roam around the streets here, with the consequence that litter is kept to a minimum.

Only vestiges of the Arakkal palace survive, bordering the west side of a small green (ask directions), where most houses are colonial in style. In the south-east corner, a plaque inscribed Abdul Rahman Mahal (Palace) identifies a house built as recently as 1938; many locals will insist that this was the Arakkal palace – it was not. Adjacent is what appears to be an ancient, free-standing belfry of a church; although certainly ancient – allegedly 500 years old – the bell calls not Christians but Muslims to prayer, in the small mosque nearby, an unusual alternative to the cries of the muezzin from a minaret. Visitors are advised to avert their eyes from the east side of the green, which is overlooked by a particularly hideous secondary school. A passage through the bell tower's archway leads from the square to the front of the school, beside which stands the twin-towered mosque facing the main street of the quarter.

Although the harbour looks attractive from Fort St Angelo, on closer inspection it has less architectural appeal than the streets behind it, and the pervading smell of rotting fish will dissuade most from staying long.

Unless the auto-rickshaw driver has been asked to wait, be sure to avoid the evening rush hour for a return to central Cannanore as local transport is hard to find and the buses will be jam-packed.

Payyambalam Beach stretches seemingly endlessly northward from St Angelo Fort; there are few fishing boats to be seen, and the sands are therefore clean. Goa's Colva Beach must have resembled this in its pre-tourist days, except that Payyambalam has the advantage of palm trees behind its entire length rather than flat paddyfields. One reason for the lack of development here is that a small crematorium is located at the town end, and Hindus do not relish the idea of a bathing resort being established in close proximity to it. Nevertheless, there are plans to build a hotel on the beach. At present, the **Government Guest House** and **Palm Grove** provide the nearest accommodation a mile away (2 km). **Choice Restaurant** in Fort Road provides reasonably good non-vegetarian food, as an alternative to the **Kamara International**.

North of Cannanore are the small towns of Chirakkal (4 miles, 6 km away) and Parassinikadavu (10 miles, 16 km), neither of which should be missed. They can be visited either from a Cannanore base on a half-day excursion, or en route northward to Kasargod.

Chirakkal

Chirakkal has two temples: that dedicated to Vishnu stands on a hill overlooking paddyfields, and is only open to Hindus. Facing a huge tank is the other, an older foundation, with a joint dedication to Shiva and Krishna. This permits non-Hindus to enter and is well worth a visit, in particular to see its magnificent *padipuram* gateway, with coffered ceiling panels carved and painted to depict the *murtis* of Vishnu. The immense 14-acre tank, the largest in Kerala, usually dries up between March and the onset of the south-west monsoon in late May.

Palace of the Kolathiri Rajas

On the west side of the tank is the former Palace of the Kolathiri Rajas, an unassuming mansion built around a central patio in Keralan vernacular style. The building is still in the ownership of the rajas' descendants, and foreign visitors are most welcome to inspect it whenever convenient. Apart from the external windows

which were added to lighten the interior, the centuries-old building has been little altered; as usual in Kerala it is the woodwork, particularly the coffered ceilings, that impresses. In spite of the mansion's undoubted charm, it seems astonishing that members of such a powerful dynasty should have occupied so unpretentious a residence.

Motel Araam

Those continuing northward from Chirakkal on National Highway 17, and seeking refreshment, are advised not to miss **Motel Araam**, at Keltron Nagar, where there is a clean, efficiently-run KTDC restaurant; there are no alternatives for a long way.

Parassinikadavu

Parassinikadavu, 6 miles (10 km) north of Chirakkal, is visited for its Snake Park and temple, one of the most fascinating in India.

Snake Park

Snake Park is generally seen first, king cobras being the star attraction. They grow to an incredible size, and their bite is always fatal; fortunately, cases of king cobras attacking man are rare. Many other varieties of snake, poisonous and non-poisonous, are exhibited, and demonstrations of milking their venom are given every hour; unfortunately, descriptions of what occurs are in Malayalam only.

One mile (2km) from Snake Park, beside the River Valapatanam, stands a major pilgrimage centre which, incidentally, is one of Kerala's most interesting locations for tourists, the **Sri Muthappan Temple** (open throughout the day). Of great appeal is the north Kerala ritual dance known as **Teyyam**, which is performed every evening. Muthappan, to whom the temple is dedicated, is an incarnation of Shiva.

This is the only temple in Kerala where *puja* takes place three times each day, the most impressive being at 3pm. The priest is made-up to impersonate the god, and wears a picturesque costume; toddy and dried fish are presented to the idol. Fortunately tourists are welcome to attend all the ceremonies, with no restrictions and without being pressed for donations – one wonders why not elsewhere in Kerala? Also welcomed are stray dogs, Shiva, being particularly fond of the canine species. KTDC operates boat trips on the river behind the complex which, viewed from the water, looks more like a hotel than a temple.

Ezhimala

The main road northward passes through the town of Ezhimala, its wedge-shaped promontory and scattering of islands to the north providing the best-protected coastline in this part of Kerala. Much of the area, however, has been appropriated by a naval academy, and is out of bounds to visitors.

Bakel, with its immense beach, lies 50 miles (79km) north of Cannanore, but as yet there is no hotel accommodation available, and, therefore, most will prefer to return to it later, continuing to Kasargod, the nearest town of any size, approximately 9 miles (15km) further on. Most of the fast trains, incidentally, do not stop at Bakel station.

Kasargod and Bakel

The only reason why any tourist might wish to stay at Kasargod is its proximity to Bakel Beach; there is little to see in the town itself. An adequate **Government Guest House** is, as usual, perched on a low hillock just outside the town centre, but the best accommodation is provided by the **City Tower Hotel**. Kasargod is very short on non-vegetarian establishments and, apart from the hotel's restaurant, **Sarbaz**, in the BHA Complex, is all that is available.

Buses take around 30 minutes to reach Bakel from Kasargod, but can be uncomfortably crowded – avoid the rush-hour at all costs. Ask to be deposited as near as possible to **Bakel Fort**, which is reached by a short path from the bus stop. The fort (small entry charge) is a mid-17th century structure erected by a Kanada chieftain on a strategically sited headland. Views from the fort across the great curve of **Bakel Beach** are breathtaking, and the area has been earmarked by Kerala state for intensive tourist development, which would take many years to complete. Although the sands are undoubtedly tempting, many problems have to be overcome. Once the headland with its great fort has been left, the beach is completely featureless, palm trees soon giving way to paddy fields which are reminiscent of the flatness of Goa's two long beaches. There is no protection from Big Wave, although it has been hinted that this problem can be overcome – presumably by increasing the depth of the sand at the point where the turbulence starts and levelling it off. Fishermen still use parts of the beach, and some of them supplement their income by digging out great quantities of sand, which they then sell for industrial purposes. When the poor infrastructure is also taken into account – the nearest airport is at Mangalore (Karnataka state), a two-hour drive away, and there are already acute water and electricity shortages – one wonders if the scheme can possibly be viable.

At present, however, a visit to Bakel's virgin beach makes a very pleasant day excursion, as long as it is borne in mind that facilities are non-existent, and all food and drink required must be taken to it. Having said that there is no accommodation at Bakel, this is not strictly true, as two bedrooms within the fort's **Tourist Bungalow** may be rented nightly. They are very basic, but it must be a pleasant experience to wake up in the morning to such a view. No refreshments are available, and the rooms are usually taken early each day. A handful of shops at Bakel Junction can supply some necessities, but there are no restaurants nearby.

Ananthapura

Ananthapura, 7 miles (12km) north-east of Kasargod, possesses the only **lake temple** in Kerala. This was the centre of worship of Ananthapadmanabha, the snake god, before the temple of Trivandrum was built.

There is little of interest on the coast north of Kasargod apart from an unusual sea water swimming pool formed on the beach 2 miles (3km) north of the small town of Manjeswaram fronting the **Kanwa Thirtha Beach Resort**.

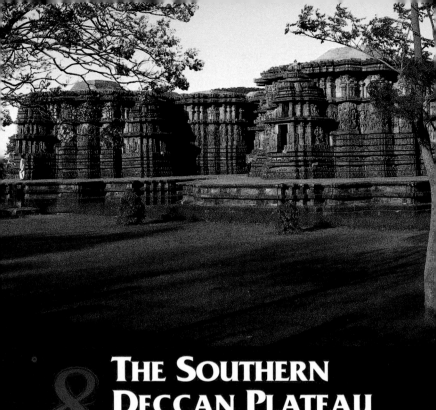

THE SOUTHERN DECCAN PLATEAU

8

The Deccan is an immense plateau lying between the Western and Eastern Ghat mountain ranges, and covering much of Karnataka and Maharashtra states. At Bangalore, it reaches a height of 3,250 feet (1,000m). Partly due to their somewhat less torrid climate, the cities of Mysore and Bangalore have prospered and are now two of India's most successful commercial cities; in addition, the former has preserved much of its history and charm, and remains a popular tourist destination. Hassan, although of little intrinsic appeal, is conveniently located for visiting the Hoysala temples of Belur and Halebid, and the Jain pilgrimage city of Shravana Belgola, where the world's tallest monolithic statue can be seen. Those who enter southern India at Madras or Bangalore airports can, of course, precede or follow their Kerala holiday with this itinerary, but in order to continue with the generally clockwise progression from Kovalam that has been followed in this book, the locations of interest are described from west to east after leaving the Kerala border and entering the state of Karnataka at Mangalore.

As long as an early start is made from Kasargod, it is possible for those with a car to bypass Mangalore where there is little of tourist interest, and proceed directly to Belur and Halebid, exploring both on the same day. A visit to Shravana Belgola, however, should be saved for the following day, perhaps on route from Hassan to Mysore. Those without a car should be able to reach Hassan by bus or train from Kasargod via Mangalore in one day.

There are flights from Mangalore to Bangalore (three per week) and Madras (daily), but not to Hassan or Mysore, which do not have airports. Those who prefer to return direct to Kerala can fly from Mangalore to Cochin (twice per week) but not to Trivandrum. There are also one bus and two trains daily from Mangalore to Hassan, Mysore, Bangalore and Madras. The daily bus from Mangalore to Hassan takes 4 hours, whilst the fastest of the twice daily trains takes $6^{1}/_{2}$ hours. This is because the rail track winds slowly upwards through the Western Ghat mountains to the plateau, providing some of the most spectacular scenery that rail passengers on any south Indian journey can enjoy. In this instance it is preferable to resist the speedier bus in favour of the slower train.

Above: The west wall of Halebid Temple, regarded as the supreme example of Hoysala art.

Mangalore

Mangalore, a commercial town on the coast just across the Karnataka state border, may be reached from Kasargod by express trains and buses in under 2 hours. The railway station is centrally located, but the main bus stand is 2 miles (3km) to the north, and the airport 12 miles (20km) away. Buses to Mangalore airport leave from near the bus station opposite the Indian Airlines office (a direct service) or from the bus station itself.

For those who stopover in Mangalore, the **Taj Manjarun Hotel** in Old Port Road is the best hotel in town, and not too far from the railway station. Roughly the same distance from the station is the somewhat cheaper **Hotel Moti Mahal**: both have good restaurants and swimming pools. If time permits, the **Kadri Temple**, north of the town centre, which is surrounded by nine tanks, displays a famous bronze **statue of Lokeshwara**, rated one of the finest in India. On the same route, which incidentally leads to the airport, the **Sultan's Battery** stands on the headland overlooking the old port; it is just one of a surprisingly large number of defence installations built by Tipu Sultan in the 18th century.

If journeying by road from Mangalore to Hassan, it is possible to visit **Manjadarbad Fort**, 28 miles (45km) before reaching Hassan. This is also the 18th-century work of Tipu Sultan. Although it is a fairly strenuous climb up the hill on which the fort stands, the views from its summit are superb.

Hassan

As already noted, **Hassan** has nothing of particular interest for visitors to see, and attracts visitors simply because of its convenient location for visiting the world-famous Hoysala temples and Shravana Belgola. The best accommodation is to be found at the **Hotel Hassan Ashok**, on BM Road, one mile (2km) from the railway station, where both continental and Indian food is served in its restaurant. The helpful management are particularly keen to promote local attractions, and can sometimes arrange visits to a coffee estate to watch young ladies harvest the beans – much more strenuous work than tea picking, needing agility both in climbing the trees and bending to collect the fallen berries from the ground. If the Ashok is full, as it frequently is, the brand new **Suvarna Residency** has a similar rating.

Those with a car who make an early start from Hassan can visit Belur, Halebid and Shravana Belgola in one day, and continue to Mysore; there are also coach tours from Hassan that include all three locations, but these involve a return to Hassan. Buses between Hassan and Belur are more frequent than those between Hassan and Halebid, from where the last returns at 6.15pm; a visit to Halebid first may therefore be more convenient for bus passengers. There are only three direct buses from Hassan to Shravana Belgola (1 $\frac{1}{2}$ hours), but more go to Chanarayapatra from where frequent buses make the short journey to Shravana Belgola.

Hoysala Temples

Three major temples survive in India from the Hoysala period: at **Belur**, **Halebid** and **Somnathpur** (near Mysore); the first two are mid-12th century work, whilst the latter was built a century later. All are similar in style, and regarded by some experts as the finest examples of Hindu architecture in India. Constructed from malleable black stone which hardens on exposure to air, the buildings rely on the quality and intricacy of their undecorated carving rather than massive towers or bright paintwork, the features of most important Hindu temples. Those who have seen the exquisite Kadamba temple at Tambdi Surla in Goa, which is contemporary with the Hoysala temples, will note certain similarities.

The Hoysalas were de facto rulers of a large part of the south-west Deccan from the early 11th century until 1310; before this they had been under the suzerainty of the Chalukas, whom they detested. Tinyaditya

(1047-78) was their first leader of note, but it was during the reign of Bittiga (1110-52) that Hoysala culture reached its zenith and the Belur and Halebid temples were built. Like his predecessors, Bittiga was a Jain, but converted to Vishnavite Hinduism, changing his name to Vishnuvardhana. He was, however, very tolerant of other religions, encouraging the rebuilding of Jain temples destroyed by Shaivite Chola invaders, and making a pilgrimage to the Jain temple at Shravana Belgola, even after his conversion to Hinduism.

Although bus passengers may find it more convenient to visit Halebid before Belur, and the interior of Halebid's temple is only well illuminated by sunlight in the morning, the magnificent external west wall of Halebid, generally regarded as the finest Hoysala sculpture of all, is not brought into sharp relief by sunlight until late afternoon. The order in which the temples are visited is, therefore, a matter of personal choice; however, for reasons of chronology and its proximity to Hassan, Belur will be described first.

Both temples are best avoided at weekends and public holidays, when Indian families throng to them, some picnicking in their grounds. Extremely thick socks (preferably two pairs) should be taken as the heat from the sun is absorbed by the stone which most visitors, particularly after mid-day, will find extremely uncomfortable to stand on following the obligatory removal of their shoes.

Belur

It is hard to appreciate that **Belur**, now an undistinguished town, was from the early 11th century the splendid capital of the Hoysala empire until this was transferred to Halebid in the 12th century. King Vishnuvardhana commissioned Belur's **Chenna Keshava Temple** in 1116, but the complexity and extent of its carving took 103 years to complete. It seems likely that the temple was built to celebrate the King's conversion from Jainism to Hinduism; alternatively, some claim that it was erected to commemorate the Hoysalas' famous victory over the Cholas at Talakad.

Although warlike, the Hoysalas were an extremely artistic people and, rare in India, their artists were permitted to sign their work. We know from his signature, for example, that a prominent sculptor, Jakanachari, was primarily responsible for designing Belur's temple. Allegedly, when the temple was ready for consecration, a small boy alarmed the architect by telling him that its idol was flawed and could not therefore be worshipped. Jakanachari vowed that if the boy could prove it was flawed he would cut off his own arm. The boy immediately struck the idol,

THE SOUTHERN
DECCAN PLATEAU

Coffee-picking, near Hassan, is a far more strenuous occupation than tea picking – trees must be climbed and fallen beans collected from the ground.

splitting open its stomach to reveal a live frog squatting within: distressed, Jakanachari amputated his arm. A typical Indian corollary to this story is that the boy proved to be the sculptor's own son whom he had not seen for some years because of his involvement with the Belur commission.

All surviving Hoysala temples are relatively small and compact; Belur's has no real superstructure at all (its *gopuram* is a 16th-century addition), but to give some height it has been erected on a platform. In other Hindu temples the *garbha griba* (sanctuary) is square in plan, but the Hoysalas turned the square round to form a diamond, and added cells that resulted in a star shape, which was then extended to the entire temple including its platform.

An outstanding feature of the exquisite carving is its realism: for example, a thread passed through the pupil of a figure's eye can be drawn out through a nostril; if, alternatively, the thread is suspended from a dancer's forehead it will fall directly on its toe. Virtually every surface is carved, but the effect is neither fussy nor heavy, so logical and finely balanced are the designs. External walls are always carved from top to bottom with horizontal bands, the lowest of which comprises elephants, representing stability; above are rows of lions (strength), horses (speed) and scrolls (beauty). At eye level,

scenes from the Ramayana and Mahabharata are depicted, together with events in the life of Krishna. Above these, *yalis* and *hamsas* (mythical beasts and birds) are surmounted by panels depicting Hindu gods.

It has been estimated that around 150 hours would be needed to examine all Belur's carving in detail, and the services of a local guide who can pinpoint the highlights is recommended. The work includes much erotica, reflecting the Jain view that sexual pleasure is a gift from the gods to be celebrated. However, modern Hindus certainly do not celebrate erotica and, particularly if ladies are present, it is very likely that the embarrassed guide will hurry past the most titillating examples.

There are entrances to the temple from the north, east and south, the most important, and the finest, being that on the east side. Its door jambs depict Rama, the god of love, and his consort Rati. Carved on each side of the door are scenes from the *durbar* of a Hoysala king, believed to be Ballala II. Particularly beautiful at Belur are the delicately framed roof bracket (corbel) figures: most are female, allegedly modelled on Rani Shantala, a musician, dancer of renown and consort of King Vishnuvardhana. Women played an important part in Hoysala's administration, and were permitted an unusual degree of freedom – including sexual.

Internally, all is rather dark

and dependent on electricity for illumination – a torch, therefore, would be an asset; there are no restrictions on photographers using flash. The profusion of sculptural detail is remarkable, and because here the work was completed, unlike at Halebid, Belur's is regarded as the finest Hoysala interior. It is also the only Hoysala temple that still functions as such.

In the centre of the **mandapam**'s ceiling, the minute carving is astonishing (a searchlight is available for hire). Look out for the lizard about to catch a fly sampling a ripe fruit, an example of the realistic minutiae in which the Hoysala craftsmen excelled. Many figures wear heavy, carved jewellery, some of which is said to be removable.

To the left, facing the sanctuary, the **Narasimba** (a reincarnation of Vishnu) **pillar** is completely carved, and bears traces of red *puja* powder. It is said that for 500 years this free-standing pillar was so finely balanced that it could be made to revolve with a light touch; unfortunately, this is no longer possible due to the wear of the pillar's base. Traditionally, the image of Vishnu, known as Chenna Kesara (the handsome god), was brought to Belur from nearby hills, but that of his consort, Mahishashuramardin, was overlooked and remains there. To help Vishnu make return visits to her from time to time a pair of shoes is kept for him within the temple.

Halebid

Halebid, which lies 9 miles (15km) east of Belur, can be reached by bus; services, however, are infrequent and vehicles are always packed. Even if a taxi has not been hired for the entire excursion it is worth considering one for this stage. As has been said, the small town also has a bus service direct to Hassan.

Halebid's original name was Dwarasamudram (Gateway to the Sea), which had been that of the lake beside which it was built. Its **Hoysaleswara Temple** was begun 10 years after Belur's temple in 1126, but although work on it continued for 86 years, the carving, particularly of the interior, was never completed.

Reminiscent architecturally of Belur, Halebid's temple is somewhat larger, comprising as it does separate shrines to Shiva and his consort. The building's north facade is approached through well-maintained gardens. Banding of the external walls is similar in style to Belur's, but its design themes differ and include battle scenes, a procession of dragons and peacocks. The top row depicts large, busty *asparas* (celestial maidens) together with Vishnu, Brahma (three-headed as usual) and Shiva. Only a few of the original 84 figure brackets have survived, and the north-east door is uncarved.

Two Nandi bulls facing the east side guard both shrines; behind them stands a small sun temple. The most splendid entrance to Halebid's temple, however, unlike Belur's is from the south side, possibly because, as alleged, this was once the royal entry and could be reached directly by a passage from the palace to the south west of the temple. Doorless as usual, the superb west wall is the glory of Hoysala, being carved from end to end with the complete pantheon of Hindu gods and their reincarnations. Some experts avow that no comparable example of Hindu art excels the quality of these sculptures.

A much lighter interior than at Belur enables visitors to inspect the internal carving more easily; this is due to the fretwork screen of the east wall which permits natural light to filter through, particularly early in the morning. Two identical sanctuaries dedicated to Shiva and his consort are separated by a small area. Brackets carved as female figures support the roofs of both pillared halls.

Halebid was sacked by two Delhi Sultans, Ala-ud-din-Khalji, in 1311 and Muhamad bin Tughlaq in 1327, and it is believed that these Muslim rulers plundered great treasures from the city. What was left of Dwarasamudram was then renamed Halebidu – meaning the old capital.

The **Kedaresvara Temple** to the north, is contemporary with the Hoysaleshwara temple, but smaller and partly ruined. Allegedly, there were once 720 Jain *bastis* (temples) in and around Halebid, but only three have survived. The most impressive is the **Parsvanathesvara Temple** to the west, built by a Hoysala general in 1123 and displaying a 14-ft (4.5m) high figure of the 23rd *tirthankara* (Jain prophet). Of greatest interest architecturally is the carved ceiling of the shrine and its unusual beaded pillars. A further temple at Halebid, the **Kedareswara**, dedicated to Shiva, is located 500 yards (0.5km) away.

Of the ancient city of Dwarasamudram, only **Potters Street** has survived. By tradition, the sister of a Hoysala king visited the city accompanied by her two sons, one of whom took the fancy of a wife (or concubine) of the King, who made advances to him but was rebuffed. The slighted lady complained to the King that his nephews had insulted her; they were both impaled and their corpses displayed at the city gate. In addition, the King banished their mother and ordered that no one should aid her; only the inhabitants of Potters Street ignored his edict, giving the distraught woman food and shelter. With a curse, she invoked the destruction of her brother and his entire kingdom, with the exception, of course, of Potters Street and its inhabitants.

Shravana Belgola

One of India's most famous sights, the immense **Statue of**

Gomateshvara, draws visitors to Shravana Belgola, the most important Jain pilgrimage centre in India. There are no buses from either Belur or Halebid and first, therefore, a return must be made by those without a car to Hassan, for buses (three daily) to Shravana Belgola; more frequent services, however, link Hassan with Chanaraypatna, a short distance from the town. There are also direct buses between Shravana Belgola and Mysore 75 miles (120 km) and Bangalore 115 miles (185 km).

Ancient rock inscriptions record that in the 3rd century BC, Chandragupta Maurya, the first great Indian emperor, renounced his throne and lived the remainder of his life as an ascetic at Shravana Belgola with his guru Bhagwan Swami. Thus was founded a centre of Jain culture that has continued as such for more than 2,000 years, succeeding Hindu dynasties showing members of the rival religion absolute tolerance. The earliest known *basti* (temple) in the town was built in the 9th century, and the last in the 19th; 35 *basti* still survive (no other Jain centre has so many) and there are 525 carved inscriptions relating to the Jain religion.

The town, now with a population of 5,000, lies between two arid hills – Indiragiri and Chandragiri, the former being the highest, and also the most important for tourists as the statue of Gomateshvara stands at its summit.

Indiragiri Hill

Shoes must be removed at the base of the hill, where the burning hot stone is an even greater problem than at either Belur or Halebid. An early start will help overcome this, but as mid-day approaches most will find it impossible to stand on the stone, even if wearing a pair of socks. Furthermore, only the fittest will be able to labour up the steep 614 steps to the 410ft (126m) high summit without some degree of exhaustion. Help, fortunately, is at hand in the form of *dholi* bearers, four men who will transport frailer visitors to the summit (and back if required) in a wicker-work sedan chair; their muscular arms and legs and, presumably, expanded lungs, enabling them to do this repeatedly without apparent stress. Some will find the 45-rupee fare requested in each direction well worth paying; if at all possible, however, it is advisable to make the return journey on foot, otherwise much will be missed.

As the climb begins, the **Parshwanatha Basti,** seen on the left, is modern work and of little interest.

After a stone gateway has been passed, the hill's largest *basti* is seen ahead; it is called the **Odegal Basti,** a reference to the *odegals* (stone buttresses)

Opposite: At Shravana Belgola the figure of Gomateshavara is the world's largest monolithic statue.

that support its walls. There are three cells, and the main shrine, of polished black stone, is dedicated to Adinatha (Rishab Anatha), the first Jain *tirthankara*.

Steps lead down and then up to a great boulder. On the right is a pillar with a floral design, erected in 981. Two more gateways are passed, the last leading to a small courtyard from where the head of the immense Gomateshvara statue can be seen rising above the *basti*'s structure.

It is believed that the statue of Gomateshvara is, at 57 feet (17m), the world's highest monolithic free-standing figure. King Vrishabha Deva, a north Indian follower of the Jain religion, gave up his position and wealth to live as a penitent, becoming the first Jain *tirthankara* and known as Adinatha. His two sons, Gomateshvara (or Bahubali) and Bharata fought each other to become his successor. On gaining victory, Gomateshvara was struck by the meaninglessness of worldly possessions and status, and presented all he had gained to his brother. There followed his 'thousand-year' contemplative penance in the jungle, during which it is said he stood motionless for such long periods that anthills were built at his feet and creepers climbed up his legs and arms.

The colossal statue, completed around 981, was commissioned from a famous sculptor, Aristanemi, by Charundaraya, a general of the Ganga King Rachamali. The statue has been carved from a single rock of pale grey granite, which probably had formed part of Indiragiri Hill.

Members of the Jain Digambara sect practise total nudity, which is why Gomateshvara is depicted naked; naked, that is, apart from the creepers around his arms and legs, a reference to the legend mentioned. The feet rest on a lotus, and anthills rise on either side, a further reference to tradition. It will be observed that the forefinger of the statue's left hand has been shortened; this, so it is said, is because the perfection of the figure would otherwise have attracted evil spirits, but another explanation is that Ramanujacharya, who converted the Hoysala king Vishnuvardhana to Hinduism, mutilated the figure to make the work imperfect and therefore ineligible for worship. Whatever the reason for this minor disfigurement, it has done nothing to diminish the perfect proportions of the statue's head and torso (its legs are foreshortened) observed from all angles. Particularly impressive is the serene expression of the face, in spite of its enormous size.

As in Ancient Egyptian art, several rules evolved which had to be followed by sculptors depicting Jain *tirthankaras*, simplicity being the keynote. All had to be shown looking straight ahead, their features had to be identical, and no embellishment that could be identified with the artist was permitted. The only exceptions from these regulations is that Adinatha, father of Gomateshvara, is sometimes given long hair, and the figures may be depicted either standing or seated. Admirers of the French artist, Matisse, may be reminded of some of his portraits.

Every 12 years, Jains from all over the world visit the hill to witness the ritual anointing ceremony (Mastakabhisheka) of the statue. For this, a great scaffold is erected at the rear, and priests pour immense quantities of materials over the head of Gomateshvara in homage, each succeeding item staining it a different hue. These include: milk, curds, ghee, flowers, coloured powders, saffron, poppy seeds and almonds, followed by gold and silver coins. The next ceremony will take place in 2005. Chemically cleaned in 1996, it is hard to believe that the pristine statue has now passed its first millennium, an event that was celebrated in 1981.

Returning to the foot of the hill, superb views are gained of the town below and its **Kalyami Temple's tank**. This was created in the 17th century, and is believed to have replaced the 'white pond of the ascetic' (the ascetic being Gomateshvara), which gave Shravana Belgola its name. Behind the town rises Chandragiri Hill.

Chandragiri Hill

Having laboured up and (or) down Indiragiri Hill, few will be ready to tackle the 3,000 ft (924m) high Chandragiri Hill immediately afterwards – particularly as here there is no *dholi* transport, and shoes must be removed once more. For hardy souls (not to mention hardy soles), however, there are a group of *bastis* within a walled area at the summit which are of interest. Even though these were built at different periods, they are all designed in similar Dravidian style. Most important is the earliest, the **Chandragupta Basti**, erected by the Buddhist emperor Ashok in the 8th century to commemorate his grandfather Chandragupta Maurya. A row of three cells is faced by a verandah, the ornate doorway of which is a later addition. On each side of the door are perforated screens and tiny sculpted scenes from the life of Chandragupta Maurya. In the central cell is the figure of Parsavanatha, the 23rd *tirthankara*.

It is said that Bhagwan Bhadrabahu, Chandragupta's guru, attained nirvana on the hill, and his footprints that have been 'imprinted' on stone were allegedly worshipped for 12 years by Chandragupta during his penance.

Visitors will be relieved to hear that the largest temple in Shravana Belgola, the **Bhandari Basti**, is located on level ground in the town centre. Sharing a decorative pedestal within its *garbha griba* (sanctuary) are 3 ft (90 cm) high figures of each of the 24 Jain *tirthankaras*, to whom the temple is dedicated. The *basti*'s name probably refers to the treasure (*bhandari*) of the Hoysala king who commissioned the temple.

As has been said, there are direct buses from Shravana Belgola to Mysore via Shrirangapatam and to Bangalore. Those with a car may find it convenient to travel from Hassan to Mysore via the Brindavan Gardens on its northern outskirts; bear in mind that the latter are illuminated between 7.00pm and 8.00pm.

From Hassan there are buses and trains to Mysore, the mid-afternoon express train being the quickest means of reaching the city.

Mysore

Mysore, the most congenial large city in India, unlike neighbouring Bangalore has proudly resisted modernization and commercialism. In consequence, it is still dominated by fairy-tale palaces, tree-lined streets and Chamundi Hill, with its ancient temples. Although Hassan and Bangalore are both situated approximately 650ft (200m) higher than Mysore, the latter is still protected from excessive heat and heavy monsoon rains by its 2,500-foot (770m) altitude. Mysore is also strategically placed for visiting Shrirangapatam, the ruined capital of Tipu Sultan; Somnathpur, where a third outstanding Hoysala temple survives; and Bandipur National Park. There are also excursions (rather tiring and hurried) to Belur, Halebid and Shrivana Belgola for those who will not be staying nearer to these important locations.

Mysore Palace

For visitors, Mysore Palace is, without doubt, the city's greatest attraction; especially on Sunday evenings and public holidays when, between 7.00 and 8.00pm, almost 1,000 light bulbs outline the exterior of the building in the manner of an English seaside pier. The palace was built as the seat of the maharajas of the former state of Mysore, the Woodyer (several alternative spellings in English are current) family, whose members still occupy part of it; the state apartments are open to the public.

Mysore's long history is attested to in the *Mahabharata*, where it is referred to as Mahishmati. In the 14th century, two brothers from Gujarat, Vijaya and Krishna Yadava, made a pilgrimage to Mysore where, according to legend, a rival king had abducted the daughter of the ruler of Hadinadu (then the name of Mysore); Vijaya rescued her, and the grateful King gave his daughter to him in marriage. Vijaya also succeeded to the King's title of Woodyer (ruler),

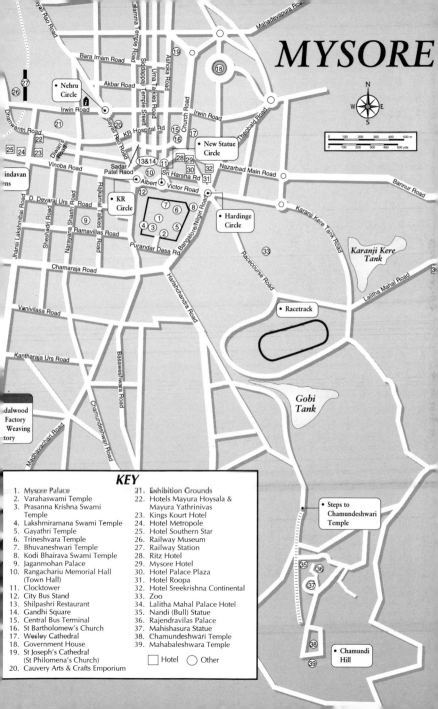

MYSORE

KEY

1. Mysore Palace
2. Varahaswami Temple
3. Prasanna Krishna Swami Temple
4. Lakshmiramana Swami Temple
5. Gayathri Temple
6. Trineshvara Temple
7. Bhuvaneshwari Temple
8. Kodi Bhairava Swami Temple
9. Jaganmohan Palace
10. Rangachariu Memorial Hall (Town Hall)
11. Clocktower
12. City Bus Stand
13. Shilpashri Restaurant
14. Gandhi Square
15. Central Bus Terminal
16. St Bartholomew's Church
17. Wesley Cathedral
18. Government House
19. St Joseph's Cathedral (St Philomena's Church)
20. Cauvery Arts & Crafts Emporium

21. Exhibition Grounds
22. Hotels Mayura Hoysala & Mayura Yathrinivas
23. Kings Kourt Hotel
24. Hotel Metropole
25. Hotel Southern Star
26. Railway Museum
27. Railway Station
28. Ritz Hotel
29. Mysore Hotel
30. Hotel Palace Plaza
31. Hotel Roopa
32. Hotel Sreekrishna Continental
33. Zoo
34. Lalitha Mahal Palace Hotel
35. Nandi (Bull) Statue
36. Rajendravilas Palace
37. Mahishasura Statue
38. Chamundeshwari Temple
39. Mahabaleshwara Temple

☐ Hotel   ◯ Other

thus founding the Hindu dynasty of Mysore's maharajas which lasted from 1399 until 1947. When all Indian titles were abolished in 1947, the Maharaja was unanimously elected the first governor of the state of Mysore; its capital, however, was moved to Bangalore and the state's name changed to Karnataka.

An early palace, razed by Tipu Sultan, was rebuilt of timber in 1800. This burned down accidentally in 1897, and was in turn replaced by the present building. Henry Irwin, the consultant architect to the Governor of Madras, was commissioned to design the complex which was completed in 1912. Visitors will find that Mysore Palace is far less crowded with visitors early in the day; Sundays are extremely popular with local Indians and should be avoided if possible (except for the external illuminations).

Entrance to the complex is only permitted from the south gate. Cameras must be left at the kiosk right of the entrance (free of charge), as no internal photography is permitted; there are, however, no restrictions on taking photographs of the exterior of the palace from its grounds. Completed in 1912, the palace is built of grey granite, most of which has been painted white and cream externally. Like most important projects in India at the time, all of which were designed by British architects, a basic Indo-Saracenic style embellished with romantic touches has been employed; ogee domes have a Mogul provenance, whilst foiled arches evoke Rajput work; unquestionably European in style, however, is the campanile. Internally, detailing owes much to the Hoysalas.

Inside, a long, pillared vestibule leads, via the **Dolls' Corridor** in which idols and palanquins are exhibited, to the **Kalyana Mandapa** (Marriage Hall). On the walls of its entrance passageway are displayed 26 canvases depicting an entire Dussehra Procession, the work of Y Naga Raja, 1945. The main section of the hall is galleried, iron pillars in groups of three supporting an octagonal stained glass dome. Designed by local artists around a peacock theme, the glass was made in Glasgow at the aptly named Saracen Foundry of Walter McFarlene. From the hall can be seen the open courtyard around which the palace is built. A **portrait gallery** of the Woodyers is followed by the **Chairs Room**, and steps then lead up to the great **Durbar Hall**.

Hung on the wall of the Durbar Hall's entrance aisle are paintings of Hindu gods by Raja Ravi Varma of Travancore. The Durbar Hall is 152 ft (47m) long and divided into three 'naves' of equal size by rows of columns. The white marble floor is enlivened between the columns with panels of semi-precious stones in the manner of Mogul pietra dura work. The central doors of silver came from the previous building.

Steps descend on the north side towards the Maharaja's private audience hall, **Amba Vilas**, a name that is sometimes applied to the entire palace. From the 'celestial' ceiling are suspended Belgian chandeliers. On important occasions, ladies occupied the upper gallery and honoured guests sat below.

During the Dussehra celebrations, the **Golden Throne** (or Royal Elephant Throne) of the maharajas is exhibited. Apparently the throne, originally of figwood and ivory decorated with mythical figures in fine metalwork, was not plated with gold and silver until the 18th century: its gold content has been estimated to weigh an extraordinary 616lbs (280kg). It is believed that the Mogul emperor Aurangzeb presented the throne to the Woodyer maharajas in 1699; for most of the year it is kept securely under lock and key.

On leaving the Durbar Hall, visitors enter a vestibule where there are two more doors of solid silver and two of teak inlaid with ivory; the chandeliers are Belgian.

In the former residential area of the old palace, the **Maharajas' Residential Museum** is open daily 10.30am – 6.30pm (additional entry charge). At the entrance it is possible to hire camel and elephant rides. It cannot be said that the museum's collection is an example of exquisite taste, which is hardly surprising in view of its early 20th-century period. Outstandingly hideous is the mother-of-pearl and solid silver furniture displayed on the first floor.

Various temples are scattered around the grounds, however, all of them are closed between 10.30am and 5pm. Immediately right of the south gate is the **Varahaswami Temple**, built by Krishnaraja Woodyer III, reusing material from an ancient Hoysala temple. The *gopuram* of this temple apparently inspired the design of the Chamundeswari Temple's *gopuram* on Chamundi Hill.

Further west is the small **Prasanna Krishnaswami Temple**, built in 1829. In the south-west corner of the palace, the **Lakshmiramana Temple**, built in the late 15th century, is the oldest of the group.

To the south east stands the **Gayathri Temple** and, facing it to the north east, the **Trineshvara Temple**, built in Dravidian style and dedicated to Shiva. This was remodelled by Dodda Deva Raja Woodyer, who was responsible for commissioning the large **Nandi bull** on Chamundi Hill.

Visitors are not permitted to explore the northern sector of the palace grounds, primarily to avoid disturbing the occupiers, descendants of the maharajas.

A brief tour northward from the palace will cover most

locations of interest in central Mysore. Situated one mile (1.5km) distant is the Jagan Mohan Palace, which makes a good starting point – but bear in mind that it is closed on Mondays and from 1.00pm – 3.00pm.

Jagan Mohan Palace

The three-storey palace was constructed in 1861 specifically for a royal wedding, but its halls were more spacious than those of the royal palace that then existed, and eventually accommodated coronations and birthday celebrations of importance in addition to the annual Dussehra *durbar*; naturally, these activities were transferred to the new palace when it was ready in 1910. The Jagan Mohan Palace's **Museum**, now primarily an exhibition of royal collections, is located at the rear of the building.

Externally, the facade of the palace, with its domes, cupolas and finials can be described as Baroque. It appears that members of the royal family were permitted to store their objets d'art in the palace, and it is these that make up most of the collection. Exhibits vary widely – encompassing fine art and memorabilia. Curiosities include a carved grain of rice and a French-made clock with toy soldiers indicating the time. Most will find the third floor display of paintings and musical instruments of greatest interest. Included are works by the ubiquitous Ravi Varma, and Nicholas Roerich. A delightful 'naive' panel portrays the rulers of England from 800-1661, the monarchs clustered around a dominant Queen Victoria. *Glow of Hope*, a painting renowned in India, is the work of Haldenkar, a Maharashtra artist. Armaments are displayed on the ground floor, just before the exit .

Albert Victor Road, which skirts the north side of Mysore Palace, is punctuated from west to east by three imposing circuses: KR Circle, New Statue Circle and Hardinge Circle. **KR Circle** is named in memory of the popular Maharaja Krishnaraja Woodyer IV and accommodates, beneath a Mogul style cupola, his marble statue, which was unveiled in 1952. A similar statue of white marble commemorating Chamarajendra Woodyer, the father of Krishnaraja IV, stands in **New Statue** (or **Chamarajendra**) **Circle** facing the north entrance of the palace. This was designed around 1920 by the British sculptor Robert Colton who spent three months in Mysore seeking references for the work. Set on a granite base, the Indo-Saracenic style canopy is of marble, but its cupola has been gilded.

To the north west of New Statue Circle can be seen Mysore's imposing Town Hall, built in 1884, and now known as the **Rangachariu Memorial Hall**. Ashoka Road passes this on route northward from New Statue Circle to the four-storey **Clock Tower**, which was built in 1927 to commemorate the 25th year of Krishnaraja Woodyer IV's reign. It was commissioned by servants and officers of the palace and is inscribed 'His Highness may be blessed with a long life and his reign rendered radiantly happy, memorable and prosperous'. The clock itself was reused from an earlier structure of 1886 which marked a visit to Mysore of Viceroy Lord Dufferin.

A short road leads diagonally north-eastward from the Clock Tower to two of Mysore's most important buildings for Christian worship, the church of **St Bartholomew** and **Wesley Cathedral** which face each other across Church Road. Neither is of particular interest internally, but St Bartholomew is the oldest church in Mysore; it is also a rare Indian example of European classical architecture, having been built in 1832 during the short reign of William IV. Its site was donated by Krishnaraja III, the church being earmarked primarily for worship by staff attached to the British Residency in Mysore. It must be said that St Bartholomew appears more like a Georgian mansion than a church – only a cross on the roof clearly defines its purpose. Prince Albert Victor, Duke of Clarence, worshipped here in 1889 as did his younger brother,

Mysore Palace is one of India's most eclectic buildings.

the future King George V, and Princess Mary of Teck, the future Queen Mary, in 1906. Much of the interior is 1930s work, including the St Bartholomew stained glass window presented by Krishnaraja Woodyer IV to mark the centenary of the church.

Further north, on the east side of Church Road, stands **Government House**, commissioned in 1805 by Major Wilks, the British Resident in Mysore. John Malcolm, who succeeded Wilks, added a hall as a wedding gift for his bride, which is still one of the largest in south India to be uninterrupted by pillars. Unfortunately, the internal furnishings and fittings were removed when the building was converted to a Government Guest House.

St Joseph's Cathedral, formerly the church of St Philomena, the name by which it is still generally known, stands at the intersection of Church Road and Ashoka Road. This is the largest church in India, its twin spires 160 ft (50m) high exactly matching the length of the building which is modelled on Cologne Cathedral. The church was commissioned as recently as 1930, in spite of its Gothic design, by Rene Feuga, Bishop of Mysore. Inside the church, soaring Gothic Revival arches continue. All is painted white, thereby avoiding the sombre appearance generally found in this type of building.

Mysore, south of the palace

Some visitors on route to Chamundi Hill may wish to visit **Mysore Zoo**, India's fourth largest. It was inaugurated by Chamarajendra Woodyer in 1892 on 10 acres of his land, but now covers 250 acres. Unlike most zoos in India, no animals are caged behind bars, most being provided with an approximation of their natural habitat. A rare white tiger and a large gorilla are the zoo's greatest attractions. Separated from the zoo by a road is the man-made **Karanji Kere tank**, an artificial lake where many types of birdlife are to be seen.

From the south-east corner of the zoo, the Lalitha Mahal Road leads to the imposing **Lalitha Mahal Palace Hotel**, nestling below the north slopes of Chamundi Hill and resembling a confection of gleaming white icing sugar. Krishnaraja Woodyer IV was a devout Hindu who remained a non-drinker and a vegetarian throughout his life; however, he had no objection to his many European guests partaking of meat and alcohol, and commissioned this former palace as a guesthouse exclusively for their use.

The building was designed in 1921 by E.W. Fritchley, who paid homage to Wren's St Paul's Cathedral by similarly focusing his main elevation on a pedimented two-storey portico with a double-drum dome rising behind it. The building was converted to a hotel in 1974, and is run as an Ashok 'Elite' hotel by ITDC. Fortunately, many internal features have been preserved including the Banqueting Hall, now a conference venue, and the Ball Room, now the restaurant; the main staircase is of white Italian marble. A modern extension has been added to the rear, and there is an outdoor swimming pool. The grounds and views from many of the rooms are a delight. Non-residents are welcome to dine in the hotel where lunchtime buffets are excellent, and to drink in the enormous bar (at a price). Most operators of premium grade tours to south India accommodate their clients in this hotel for its luxurious ambience, even though it is not, as has been seen, conveniently located for the city centre. However, the Lalitha Mahal is well placed for reaching the summit of Chamundi Hill.

Chamundi Hill

Lying due south of Mysore Palace, the 3,450 foot (1062 m) high **Chamundi Hill** dominates the entire area. Temples and statues have been erected on the hill since the 1st century, and these remain Mysore's structures of greatest historic interest. An early start is recommended as the **Chamundeshwari Temple** is closed 12.00 – 5.00pm. Bus No. 101 from the City Bus Station (immediately north of the palace) goes all the way to the summit of

the hill, an 8 mile (13 km) journey; taxis are also permitted to continue to the summit, but not auto-rickshaws. Pilgrims on foot take a different route, via 900 steep steps, which cuts their journey distance to 2 $^1/_2$ miles (4km). Most tourists however, will prefer to make only the downhill return journey by the steps which pass the famous Nandi statue one third of the way down.

At a roundabout on route to the hill's summit, a statue has been erected of the scowling, buffalo-headed demon, Mahishasura, who has given Mysore its present name. By tradition, Chamundi defeated Mahishasura after a 10 day battle, which is celebrated in the city every autumn by the Dussehra Festival. In one hand, the demon grasps his scimitar, in the other a cobra. It is said that in order to placate the demon and dissuade him from returning, the inhabitants renamed their city Mahisur (Town of the Buffalo).

From the north side, a short road descends to **Rajendra Vilas**, a summer palace built around 1905 by Krishnaraja Woodyer IV. Though basically Indo-Saracenic in style, the European influence is apparent. Until recently the building was operated as a hotel, and it is expected that the Taj Group will reopen it as such once more in the near future. No doubt the splendid, mirrored foyer will be preserved.

A large car park for taxis and

buses has been laid out near the Chamundeshwari Temple, the hill's greatest attraction. Before continuing, it is worth spending a short time in the adjacent **Godly Museum** where visitors are warned against committing many sins that most will have committed already without realizing it.

Chamundeshwari Temple

All are permitted to enter the temple, but photography is not allowed; shoes must, of course, be removed and deposited at the *chappie* kiosk nearby.

Chamundi, an aspect of Shiva's consort Parvati, is the patron deity of the Woodyer dynasty. After her defeat of Mahishasur it is said that she decided to live on Chamundi Hill, which is named after her. **The Chamundeshwari Temple**, dedicated to the goddess, was built in the 12th century in the Dravidian style. Much of the building, however, was altered during renovations by Krishnaraja Woodyer III in 1827, particularly by the addition of a cream-painted tower (*gopuram*) 130 feet (40m) high above the gateway and another (*vimana*), which is much shorter, above the sanctuary.

The same maharaja also presented the temple with a solid-gold ornament inscribed with 30 verses in Sanskrit, known as the *Nakshatramalika*, which is housed within the sanctuary. It may be noted that the architrave to the sanctuary's entrance is of brass, another gift of Krishnaraja Woodyer III.

South of the Chamundeshwari Temple is a small and less important but much more venerable **temple** dedicated to Mahabaleshwara, an aspect of Shiva, and built by the Cholas around 2,000 years ago. The original Shiva *lingam* of silver, now plated with gold, survives within the sanctuary. Above the door on the right, are many inscriptions, the oldest dating from 950 during the rule of the Gangas.

Nandi (Bull) statue

Shoes should be retrieved before descending the first flight of steps (600) indicated 'Way to Bull'. It is believed that the reclining figure of Nandi, Shiva's bull, was carved during the reign of Dodda Deva Raja, which began in 1695. It is certainly monolithic, being carved from a single black boulder, but the tradition that the 16 ft (5m) high statue was completed in one night seems dubious. Extremely popular with the inhabitants of Mysore, this wistful Nandi has become the city's emblem and is usually garlanded with flowers presented by pilgrims on their way up to the temple. Particularly charming are the bull's richly carved bands of necklaces, the lowest comprising small bells.

The final flight of 600 steps,

Opposite: The Bull (Nandi) Statue on Chamundi Hill attracts tourists and worshippers alike.

also begun in the reign of Dodda Deva Raja, descends to the road, from where auto-rickshaws can be hired to the town centre. There are shelters to protect temple visitors from the sun while waiting; around them, monkeys cadge titbits. Rather than returning to Mysore centre, some may find it convenient to continue directly westward to the Government Silk Weaving Factory and (of greater interest) the adjacent Sandalwood Oil factory.

The **Government Silk Weaving Factory** is located on the corner of Sarjavanika Hostel Road and Madhavachari Road. It is one of four similar factories in Karnataka where silk is woven by power looms into fabric for saris – 350 per day being produced. Visitors are permitted to enter the showroom, but not the factory itself. It closes between 12 noon and 3.00pm. A more interesting proposition is the Government Sandalwood Factory, a short walk away, where production stages may be observed.

Sandalwood Oil Factory

The white sandalwood tree, grown around Mysore, takes 40 years to reach maturity, and this factory, built in 1916, claims to be the only one in the world where oil is extracted from it. There are 24 stills, each of which processes 242lbs (110 kg) of powdered wood per week by means of hot steam created by burning coal. All have been in use for 50 years, but only six stills at a time are operated. The sandalwood oil is stored in drums, 90 per cent of which are exported.

Incense sticks are made (by hand) in a separate part of the factory, primarily by women and children. Six-inch long bamboo sticks are dyed red or green at one end, the other end is covered in a paste of sandalwood dust; some are then dipped into powdered jasmine (from France) or rose (from Madras), thus providing three varieties of perfume. Each worker can produce 10,000 sticks per day, always by hand, and one tonne of wood every week is used at the factory in making the sticks. Families also make sticks in their homes, which they then sell privately; in certain quarters of Mysore, the pleasing aroma of sandalwood pervades many streets. A shop outside the factory sells sandalwood products, including soaps manufactured in Bangalore. The factory is closed between 11.00am and 2.00pm.

Railway Museum

A straight road leads northward from the factory to the Vinoba Road/Jansi Lakshmibai Road junction, around which most of Mysore's higher grade hotels congregate. Nearby, behind Mysore Railway Station, is the Railway Museum (closed Monday and 1.00 -3.00pm). Displayed are steam engines and signalling equipment, that were operated by Mysore State

Railway from 1881 until 1951, when all of India's regional lines were nationalized. Of great interest is the Maharani's luxurious coach, built in 1888.

Accommodation

Mysore is well supplied with hotels of all grades, budget accommodation being concentrated on Dhanwantri Road east of the Diwans Road junction and, more centrally, west of Gandhi Square. Middle-grade accommodation is found north of Hardinge Circle on Shri Harsha Road, Church Road and Nazarbad Main Road. Recommended are the **Hotel Sreekrishna Continental, Mysore Hotel, Hotel Roopa** and **Hotel Palace Plaza**; the old-world **Ritz Hotel** is also recommended but only has four rooms. Of the top grade hotels, the splendid **Lalitha Mahal Palace Hotel**, on the outskirts of Mysore, has already been mentioned. Of the cluster south of the station, that with most character is the **Hotel Metropole**, a former guest house of the maharajas. Bedrooms are enormous, with wide verandahs, but there are only 18 of them which is why the hotel is nearly always full. Its Regency Restaurant is good value, and barbecues are held in the grounds every evening. Opposite, the **King's Kourt Hotel** has more rooms; it is entirely air-conditioned and the food is reliable. Much more expensive is the nearby **Southern Star** with a swimming pool, restaurant and coffee shop. Here, the Gardenia Restaurant is extremely popular, but as it is not very large, reservations for dinner are advisable.

Restaurants

Excellent food at reasonable prices is served in all the top Mysore hotels referred to above, the finest (and naturally the most expensive) being that of the **Lalitha Mahal Palace Hotel**. A recommended, centrally-located restaurant with a cosmopolitan atmosphere is the **Shilpashri** on Gandhi Square, where the rooftop terrace is extremely popular for evening drinking and dining. Do not confuse this with the unappealing terrace restaurant of the Hotel Durbar opposite.

Shopping

Those seeking souvenir 'handicrafts' will enjoy the huge **Cauvery Arts & Crafts Emporium** on Sayaji Rao Road, where quality is guaranteed and prices are fixed; although great bargains are few, the emporium does provide an approximate guide to what the price of an item should be. Mysore's best western style shopping street is, however, **D. Devaraj Urs Road**, one of the most agreeable in India and certainly a better bet than Bangalore's renowned Commercial Street. Surprisingly, most Mysore city maps ignore the street's existence, even though it is within easy walking distance of the top hotels around Vinoba Road, from which it runs northward. Men will find top class tailoring and materials for made-to-measure shirts and trousers at e.g. Gwalior and Raymonds, whilst ladies can order exquisite blouses of cotton or vivid silk at several establishments. A great bargain in India is optical goods, where around 80 per cent savings against western prices can be expected, for example, on made-to-prescription bifocals: Optoline, next to the Andhra bank, can be recommended for these.

Sightseeing tours of Mysore

Many visitors to Mysore have only a very limited amount of time available, and for them, a sightseeing tour usually lasting from 8.30am – 8.30pm maybe convenient. It is likely to include: the Jagan Mohan Palace, the Zoo, Chamundi Hill, Mysore Palace, St Bartholomew's Church, Shrirangapatam and Brindavan Gardens, for the evening illuminations – plus, of course, the obligatory and often time-wasting visit to an emporium. All is rather too rushed, particularly at Shrirangapatam, which in itself deserves half a day; moreover, Somnathpur's Hoysala temple is never included.

Shrirangapatam

This former capital of Tipu Sultan is included in most

Mysore city tours, but needs at least half a day to itself for thorough exploration. Many buses leave Mysore's City Bus Station on KR circle, for Shrirangapatam, which is located around 10 miles (16km) to the north; trains from Mysore to Bangalore also stop there. Points of interest are fairly well-scattered, and most will need an auto-rickshaw or taxi on arrival.

The Fort

In 1454, Timana, a Vijayanagar leader, was granted the governorship of Shrirangapatam, and built its first fort, reusing material from 101 Jain temples that he had demolished, and allegedly financed by discovering a cache of treasure. The last Vijayanagar ruler surrendered to the Maharaja of Mysore in 1610, and Shrirangapatam became the capital of the Woodyer dynasty until Hyder Ali, the Commander-in-Chief of the Woodyer army, seized power from the weak Chika Krishna Raja Woodyer in 1761. He soon enlarged the fort but, in 1791, Tipu Sultan rebuilt much of this work and constructed his palace within its walls. Between 1659 and 1799 the fort suffered seven sieges.

The main entrance, the **Elephant Gate**, survives to the south, but the Water Gate was breached by the British on 4th May 1799; its position is commemorated by a stone obelisk. Of particular interest within the fort are the Ranganata Temple,

the mosque, the dungeon and the site of Tipu's death. Nothing, however, survives of Tipu's splendid palace.

The Gangas built the first temple within the fort in 894, at a time when the entire island was covered with jungle. In 1120, this was expanded by the Hoysalas who replaced most of the original temple. Timana, the builder of Shrirangapatam's earliest fort referred to above, added a pillared hall (*navarana*) to the temple in the mid-15th century. Stylistically, therefore, the **Ranganata Temple**, one of the oldest Dravidian examples in Karnataka, is a combination of Hoysala and Vijayanagar styles; as may be surmised, however, the tall *gopuram* of the gateway is a more recent addition. Within, carving on the two pillars facing the entrance, the ceiling and the domes depicts each of Vishnu's 24 *murtis*. The temple is dedicated to Vishnu as Ranganata, and in the sanctuary the god's immense black stone idol reclines on Adisesha the seven-headed serpent, whilst at his feet the local river goddess Cauvery holds a lotus.

Although they were both devout Muslims, Hyder Ali and his son Tipu Sultan showed great respect for Hinduism. Hyder Ali donated the great juggernaut that stands outside the temple, and Tipu Sultan presented the temple with a sword and ritual vessels of silver. A favoured wife of Tipu was a Hindu and even though, as a Muslim, the Sultan could not join her within the temple, he frequently prayed outside. It is also said that in accordance with Hindu tradition Tipu would never sit at table until he had heard the temple bell ring.

Tipu's favourite mosque, **Majid-i-Allah,** lies to the southeast of the temple and was built, so it is said, at the request of a fakir. An unusually tiny dome and two lofty minarets (each with 200 steps to the top) give the cream painted mosque an unconventional external appearance; equally unconventional is the first floor location of the sanctuary. The 99 names of Allah are inscribed in Persian, together with the mosque's construction date of 1787. A former *madrassa* (school) on the north side has been converted to kitchens; the adjacent tank is now dry.

North of the Ranganata Temple, a marble stone indicates the steep steps which descend to the dungeon in which British officers captured by Hyder Ali at Pollilore were imprisoned 1780-84. Unlike his father, Tipu Sultan showed little mercy to those whom he captured, and it is said that his prisoners were shackled so that river water lapped their feet. Another accusation is that Tipu, 'the Tiger of Mysore', kept tigers to whom those who particularly displeased him were thrown.

The open area to the east was formerly the Parade Ground,

which faced Tipu's palace. To the north east, the site of Tipu Sultan's death is marked by a stone obelisk. Tipu had been cut off, surprised by the rapid success of the British and assault, he was placed, badly wounded on a palanquin which served as a stretcher. A soldier, described as European and probably British, attempted to steal the Sultan's bejewelled dagger belt, but Tipu managed to repel and stab him; the soldier thereupon shot Tipu in the head. It was not quite, therefore, the glorious death in battle that is generally assumed.

Daria Daulat Bagh

Tipu's summer palace, the Daria Daulat Bagh (Wealth of the Sea Garden), more closely resembles a grand summerhouse than a palace. Two storeys high, it was constructed in 1784, seven years before Tipu's main palace within the fort. Following Tipu's defeat, the Daria Daulat Bagh served as the residence of its British Commandant, Colonel Arthur Wellesley, the future Duke of Wellington. The palace is open 10am-5pm, but closes on Fridays.

The palace is approached through a formal four-part garden (bagh), which is embellished with slender cyprus trees. Externally, the timber building is unusually simple in appearance, although the green painted bamboo screens are not an original feature, being added to protect the painted interior from the weather.

In contrast, the interior of the palace is richly decorated in Saracenic style. Side walls comprise *jarokhas* (balconies), columns and foliated arches, reminiscent of a Rajput palace; everything is plastered and painted with a floral design. However, it is the west wall's painted battle scenes, that are exceptional.

The original paintings had been in poor condition for some years when Colonel Wellesley took up occupancy, and he ordered their restoration. However, they were subsequently whitewashed over, and not replaced until the 1850s, when Governor-General Lord Dalhousie during a visit to the summer palace commissioned their repainting by a local artist who 'remembered' the originals. The present work, therefore, is a third representation. Naive in style and with imperfect perspective, the paintings nevertheless display a colourful vivacity and incorporate interesting details.

Hyder Ali had been assisted by the French in deposing the Woodyers in return for promising to aid them in the Wars of the Carnatik against the East India Company. As a consequence of this alliance, Hyder Ali and Tipu Sultan between them waged the four 'Mysore Wars' with the English: 1767-69, 1780-84, 1790-92 and 1799. Hyder Ali was able to dictate his terms for peace at the end of the first war, partly because the English had been let down by their ally, the Nizam of Hyderabad. The second and longest of the wars was begun by Hyder Ali, backed by the Marathas and aided by his son Tipu, who together defeated Colonel Baillie's troops at Pollilore, near Kanchipuram, in 1780 (the main event depicted in the wall painting). Hyder Ali died two years later, and it was the self-proclaimed Tipu Sultan who made peace with the English by signing the Treaty of Mangalore.

The third Mysore War took place during the French Revolution and it is recorded that Tipu referred to himself on occasions, probably humorously, as Citoyen (Citizen) Tipu, in the egalitarian manner practically obligatory in France at the time. It appears that this war was caused by General Lord Cornwallis dropping Tipu Sultan from the East India Company's list of 'friends', on suspicion (justified) of his collusion with the French. Tipu was successful in two campaigns, but was besieged at Shrirangapatam in 1792, where he was forced to surrender half his territory and hand over to the English two of his sons, aged 8 and 10, as hostages. Tipu had far less political acumen than his father, and ill-advisedly strengthened his alliance with France. In 1799, Lord Mornington (Baron Wellesley) decided to put an end to this thorn in the British flesh and so began the fourth, final

and shortest of the Mysore Wars, which lasted just four weeks and resulted in Tipu's death. Before his defeat Tipu caused consternation amongst his opponents by asking Napoleon to come to India to help him. However, the French general, otherwise engaged in Egypt and soon to become First Consul of France, declined the invitation. After the battle, Lord Mornington immediately returned the Woodyers to power as maharajas of Mysore.

The two battle scenes are captioned in rather eccentric English, of which Lord Dalhousie is unlikely to have approved. In the first battle, Hyder Ali is seated on an elephant, Tipu on a horse below him, both smelling flowers. The English are depicted with mutton-chop side whiskers, the French with moustaches (all in red uniforms). In the second battle scene, the Nizam of Hyderabad is shown on the back of a lion; he led the Deccan force, but arrived too late to save the English, who are grouped in a phalanx, protecting ammunition. Their leader, Colonel Baillie, is being transported in a palanquin. Durbar scenes decorate the east wall.

Inside the palace, a small **museum** exhibits memorabilia of Tipu Sultan which include a large portrait of Tipu (aged 30) by John Zoffany, 1780, paintings of six of Tipu's sons by Thomas Hickey, 1801, and a drawing of a seventh son.

Paintings of Tipu's forts demonstrate the enormous number that he built. His gold-embroidered tunic, coin collection and ebony furniture are also on display. He adopted tiger stripes as his insignia, and frequently incorporated them in the design of personal items. A popular exhibit at the Victoria and Albert Museum in London is Tipu's Tiger – a beautifully-painted moving wooden model (1790s), depicting a tiger and its victim, a British soldier, which simulates the growls of the tiger and the cries of the soldier.

Gol Gumbaz

Tipu was extremely fond of the east end of the island on which Shrirangapatam stands, and it was there, around 2 miles (3km) from the fort, that he built a mausoleum for his father, known as Gol Gumbaz, soon after his death in 1782. Like the Daria Daulat, it also stands in a formal garden.

The mausoleum is a square building set on an arcaded platform and surmounted by a bulbous dome. Black hornblende pillars, which are regularly polished with coconut oil to maintain their shine, create the arcade and support a parapet with minarets at each corner. Directly below the dome, another parapet has much smaller minarets at its four corners. Intricate, cream plasterwork decorates the building. Buried beneath the pavement of the arcade are female members of Tipu's family.

Lord Dalhousie presented the mausoleum chamber's double doors of ebony inlaid with ivory around 1852. Within the mausoleum's chamber, decorated with tiger stripes, are the tombs of Tipu Sultan covered in tiger stripe material and inscribed: 'The light of Islam has left this world, a martyr for the faith of Mahomed'; Hyder Ali, draped in purple; and Fatima Begum, Tipu's Hindu-born mother, covered with a green cloth. In the courtyard are the tombs of Tipu's wife, Ruqia Begum, his sons and military commanders.

Facing the Gol Gumbaz is a memorial to Colonel William Baillie, who was captured by Hyder Ali in 1780, and died two years later a prisoner of Tipu Sultan; it was erected by his nephew in 1816.

Brindavan Gardens

These ornamental gardens, 12 miles (19km) north west of Mysore and 9 miles (15km) south west of Shrirangapatam, are usually the final destination in Mysore City tours, so that their evening illuminations can be seen. If timing is convenient, those travelling to Mysore by road from Hassan can visit the gardens on route by making a short diversion. Whilst the gardens are pleasant enough and highly regarded by Indians, they are not sufficiently spectacular to be a compelling draw for foreign tourists.

As usual, the gardens have been laid out to one side of a dam. This example 1.6 miles (2.6km) long, was completed by the British in 1932 and named the **Krishnaraja Sagar Dam** in honour of Maharaja Krishnaraja IV; it is the largest project of its type in Karnataka. Earlier efforts to construct a dam here, including an attempt by Tipu Sultan, were failures.

From Mysore's City Bus Stand, bus 150, a half-hourly service, transports passengers to the edge of the dam in around 40 minutes. As most prefer to visit the gardens in the evening, buses from 5.00pm onward will be packed. The last one returns to Mysore at 9.30pm. Tickets for the gardens must be purchased at the entrance to the dam, which must be walked across in order to reach the gardens, one mile (1.5km) distant. To the west lies the **Krishnaraja Sagar (Lake)** encompassing 50 square miles (130 sq km). The ornamental gardens are terraced, with water flowing through their centre. Boats may be hired. At the far end of the gardens, 'Musical Fountains' entertain for half an hour every evening, performances beginning 30 minutes after the garden's illuminations have been switched on.

It must be pleasant to wake up in the morning within the gardens, and there are two hotels where visitors can stay; guests who have booked a room are permitted to cross the dam by motor vehicle to their hotel. The **Hotel Krishnaraja Sagar** is a beautiful old building with comfortable rooms, a bar and an international restaurant which all, of course, may use. Tea served on the verandah at sundown is most popular. Like Mysore's Metropole Hotel, the Krishnaraja Sagar is a member of the Ritz group and, also like its sister hotel, it is often fully booked in the season. Much cheaper accommodation is available at the state-run **Hotel Maurya Cauvery** nearby.

Somnathpur

Lying 20 miles (33km) east of Mysore and a similar distance south-east of Shrirangapatam, Somnathpur possesses the third of Karnataka's famous Hoysala temples, but due to its rather isolated situation it is never included on Mysore City tours. Somnathpur village can be reached direct from Mysore by several buses that depart from the north side of Nazarbad Main Road, diagonally facing the Ritz Hotel. More buses, however, go to Bannur or Narsipur, from either of which additional services make the short journey to Somnathpur. Those who have seen the temples at either Belur or Halebid will know roughly what to expect as Somnathpur's **Prasanna Chenna Kesava Temple** is almost contemporary with them and was probably designed by the same architect, Janakachari.

There are, however, some major differences.

Somnatha (from whom Somnathpur is named), was a member of the royal family and a philanthropic and highly religious minister of Narasimha III. To honour three gods particularly revered by his family, Chennakeshava, Janardhana and Venugopala, he built a temple dedicated to them, which was completed in 1270, the last of the great Hoysala temples.

The building stands in a courtyard which is enclosed by a 64-cell cloister. Its plan follows the usual star shape, walls have banded decoration and the temple is set on a plinth. However, there are three sanctuaries rather than two and, uniquely, their identical *vimana* towers have survived, resulting in an appreciably higher structure. From the points of the pedestal's 'star' protrude small carved elephants and gods.

Somnathpur has been little altered since it was built, all the decoration was completed, and its location, more isolated than Belur or Halebid, has resulted in fewer visitors. For these reasons it is certainly worth visiting, even if the two more famous Hoysala temples have already been seen.

9 BANGALORE

Although located some way from Karnataka's border with Kerala, Bangalore is easily reached from Mysore, and some with time to spare may wish to explore India's fastest-growing city. If, however, a choice has to be made between Bangalore and Mysore, most tourists will find that the latter has significantly more to offer. Bangalore is the only city in the south Deccan with an airport (domestic) and there are direct flights to the Kerala cities of Cochin, Calicut and Trivandrum; there are also services to nearby Mangalore, Coimbatore and Madras, in addition to India's major cities.

Bangalore's congenial all-year-round climate, due to its height (3,250ft -1,000m) and location, is unusual for an Indian city: not only are temperatures bearable in the hot season, but rainfall is much less dramatic during the monsoons. This, together with an abundant supply of spring water, has led to the city's popularity as a centre for skilled industries, machine tools and electronics being prominent. Bangalore is also renowned for the manufacture of fabrics, especially silk, and its region is still a major producer of coffee. Since the 1980s, many commercial organizations have transferred their operations to Bangalore from Calcutta, to escape the Marxist policies of its administrators, and from Bombay, due to the high cost of land. Unfortunately, this rapid expansion has destroyed a great deal of the charm of Bangalore, which had been highly regarded by the British who felt more at home here than in any other large Indian town. Winston Churchill was particularly fulsome in its praise. Now, the streets are as congested and the air is just as polluted as in other Indian cities and, in addition, prices have risen spectacularly. Bangalore's westernization is particularly noticeable in the emancipation of women and the café society that has developed, based on 'pubs' and smart restaurants, where the food is as likely to be 'continental' as Indian. A yuppy element is more noticeable in Bangalore than in any other Indian city, including Bombay, and the language in which the young executives communicate is generally English.

Evidence of international trade in the region as early as the first century BC has been discovered in the form of Roman coins, but the origin of Bangalore's name is greatly disputed, many alternatives being suggested. However, an inscribed temple stone records a 9th-century battle in the area and refers to a village of Bangalura, from which it seems likely that the name of the present city evolved. In the Kannada language, which is spoken throughout Karnataka, *bengallu* means granite, whilst *ura* means place, and this may be the linguistic origin.

What is certain, however, is that Bangalore was founded in 1537 by Kempe Gowda I, a vassal of the Vijayanagar ruler Achuta Raja. Allegedly, whilst hunting, Kempe Gowda's dog was chased by a hare, and its bravery convinced him (or his astrologer) that this was a propitious sign that a new city should be founded on the spot. Its limits were defined by the extent to which bullocks could pull carts in four directions before stopping through exhaustion. At each point where they came to a halt, Kempe Gowda built a watchtower: all four have survived, and are, apart from the Someshwara Temple, the oldest structures to be found in the city, which is noticeably short of ancient monuments.

Muslims first ruled Bangalore in 1638, when the Sultan of Bijapur's powerful army marched in. Fifty years later, the Moguls,

Opposite: *Vidhana Soudha, Bangalore's Parliament*

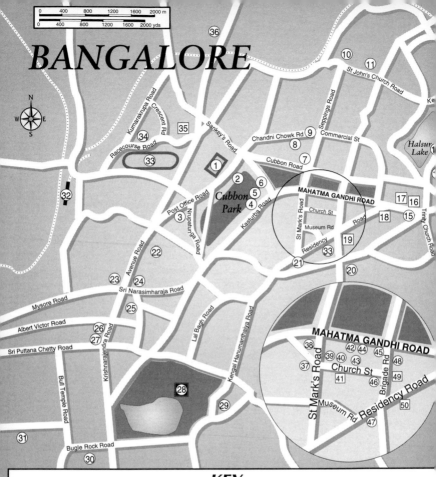

BANGALORE

KEY

1. Vidhana Soudha (Parliament)
2. High Court (Athara Kutcheri)
3. Mythic Society
4. Venkatappa Art Gallery
5. Government Museum
6. Visvesvarava Museum
7. St Andrew's Kirk
8. St Mary's Basilica
9. Russel Market
10. St Francis Xavier's Cathedral
11. St John's Church
12. Kempe Gowda Tower (NE)
13. Gurudwara
14. Someshwara Temple
15. Trinity Church
16. Taj Residency Hotel
17. Oberoi Hotel
18. Hotel New Victoria
19. Hotel East West

20. Central Cottage Industries Emporuim
21. Casa Piccolo Restaurant
22. Ranganatha Temple
23. City Market
24. Jama Masjid
25. Fort
26. Venkatramanaswamy Temple
27. Tipu's Summer Palace
28. Lal Bagh
29. Kempe Gowda Tower (SE)
30. Bull Temple
31. Gavi Gangadeswara Temple
32. City Railway Station
33. Racecourse
34. Janardhana Hotel
35. West End Hotel
36. Bangalore Palace
37. British Library

38. St Mark's Cathedral
39. 'Nineteen (19) Church Street Restaurant
40. Government of India Tourist Office
41. Highgates Hotel
42. Higginbothams
43. Coconut Grove Restaurant
44. Gangaram's Book Bureau
45. Cottage Arts
46. NASA & Oasis Bar
47. Shanbag Cafe
48. Cauvery Arts & Crafts Empor
49. Hotel Curzon Court
50. Gateway Hotel

 □ Hotel ○ Other

at last making incursions into south India, took the city but, in 1687, their governor Kasim Khan leased Bangalore to Chikka Deva Woodyer, Maharaja of Mysore, whose successors became its rulers. The remainder of Bangalore's history closely follows that of Mysore, with the brief appearance of Hyder Ali and Tipu Sultan, followed by the British occupation and Indian rule at independence. In 1956, Bangalore became the state capital of Mysore, which was renamed Karnataka in 1973.

Within a short period, as was their habit in India, the British had built their Cantonment; this was located 1.5 miles (2.5km) north east of the old city, from which it was separated by open land. Pestilence forced the transfer of troops to Bangalore from Srirangapatam to occupy new barracks, and their parade ground, two miles (3km) long, formed the centre of the Cantonment.

In 1831, the British took over the administration of the city from the Woodyers, more troops were brought in, and Bangalore became the regional headquarters. Civilians now followed the military, primarily comprising soldiers' families and merchants.

Residential areas were developed north and south of the Cantonment, and many of their bungalows have survived. Imposing civic buildings, including the present High Court, were also constructed, and a railway was brought to the city.

Arriving in Bangalore

Conveniently, the **City Railway Station** and the **City Bus Stand** face each other. As usual, the surrounding area is where the cheaper hotels are to be found, but it is not very convenient for sightseeing, and Bangalore taxis are expensive by Indian standards. Unless loaded down with luggage, the more centrally located Residency Road can be reached by buses from the Bus Stand; in this area, hotels in the middle and upper price range are to be found. Bangalore's airport is located unusually close to the city centre (7 miles, 11km away), and there is a bus service (irregular) between them. Auto-rickshaws are significantly cheaper than taxis, and some effort here is made by the authorities to ensure that meters are used; however, non-locals may have the usual exasperating problems with cheats.

Sightseeing

Six-hour **circular tours of the city**, operated by the Karnataka State Tourist Development Corporation (KSTDC), leave in front of the state tourist office at 7.30am, ending at the railway station; a similar afternoon tour leaves the railway station at 1.30pm, returning to it later. However, these will not suit everyone as a great deal of time is spent in museums that are less than riveting, in addition to the usual wearisome 'crafts' emporiums. It is far preferable to hire a taxi for a day and make a more

leisurely inspection of the city. All the following locations can be seen in one day without too much difficulty and are described in sequence. Bangalore's state museums are grouped together, and as a taxi is not needed to travel from one to the other, these are treated separately.

Fort

At the junction of Krishnarajendra Road and Mysore Road, the City Market faces the **Jama Masjid**, Bangalore's largest mosque. This area marked the centre of Kempe Gowda's original, 16th-century city, which was dominated by his mud-built fort. Within, the Woodyers soon constructed a smaller citadel, but Hyder Ali replaced this with a large, moated enclosure of stone. Tipu Sultan later added his own palace to the south. Most of the fortress was demolished by the British during the third Mysore war, but fragments of the wall, one of the two fortified gates, two temples from the Woodyer period and part of Tipu's palace have survived.

The fort is entered from the east side of Krishnarajendra Road, where a plaque on the wall commemorates the final battle in the third Mysore War, which marked the defeat of Tipu Sultan: 'Through this breach the British assault was delivered March 21st 1791'.

Opposite: Rearing steeds adorn Bangalore's Ranganatha Temple.

Within the fort, facing its entrance, is a small **Ganesh Temple** which never seems to be open. Carved on its roof structure, a double-headed peacock, the emblem of the Woodyer family, indicates that the building is a survival from their earlier citadel. Although a devout Muslim, Hyder Ali permitted this Hindu temple to remain, through respect for his wife's religion. Part of the ramparts can be climbed to their battlements, from where can be seen the immense Victoria Hospital, built on part of the west wall's moat, which had to be filled for it. From the battlements it is still possible to reach the dungeons in which British prisoners-of-war were held by Tipu. The most impressive part of the fort is its north-facing **Delhi Gate**, a rebuilding in granite of an earlier structure. Islamic in style, delicate plaster decoration has survived.

Venkataramanaswamy Temple

This granite temple to Vishnu in Dravidian style, (closed 12-6pm) stands further south along Krishnarajendra Road, at the Albert Victor Road junction. Constructed outside the Woodyer fort in the late 17th century, the temple eventually fell within Hyder Ali's larger enclosure and survives as the oldest structure in the area; both *gopuram* towers, however, are modern additions. The banded pyramidal *shikara* above the *vimana* tower is original work, although much of the temple needed restoration after being damaged during the British assault.

Bas-reliefs of Vishnu, Brahma and Shiva embellish the external walls, and lion brackets in sets of four decorate the columns of the *mandapam*. A small temple to the monkey god Hamuyan stands in a corner of the courtyard.

Tipu's Summer Palace

Immediately south of the temple stands the most interesting Islamic building in Bangalore, all that survives of **Tipu's Summer Palace**. Tipu Sultan completed this in 1789, and those who have seen his palace in Shrirangapatam will note many similarities. Located within his father's fort, the two-storey open structure, built mostly of timber, served primarily as Tipu's audience chamber. Originally, the palace was fronted by a courtyard, in the centre of which stood a fountain, but this, together with the remainder of the complex, has been lost. Stairs lead to the upper storey where, from the seat of state on its central balcony, Tipu held audience with his subjects gathered below. Most walls were gilded and painted, but only traces of this have survived. It is still possible, however, to appreciate the delicacy of the carving, particularly on the fluted pillars and the beaded balustrade; the inscription on a wooden beam 'An abode of Happiness and Envy of Heaven' is witness to the former splendour of the building.

Returning northward, Krishnarajendra Road becomes Avenue Road. To the east, in the centre of a lively quarter is the Ranganatha Temple.

Ranganatha Temple

Built by Kempe Gowda II early in the 17th century, although much restored, this Vishnu 'snake' temple retains much original carving. Worth noticing are the enormous horses supporting the roof brackets, and the avatars of Vishnu, sculpted and painted on the roof of the sanctuary. On both sides at the rear are carved snake stones, one of them allegedly the work of Kempe Gowda himself. Further east, the maze of roads ends at Narasimharaja Square, where the KSTDC Information Office faces the Corporation Office. Ask the driver to follow the road ahead (one way only) through Cubbon Park.

Cubbon Park

The park was laid out by the British in 1864, and named to commemorate the popular Commissioner of Mysore (1834-61). Its 300 acres are a remnant of the swathe of open land that originally separated the old city from the Cantonment. As car pollution increases, the existence of this 'lung' in the city centre has assumed even greater importance. Officially, it is now known as **Chamarajendra Park**, but the original name is still more commonly used. Informal in style, with splendid trees providing shelter from the sun for office workers on lunchtime breaks as well as picnickers, the park is criss-crossed with paths and short roads. In the south-east corner, **Jawahar Bal Bhavan**, an area set aside for children (no adults admitted unaccompanied by a child), incorporates a children's theatre/cinema, a fairground and a miniature steam train, which puffs around the park from 3 to 7pm (not Mondays). Towards the north end of the park is the red-painted High Court building with, at its rear, an 1866 statue of Cubbon, the work of the Italian sculptor Baron Marochetti, whose work at Windsor was much admired by Queen Victoria.

High Court

This long building was designed specifically to house the Revenue and General Secretariat departments of the British administration when Tipu's Palace became too small for them. Opened in 1868, the building was known as the Athara Kutcheri (Eighteen Courts), a reference to the eighteen departments accommodated within. In 1956, the departments were transferred to the new, much larger Secretariat opposite, demolition of the Athara Kutcheri being proposed. Fortunately, local objectors saved the building which was converted to serve as Bangalore's High Court, but its original name is still in common usage. Within, Cubbon is commemorated on a ceiling by a medallion portrait. The Legislative Council formerly met in the Central Hall.

Vidhana Soudha Secretariat

Facing the Law Courts across Vidhana Vidhi is the present Secretariat and Legislature of Karnataka State, the **Vidhana Soudha**.

The building, which may not be entered by members of the public, is spectacularly floodlit on Sunday evenings – Bangalore's answer to Mysore Palace! India's largest legislative building was constructed of granite and porphyry in 1956 at enormous cost, to coincide with Bangalore's new status as capital of Karnataka.

Sensitive to Russian criticism that India's administrative buildings were 'too European' in style, typical architectural features from different parts of the country have been incorporated. The main porch, with its 'sunshade' and pillars, is south Indian Dravidian, whilst *jarrokha* balconies on either side of it evoke Rajasthan palaces. Hindu pillars support three long tiers of loggias, which stretch above an arcade. The 65 ft (20m) high dome is surmounted by four gold lions in the manner

of the capitals of Ashok pillars, whilst smaller cupolas are Indo-Saracenic in style. Above the entrance is inscribed 'Government Work is God's Work'. Not all those in receipt of tax assessments, for example, might agree wholeheartedly with such a sentiment.

From the Vidhana Soudha, Post Office Road and Nrupthunga Road (branching off it) return southward, passing various colleges and government buildings. These are of little interest to tourists apart from the **Mythic Society**, on the west side of Nrupatunga Road at its north end.

Mythic Society
(Daly Memorial Hall)

Reminiscent of a small English classical church, the now little-used name of the hall commemorates Sir Hugh Daly, Resident of Mysore and president of the Mythic Society, for which the building was erected in 1917. A pedimented Corinthian portico fronts the road. Within the hall is a reference library and a reading room. Paintings of patrons, including three maharajas, line the walls.

From Nrupatunga Road, Kasturba Road runs diagonally north eastward skirting Cubbon Park. At its far end, on the west side, are a cluster of state museums which can be seen without the services of a waiting taxi. These are: the **Venkatappa Art**

Opposite: St Andrew's Kirk, one of the few Scottish churches in India.

Gallery, closed Wednesday; the **Government Museum**, also closed Wednesday; the **Visvesvarya Museum**, closed Monday; and the **Aquarium**, closed Tuesday.

Where Kasturba Road joins MG Road a statue was erected, in 1906 to commemorate Queen Victoria. Designed by Sir Thomas Brock, the marble figure standing on a granite pedestal was a copy of a statue at Worcester.

St Mark's Cathedral

Bangalore's present cathedral, at the west end of MG Road, was built in 1927. However, it had been founded in 1808, and was completed on the same site four years later – to much criticism. This building, which could only accommodate a congregation of 500, was accused of being the ugliest ever erected; low-roofed and with yellow painted walls, its appearance was said to resemble a Bryant and May matchbox. The Lord apparently concurred as a tower, added in 1901, collapsed the following year, and in 1923 the nave was burnt to a cinder.

It cannot be said that the present cream-painted building is an entirely successful example of Baroque Revival architecture. Round-headed arches support the pediment of the south porch, rather than slender columns, resulting in a heavy appearance. The balustrades are delicate enough, but the shallow dome can only be appreciated from a distance, a common problem with domes which few architects overcome.

Entry is gained from the south door of the nave. Within, all is painted white, colour being provided by stained glass: floral designs in the clerestory and Christ enthroned above the west entrance being particularly noteworthy.

Immediately north of the cathedral, on the north side of Cubbon Road, stands **St Andrew's Kirk**, the only Scottish church in Bangalore. Of plain design, a stained glass window depicting Christ with the Apostles, and a pipe organ installed in 1881, are the chief features of interest.

Continue directly northward, passing the Bus Stand to Chandni Chowk Road where, on the south side, stands Bangalore's Roman Catholic Basilica.

St Mary's Basilica

The cathedral, completed in 1882 by Rev. L.E. Kleiner, replaced a small chapel which had been built by the Abbé Dubois in 1818. Pope John Paul VI raised it to minor basilica status (the sixth in India) in 1973. Gothic revival inside and out, the building is entered from its south door.

A pale blue and white colour scheme creates a cool interior. Painted vines decorate the capitals of the columns, colourful ceramic figures embellish the altars in both chapels of the sanctuary. Mass is usually celebrated in the rather ugly building to the south.

The east end of Chandni Chowk Road faces **Russell Market**, a centre for good-quality meat, vegetables and fruit. Originally an open-air market with stalls sheltered by trees, Russell Market was created on the bed of a dried-up lake in 1927; its name commemorates a Civil Services Officer T.B. Russell, who was in charge of the project.

A short walk from the south-east corner of the market leads to Bangalore's famous **Commercial Street** which stretches eastward, parallel with MG Road. Although this is Bangalore's best-known shopping thoroughfare, prices are comparatively high and there are not many shops from which tourists would wish to make purchases, an exception being, perhaps, **Mysore Handicrafts Emporium** where good quality artefacts are to be found.

Seppings Road leads from the north-east corner of Russell Market to **St Francis Xavier's Cathedral**, a granite cruciform structure built for Roman Catholic worship. The interior, in Byzantine style, is very different from other churches in Bangalore.

The cathedral overlooks St John's Church Road, which leads eastwards to **Halsur (or Ulsoor) Lake**, where it becomes Kensington Road and skirts the lake. Boats of many types can be hired at the north end from the Boat House, beside which is a public swimming pool. A leafy artificial island in the lake can be visited by boat. Perched on a rock overlooking the lake at its south-east end is a **Kempe Gowda Tower**, the most easterly of the four towers erected by Kempe Gowda I to mark the limits of his city. Built circa 1537, the rather bulbous, pyramidal structure is supported by short Hindu columns.

At the southern tip of the lake, on its east bank, is a **Gurudwara** (Sikh Temple), rare in southern India. Further south, Halsur Road leads eastward to Bangalore's most ancient monument.

Someshwara Temple

This temple is known to predate Bangalore itself, as its sanctuary has survived from the Chola period (907-1310). Kempe Gowda I extended the building in Dravidian style, so that most of it is now 16th-century work. For five years, Kempe Gowda was unfairly imprisoned by his suzerain the Vijayanagar ruler, and may have been inspired by the great Shiva temples at Hampi, the Vijayanagar capital. The outer wall is decorated with figures that represent the signs of the zodiac; the cross-legged man leaning on a stick was allegedly modelled on Kempe Gowda. Within, the pillars of the *mandapam* are carved to depict riders on prancing horses.

National Highway 4 leads southward to the MG Road/Trinity Church Road junction. On its south-west corner is the second church to be built in Bangalore.

Trinity Church

As St Mark's Cathedral, the first Bangalore church, could only accommodate 500 worshippers, a new building was soon needed to cope with the rapid expansion of the city's European population, both civil and military. Primarily, however, Holy Trinity served as a military church. The architect was a Major Peak, who opted for the classical style. Beneath the foundation stone, laid in 1848, is a 'time capsule' which includes coins and a parchment record of the ceremony. A year earlier, the church bell had been cast in London, and this is still rung for Sunday services.

Trinity Church is entered via a porch supported by Ionic pillars. Mosaic tiles and a stained glass Baptism of Christ window in the chancel add some colour to the otherwise monochrome interior. Although the British military considered Bangalore to be one of India's healthier postings, many soldiers died from local diseases (only a few were killed in battle), and they are commemorated by impressive plaques along the walls of the nave.

The long MG Road stretches east to west, fronting the church.

Mahatma Gandhi (MG) Road

This thoroughfare, Bangalore's most important, formerly marked the southern stretch of the British military parade ground and was called South Parade. Much of its north side fronts parkland. Commercial properties, apartment blocks, silk emporiums and hotels now dominate the two mile long road. Many of Bangalore's top and medium grade hotels and restaurants can be found in the triangle formed by MG Road, Residency Road, Museum Road and St Mark's Road. At the east end are Bangalore's finest hotels, **The Oberoi**, with beautiful grounds and outstanding food, and the Taj Residency. Unlike the Oberoi, the **Taj Residency** permits non-residents to use its swimming pool, for a daily charge. Almost facing each other, at the Brigade Road intersection, are **Cottage Arts** and **Cauvery Arts and Crafts Emporium**, both specializing in crafts from all regions of India. Further west along MG Road is a branch of the **Higginbothams** chain of bookshops and **Gangaram's Book Bureau**.

For those wishing to catch up on UK events, the **British Library**, 29 St Mark's Road, a turning off MG Road, permits visitors to peruse (usually one week old) English newspapers.

A south-westward route follows St Marks Road, Residency Road and Lal Bagh Road to Lal Bagh.

The Glasshouse at Lal Bagh Gardens was opened by the future Edward VII in 1890.

Lal Bagh

This garden, one of the most famous in India, is believed to have been laid out for Hyder Ali, and named *lal* (red) to record his love of red roses. Tipu Sultan increased the original area of 40 acres, and imported plants then unknown in India. The floral beds are Mogul in style, one species being allocated exclusively to each plot. Straight gravel paths and fountains at their intersections emphasize the formality.

From the main entrance facing Kengal Hanumantaya Road, the visitor is confronted by a huge granite outcrop which can be climbed. It is 3,000 million years old and one of the oldest examples of rock in the world. In 1916, Dr W.F. Smeeth of the Mysore Geology department named it the Peninsula Gneiss. Such outcrops are common throughout India, but this is one of the most spectacular. Surmounting the summit is the southern watchtower erected by Kempe Gowda in the 16th century.

By 1856, Lal Bagh had been expanded to 240 acres (97.2 hectares) and the British introduced horticulture and a superintendent from Kew as manager. In 1890, the Prince of Wales, the future Edward VII, opened the Lal Bagh glasshouse which had been modelled on the Crystal Palace. This survives, in splendid condition, north east of the Peninsula Gneiss, and may be entered; however, it no longer houses plants but has become a fashionable venue for functions.

An extensive lake occupies the south end of the garden, and many waterfowl can be observed. Today, Lal Bagh boasts more than 1,000 subtropical and tropical specimens, some of which can be found nowhere else in India. Flower shows are held in January and August.

Bugle Rock Road runs westward from the south side of Lal Bagh to the Bull Temple.

Bull Temple

Carved from a single black boulder, this 20 ft (6 m) long bull (*basava*) has given its name to the district of Basavangudi in which it stands. The figure, of course, represents Shiva's mount Nandi, and is reminiscent of Mysore's bull on Chamundi Hill. By tradition, the figure was created to calm an aggressive bull which had caused much damage in the locality. When finished, however, it gradually expanded in size, and only stopped growing when the Shiva temple was built next to it. Behind Nandi is a figure of Ganesh; Shiva is represented in the sanctuary by a *lingam*. Within the temple, an inscription relates that the River Vrishabhariti has its source at Nandi's feet. Towards the year's end, a peanut festival is held in the locality, samples of the new crop being offered to Nandi.

Just north of the temple, **Bugle Rock**, surmounted by a small pavilion, marks the spot where a section of Tipu Sultan's army regrouped immediately prior to the British assault on Bangalore Fort towards the end of the third Mysore War.

Bull Temple Road stretches due north for half a mile (1km) before a left turn leads to the 'cave' temple.

Gavi Gangadheeshwara Temple

As usual, this temple is closed 12 noon to 5.00pm, but a side gate is normally left open. It is best approached from the road to the rear, via the **Harihareswara Temple**. Kempe Gowda I built the structure, so it is said, in thanks to Shiva for his release from the Vijayanagar prison. *Gavi* means cave, a reference to the cave in which the shrine of Gangadheeshwara, an aspect of Shiva, is worshipped.

Two sanctuary domes rise above the cave, and a Nandi guards the temple. Finely carved figures of gods displayed in niches include a rare depiction of Agni, the god of fire, and Shiva's consort Parvathi. At the Festival of Makara Sakranti, 13/14 January, the rays of the setting sun strike the Shiva *lingam* within the cave via an archway, two barred windows and another Nandi.

Many roads lead north eastwards to the city centre.

Bangalore Palace

North west of the city on the east side of Sankey's Road, the picturesque former palace of Maharaja Srikantadatta Woodyer, in English mock-Tudor style, incorporates features reminiscent of Windsor Castle. Neither the palace nor its grounds are usually open to the public, and few tourists will find the 2 mile (3 km) journey from Bangalore centre worthwhile. However, the state has plans for acquiring and developing the palace and its extensive grounds. Check the current situation.

Museum Complex

Bangalore's museums and aquarium are located conveniently adjacent to each other. Of greatest interest to most foreign visitors is the **Government Museum**, founded in 1866 and one of India's oldest museums.

On the ground floor are Hoysala, Vijayanagar and Shravana Belgola sculptures, and exhibits from India's earliest periods. Tipu Sultan's canons and a model of his fort at Shravana Belgola, which was almost entirely demolished by the British, are of particular interest.

Upper floor (east side): Paintings from the Tanjore School, incorporating semi-precious stones, gold-leaf miniatures from Rajasthan and Gujarat, and musical instruments.

Restaurants	Bars
Taj Residency, 41/3 MG Road ☎ 558 4444 Fax: 558 4748 Memories of China (particularly buffet lunch).	Black Cadillac, Residency Road Oasis, Church Street

Restaurants

Taj Residency, 41/3 MG Road
☎ 558 4444 Fax: 558 4748
Memories of China (particularly
buffet lunch).
'19 Church Street'. Good Italian food.
Coconut Grove, Church Street.
Shanbag Cafe, Residency Road.
Outstanding thalis.
Casa Piccolo, 131 Residency Road.
Reliable steaks (beef).

Bars

Black Cadillac, Residency Road
Oasis, Church Street

Airlines

Indian Airlines, Housing Board
Buildings, Kempe Gowda Road
☎ 221 1914

British Airways, St Mark's Road
☎ 221 4034

Upper floor (west side): natural history exhibits – of little appeal unless attracted by dusty skeletons and stuffed creatures.

Venkatappa Art Gallery

Lying immediately west of the Government Museum, the gallery's name commemorates a famous Karnataka artist whose work is displayed on the ground floor. On the floor above are exhibited works by contemporary local artists. Those interested in modern Indian art may wish to spend some time here.

Visvesvaraya Industrial and Technological Museum

Located on the other side of the Government Museum, this museum of Indian technological achievement is of great appeal to Indians – primarily Indian schoolboys who like to make things work.

Onward travel

Travellers arriving from or continuing to Madras from Bangalore can either take a 45-minute flight (3-5 flights per day) or an express train. The fastest train (5 hours 10 minutes) is the mid afternoon *Shatabdi Express* (not Tuesday) which links Bangalore with Mysore and Madras (no first class, but air-conditioned). The early afternoon *Brindavan Express* is, however, much cheaper, although it takes almost an hour longer. A direct train from Trivandrum, the *Kanyakumari Express*, currently leaves Madras at 9.00pm, reaching Trivandrum at 9.00pm the following day.

10 MADRAS, KANCHIPURAM AND MAMALLAPURAM

The closest airport to Kerala with scheduled flights operating between India and Europe is the international airport at Madras, even though it is around 375 miles (600km) distant. Many visitors to Kerala, therefore, arrive at and depart from Madras, and while they are in the area some of them naturally wish to explore its attractions. Madras, India's fourth largest city, only really warrants a couple of days of the average tourist's time, but it forms the apex of Tamil Nadu's 'golden triangle' comprising Madras, the shore temple beach resort of Mamallapuram, and the ancient temple city of Kanchipuram.

The monsoons that affect the Coromandel coast are significantly different from those encountered on Kerala's Malabar coast, although temperatures do not vary greatly. Summer and

Above: The Five Pandava Rathas at Mamallapuram.

Autumn monsoons reach both coasts, but whereas the former brings relatively light rainfall to Madras whilst Kerala is being soaked, October and November receive a great deluge from much of which Kerala is protected. On occasions, the autumn monsoon fails, creating major water and power shortages throughout Tamil Nadu. If, for some reason, a tourist is still in Kerala on 28th or 29th May, when the summer monsoon arrives as regularly as clockwork, the downpour can be minimised by crossing to India's east coast.

Madras (Chennai)

Those arriving at Madras by air can book taxis or a minibus that calls at the leading hotels, from the prepaid counter at the international airport terminal. For budget travellers there are trains from Tirusulam station, beside the air terminal, to Egmore Station which is handy for a number of economy and medium grade hotels. The international and domestic airports are both located 10 miles (16km) south of the city centre.

Long-distance trains generally terminate at Madras Central Station just south west of George Town, where the hassle created by porters, who almost fight to carry a tourist's luggage, can be annoying. The terminal for long-haul buses on Esplanade Road is just behind the High Court, to the south east of George Town.

Official sightseeing tours of this enormous city, the fourth largest in India and the state capital of Tamil Nadu, take only six hours, a good indication that Madras is hardly a tourist mecca. A young city by Indian standards, its foundation in 1611 also marked the foundation of the British Empire. Fortunately, the most important early buildings of the East India Company have survived, within Fort St George, and are the greatest tourist attractions that the city has to offer – certainly as far as British tourists are concerned.

Fort St George

The original walls of Fort St George were completed on 23 April 1630, St George's Day, which is how the enclosure gained its name. It surprises many that William Shakespeare had died, also on St George's Day, just 23 years earlier. The walls protected the East India Company's 'factory', as European trading settlements were referred to at the time. Its function was to serve as a base for English agents to prevent local merchants from controlling prices of goods on the Coromandel coast. Competition from Dutch, Portuguese and French agents was fierce, which is why the fortification was necessary. As early as 1601, the East India Company had begun trading on the coast, and within ten years it had established a station at Machilipatnam, a few miles north of present day Madras. Eventually, however, the station's managers Andrew Cogan and Francis Day learned that the prices demanded for cloth and spices were much lower at the coastal village of Madraspatnam, further south, and decided to relocate there. The land was owned by the last Vijayanagar emperor, Venkata III, who in 1639 leased the company, through his representatives in Madraspatnam, a desolate strip of sand on which to build. Initially around 100 square yards (85 sq m) in extent, the enclosure was gradually extended until it finally encompassed 42 acres (17 hectares). In 1666, most of the wall was rebuilt and the moat extended; all were strengthened in the 18th century. The first building within the walls was called Fort House, but this no longer exists, having been replaced by a new Fort House built to the east of it as a residence for the first governors of Madras. This does survive in part, but only as the core of the Secretariat building, the most important structure in Fort George, and which also houses the Legislature of the Tamil Nadu state government. The Secretariat faces the main entrance to the fort, on Kamarajar Salai (formerly Beach Road) and is the best point at which to begin a tour of the complex. Taxis are usually permitted to park at the rear of the building.

Secretariat/Legislature

In spite of encompassing the second Fort House, the oldest British-built structure in India (nothing of which can be seen by the general public), the symmetrical facades of the **Secretariat** are early 20th century work. However, they do incorporate 16 columns of black granite known as charnockite to commemorate Job Charnock, an 18th century governor of the fort. These represent half of the 32 original columns that had been erected as a colonnade in 1732. Inside, the impressive Assembly Hall of the Legislature was developed from the Secretariat's Council Chamber; in theory, this may be viewed by applying in advance to the Speaker's Office, but the procedure will be too time-consuming for most visitors.

To the right of the facade facing the main gates is the cupola that was brought here from the Parade Ground, and beneath which had stood a statue of Lord Cornwallis. Its eight black columns of charnockite are from the same set as the Secretariat's. In front are specimens of the fort's original cannons.

Fort Museum

Immediately north of the Secretariat, separated from it by a street, is the *Fort Museum*, one of India's best. It is open 9.00am to 5.00pm but closed on Fridays. The museum opened in 1944 in what had been the Exchange Building, constructed in the

18th century; exhibits are dispersed on its three floors. At the foot of the stairs, facing the entrance, is the statue of Lord Cornwallis, transferred here from its cupola seen outside. Ground floor rooms originally accommodated warehouses and the city's first bank, The Bank of Madras, which, after several mergers now forms part of the State Bank of India, one of the largest banks in the world.

Uniforms and armaments are displayed left of the entrance. To the right are medals, porcelain and Indian postage stamps. Of particular interest is a model of the fort, together with the huge locks of its gateway. The Long Room, on the first floor, serves primarily as a portrait gallery of British governors of Madras. This was formerly the Public Exchange Hall, an informal coffee house where merchants met to discuss trade, occasionally overlooked by the governor from his private gallery above. On the second floor, memorabilia of the French in India includes clocks and furniture from the Louis XIV period. In another room are exhibited old prints depicting the fort. India's first lighthouse functioned on the roof of the building until 1841, but no trace of it remains.

The flagpole of Fort St George stands to the south of the Secretariat; it is India's highest at almost 150ft (47.5m) and dates from 1687, when Governor Elihu Yale hoisted the English flag from it to mark his country's first territorial acquisition in India.

Old Fort House

Behind the museum, the Old Fort House is the third building in the complex to have been so named; constructed in the 18th century, it now serves as the headquarters of the army's area commander. Facing this is the extension to the rear of the Secretariat which accommodates the Legislature and, further south, St Mary's Church.

St Mary's Church

Consecrated in 1680, St Mary's Church is the oldest Protestant foundation in India, possibly in Asia. Its original architect was the East India Company's Chief Engineer William Dixon who, mindful of possible attack, specified 4 foot 4 inch (1.33m) thick walls and a curved 2 foot (0.6m) thick roof, designed to repel cannonballs. Governor Elihu Yale, soon to give his name to Yale University in the United Sates, was an important benefactor to the fund for constructing the church. Dixon's building took the form of a plain rectangular box which was embellished in 1759 with a Gothic Revival tower and turrets. He also added a new entrance reached by a flight of steps for the exclusive use of the Governor and council members on important occasions.

The church is entered from the north porch. It is alleged that the artist responsible for

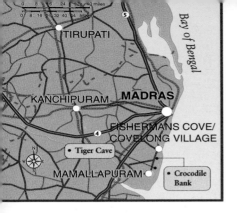

the Last Supper scene above the high altar was a 16th-century student of Raphael, and Raphael is personally credited with painting the chalice. Walls are decorated with marble plaques and monuments, typical of a venerable English parish church: most of those commemorated were military personnel. The finest monument, however, is to the missionary Schwartz who tried to negotiate a peaceful settlement between the English and Hyder Ali. He is depicted on his deathbed, surrounded by friends, while an angel waits for him patiently above.

Displayed in a glass case are historic church records, including the marriage of Robert Clive (Clive of India) to Margaret Masekeylene, Elihu Yale to Catherine Hynmers, and the baptism of Job Charnock's three daughters born to his Indian wife; Charnock later founded the city of Calcutta. William Hastings and his wife-to-be worshipped at St Mary's, as did Arthur Wellesley, the future Duke of Wellington, who served here as best man at a wedding.

Immediately after leaving St Mary's, note the burial stones just north of the west end of the church. Of particular interest is the damaged stone of 1652 inscribed in Latin to commemorate Elizabeth(ae) Baker. She was the wife of the first President of Madras, Aaron Baker, and died in childbirth on the voyage from England to join her husband in a land that she would never see. This is believed to be the oldest British inscription in India to have survived. The tombstone of missionary Schwartz can also be seen. During attacks on the fort by the French and Hyder Ali the tombstones were used a gun mounts.

Three historic 18th-century buildings stand in line to the south of St Mary's. **Writers' Building** accommodated clerks on their arrival from England. One of them, Robert Clive, a melancholic, made the first of many unsuccessful suicide attempts in this building soon after arriving as a humble clerk in 1744; eventually he slit his throat with a razor, dying at his London home, 45 Berkeley Square, in 1774. However Clive, of course, gave up 'writing' and fought valiantly against the French when they attacked the fort. Prospering, by 1753 he was able to rent from a wealthy Armenian merchant the adjoining mansion, now known as Clive House, for the exclusive occupancy of his wife and himself. It now accommodates the Pay Accounts Office, but one room on the ground floor, 'Clive's Corner', has been set aside as a small museum; exhibits are primarily paintings and prints relating to Clive's exploits.

Further towards the sea is the detached **Wellesley House,** built in 1796 and allegedly the residence of Arthur Wellesley during the brief period when he and his regiment prepared for the final battle with Tipu Sultan. Sadly, it has been allowed to fall into ruin. Just beyond this building is the San Thome Gate.

A return north westward leads to the **Parade Ground,** laid out in 1715. It was here that the original Fort House had been erected in the 17th century. On three sides survive the 19th-century British Army barracks, now occupied by Indian soldiers.

George Town

North of the fort, George Town, a roughly square area of 850 acres was created in the late 18th century, its street plan being one of the first to be designed in a grid pattern: New York's was to follow shortly. In 1781, the East India Company levelled an Esplanade immediately north of Fort St George to provide its cannons with an unobstructed line of fire. The land for it had been settled formerly by Indians and was called Black Town by the English, to distinguish it from White Town where their expatriates lived. Its real name, however, was

Chennapatnam in honour of Chennappa, the father of the two brothers who had administered this community of weavers on behalf of the last Vijayanagar Emperor.

After demolishing the settlement, the English constructed a new Black Town (the present Georgetown) for its former inhabitants, a little further to the north. In 1906, the Prince of Wales, later George V, visited India and Black Town was renamed George Town to commemorate the event. As Madras grew, the local Tamil people assigned the name Chennai (after Chennapatnam) to the entire city, whereas the British stuck to Madras (after Madrasapatnam). In recent years, it has been decided that the official name of the city should be Chennai. However, to avoid confusion, the better-known name, Madras, will be adhered to throughout this book. Although rarely visited by tourists, the north half of George Town is the least altered, its courtyard houses, still decorated with carved wooden doors and windows. Many inhabitants are descended from the earliest settlers of Madras.

To the south, 50 acres of narrow lanes form the city's largest market **Kothwal Chavadi.** Although officially a wholesale market, anyone may purchase – and save quite a few rupees. N.S.C. Bose Road delineates the southern boundary of the market, but immediately to its south are separate **Fruit and Flower Markets** – well away from the pungent aromas found in some parts of the Kothwal Chavadi. Around dawn, vehicles arrive with goods for all the markets, and it is then that the scene is at its liveliest.

Behind the Flower Bazaar Police Station stand the twin **Chennakesvarar** and **Chennamallikesvarar Temples,** built in 1762, by official patronage. Their predecessors had stood in the earlier Black Town and were lost when this was demolished. Almost 50 religious buildings of various faiths have survived in George Town, all constructed between 1639 and 1839.

The name of **Armenian Street,** to the east of Kothwal Chavadi, commemorates the Armenians that settled in India in the 13th and 14th centuries. Their church, the **Armenian Church of the Virgin Mary**, was built on a former burial ground in 1772. A free-standing belfry accommodates six bells, the greatest number in any Madras church.

Adjacent to this church is the Roman Catholic Cathedral of **St Mary of the Angels**. Founded in 1658 as a small church by Ephraim de Nevers, a Capuchin friar, the building was reconstructed in 1692, but extensive remodelling has taken place since. De Nevers had also been responsible for founding St Andrew's Church within Fort St George, and when this was demolished in 1792 its bells and some furnishings were incorporated in the cathedral. The cruciform building, painted cream and grey, is set within surprisingly extensive grounds.

Just outside the south-west corner of George Town, **Madras Central Railway Station** is a red brick Indo-Saracenic edifice, built early in the 20th century.

Towards the south-east corner of George Town, Prakasam Road meets N.S.C. Bose Road, and the junction is known as **Parry's Corner**. The offices of Thomas Parry, now accommodated within Dare House, have stood here for more then two centuries, and the company is India's second oldest. A pillar marks a northern boundary of the Esplanade.

High Court

This enormous legal campus, in the Indo-Saracenic style, was built over the Esplanade between 1888 and 1892. It is said that apart from the Royal Courts of Justice in London, this is the largest law court building in the world. The court rooms are open to visitors Monday to Saturday 10.45am to 1.45pm and 2.30 to 4.30pm. Court 13 is outstanding, with pattern-embossed and silvered wall panels, a vividly painted ceiling and stained glass windows, together with carved woodwork brought from the former High Court on North Beach Road.

Indo-Saracenic civic buildings

are virtually synonymous with Madras, and many examples will be seen in the city. Most were built in the 1870s, the prime exponent of the style being R.A. Chisholm. It was created earlier, however, by Major Mant, known as 'Mad Mant', who died before he was able to complete many commissions. Basically, the style incorporates Islamic form with Hindu and Islamic details, sometime incorporating a touch of Byzantine. In spirit, therefore, Indo-Saracenic attempts to emulate Mogul architecture, but failed to synthesize its various disparate elements as the Moguls had done. Walls were invariably plastered and painted pink to imitate the red sandstone of north India. Eventually, Indo-Saracenic architecture spread to most large cities in India, becoming a symbol of respectability for important buildings in the way that the Gothic Revival did in England.

The central cupola of the High Court is surmounted by a red-domed structure, added in 1894 as the Madras lighthouse and which remained in operation until 1977. It had been preceded by the **Esplanade Lighthouse** which surmounted the Doric pillar to the south-east of the building. This was the second Madras lighthouse to be constructed, operating from 1841 to 1894; before its construction, the city's lighthouse, its first, had been located within Fort St George.

Also within the campus, the **Law College**, flanked by minarets, occupies much of the site of the cemetery of Fort St George; this too disappeared when the Esplanade was laid out in 1781. Behind the college, an obelisk records the burials in the cemetery of David, the son of Elihu Yale, who died aged four, and of Edward Hynmers whose widow was to become Yale's wife and the mother of David.

Rajaji Salai, formerly North Beach Road, runs northward to the harbour, passing some impressive buildings. Most historic of these is **Bentink's Building**, a structure in which, allegedly, were accommodated the sons of Tipu Sultan after they had been taken hostage by the English and made wards of Sir John Doveton. The Supreme Court sat here from 1817 until 1862, when it became the seat of the High Court for thirty years. The unoccupied cupola in the grounds originally sheltered the Lord Cornwallis statue on the Parade Ground of Fort St George; this was replaced by the present cupola, which now stands outside the Fort Museum.

R.H. Chisholm designed the **General Post Office**, with its twin towers, which opened in 1875. The State Bank of India and the surprisingly exuberant Magistrate's Court are further examples of Indo-Saracenic work.

Skirting the harbour, **Burma Bazaar** comprises small shops selling foreign goods that are

KEY

1. Fort St George
2. Scretariat & Legislative Assembly
3. St Mary's Church
4. Fort Msuseum
5. Kothwal Chavadi
6. St Mary's Cathedral & Armenian Church
7. Chennakesvarar and Chennamallikesvarar Temples
8. General Post Office
9. Beach Railway Station
10. State Bank of India
11. Hotel Surat
12. Tamil Nadu State Bus Stand
13. Thiruvalluvar (TTC/JJTC)Bus Stand
14. High Court
15. Central Railway Station
16. St Andrew's Kirk
17. Egmore Railway Station
18. Impala Continental Hotel
19. Chandra Towers Hotel
20. Sri Durga Prasad Hotel
21. Pantheon Complex – Museum/Art Gallery
22. Ambasador Pallara & Kanchi Hotels
23. UK High Commission
24. Hotel Taj Coromandel
25. Valluvar Kottam
26. Residency Hotel
27. St George's Cathedral
28. Hotel Madras International
29. Spencer Plaza
30. Connemara Hotel
31. Higginbothams/Dasa
32. Rajaji Hotel
33. The Victory War Memorial
34. Madras University
35. Aquarium
36. Chepauk Palace
37. Presidency College
38. Vivekananda House
39. Lighthouse
40. Hotel President
41. Nilgiri's Nest Hotel
42. New Woodlands Hotel
43. Hotel Savera
45. Welcomgroup Chola Sheraton
46. San Thome Basilica
47. Kapaleeswarar Temple
48. Luz Chruch
49. Welcomgroup Park Sheraton
50. Theosophical Society
51. Little Mount Church
52. Gundy National Park
53. St Thomas Mount

☐ Hotel   ○ Other

GEORGE TOWN

Mint Street
NSC Bose Road
Walltax Road
Prakasam Road
Armenian Street
North Beach Road
Harbour Station Road
Rajaji Salai

Vepery High Road

Rithardon Road

EVR Periyar High Road
GH Road

(Poonamallee High Road)
McNichols Road

Gandhi Irwin Road

Kennet Lane
Cooum River

The Island

Anna Salai (Mount Road)
Adams Road

Harris Road

Pantheon Road
Montieth Road

C-in-C Rd
Binny Rd

Greams Road
College Road

Sterling Road
Nungambakkam High Road
St George's

Village Road

Anna Salai (Mount Road)
Woods Road
Peter's Road
General Patter's Road

Wallajah Road

Bharathi Salai (Pycroft's Road)

Kamaraj Salai (South Beach Road)

White's Road

Gemini Flyover

Kodambakkam High Road

Sri Mahamed Usman Road
Bazullah Road

G Narayanaswami Chetty Road
Sri Tyagaraja Road

Venkatanarayana Road

Lloyd's Road

St George's Cathedral Road
Mount Road (Anna Salai)

Royapettah Baza

Peter's Road

Lloyd's Road

Dr Radhakrishnan Salai

Besant Road

Triplicane High Road

Anna Square

Triplicane High Road
Mylapore Bazaar Road

Eldham's Road

Luz Church Road

Kutchery Road

MYLAPORE

Chamiers Road

TTK Road (Mowbray's Road)

St Mary's Road
Mada Church Street

RK Mutt Road

Gandhi Mandapam Road

Greenway's Road

Adyar River

Marina Beach

Bay of Bengal

TO:
• Airport (10km)

TO:
• Mamallapuram

Sardar Vailabhai Patel Road (Elliot Beach Road)

Elliot's Beach

MADRAS

Parry's Corner

| 0 | 200 | 400 | 600 | 800 | 1000 m |
| 0 | 200 | 400 | 600 | 800 | 1000 yds |

N
W   E
S

difficult to obtain in India, together with reproductions that are made locally. Burmese refugees began the enterprise, which is how the Bazaar gained its name. Although the atmosphere of fierce bargaining is lively, western tourists are unlikely to find goods at bargain prices.

At this point tourists can decide whether to explore central Madras, which is likely to be significantly hotter than the coastline, or proceed southward, hugging the coast. Those who will be continuing from Madras to Fisherman's Cove and Mamallapuram will find it more economical, both in time and money, to view the coastal sector on route. Most will be staying at a reasonably centrally located Madras Hotel and may prefer to return to it to escape the afternoon heat, particularly if their hotel is air-conditioned or possesses a swimming pool.

Many of the buildings of central Madras, although exceptional in south India, are of no particular interest to British visitors who will have seen similar examples in their own country, but St Andrew's Kirk, the Pantheon Museum/Art Gallery complex, the Valluvar Kottam memorial and St George's Cathedral are worth making an effort to see, and should not take up more than two hours. Remember that the museums close at 5.00pm and on Fridays.

St Andrew's Kirk

Located immediately north of Egmore Station, this Georgian-style Presbyterian church is architecturally one of the most pleasing in Madras. It was completed in 1820, almost a century after St Martin-in-the-Fields church in London, by James Gibbs (1682-1754), with which it has been compared. Although Gibbs was much criticized for locating his tower with its steeple at the entrance to the church – an innovative feature – this format soon proved popular in the British colonies, particularly North America. Very unlike St Martin's, however, is the castellated west porch. Within, the dome above the crossing is supported only by Ionic columns; it is painted to represent the heavens, gold stars glittering from a deep blue sky. The organ and the circular pews of mahogany are original fixtures.

South west of the church, on Pantheon Road, is the most important museum in Madras.

Pantheon Complex (Government Museum, National Art Gallery and Connemara Library)

(Open Saturday to Thursday 9.00am to 5.00pm)

In 1793, twenty-four worthy British residents of Madras founded the Pantheon Committee to improve the social life of expatriates. They were presented with a 43-acre estate by civil servant Hall Plummer on which was built the Public Assembly Rooms, which became the venue for glittering social events in the early 19th century. The Madras government eventually purchased the estate and opened the Government Museum in 1854. Those with limited time should make for the outstanding Archaeology section, in particular the 2nd century Buddhist sculptures from Amravati. Geological exhibits are more interesting than those normally found in Indian museums; look for the million-year-old fossilized skull of an elephant, and the explanation of just how the rod of carbon is so tightly enclosed by wood in a pencil. In front of the museum is the circular, domed **Museum Theatre**, built in 1896, where local Madras groups perform.

If time permits, it is worth popping into the adjacent **Connemara Library** to admire its exuberant interior. The building, designed in Indo-Saracenic style by Henry Irwin, is contemporary with the Museum Theatre; its name commemorates the Governor of Madras at the time. As this is a national library, one copy of every book published in India must be sent to it.

Architecturally, the most impressive of all the Pantheon buildings is the **National Art Gallery**, which faces the main road. It was constructed of pale pink sandstone in 1906, but did not become the Art Gallery until 1951. Unusually for the period, the design is pastiche Mogul rather than Indo-Saracenic – and very successful it is too. Unfortunately, the interior is poorly lit and unkempt. Of greatest interest are the Tanjore paintings on glass and the Mogul miniatures. Also forming part of the Art Gallery's collection, but housed in a separate building behind it, are the renowned south Indian bronzes from the 10th to the 13th centuries. The star of the show is the exquisite Chola figure of a dancing Natraj.

Pantheon Road crosses the River Cooum, the most northerly of the two rivers that run parallel through Madras to the sea. Greams Road then runs southward to Anna Salai, from which is approached Kodambakkam High Road and the Valluvar Kottam.

Valluvar Kottam

This is one of south India's modern memorials that should not be missed. It was built in 1976, almost 1,000 years after Thiruvalluvar, to whom it is dedicated, had died. Thiruvalluvar, the 'Tamil Shakespeare', was a philospohical poet, and his greatest work, known as *Thirukkurral* (the Voice), is inscribed in its entirety on 133 granite slabs. These line a corridor within the auditorium which seats 4,000, and is said to be Asia's largest; it is certainly the foremost centre of cultural activities in Madras.

Of greater interest to most tourists, however, is the carved granite chariot 101ft (31m) high, a replica of the Chola/Pallava carved chariot of Thiruvarur temple in central Tamil Nadu.

Eastwards, Kodambakkam High Road leads to St George's Cathedral Road, which runs beneath the Gemini Flyover of Anna Salai.

St George's Cathedral

Designed in Ionic style throughout, **St George's Cathedral**, the largest church in Madras, was constructed in 1815. Its spire is said to be a replica of that of St Giles in the Fields, built in London 82 years earlier. The bells of the cathedral are the only examples in Madras that play a tune.

Within are commemorated Bishop Reginald Heber, his figure carved by Sir Francis Chantry, and a baby whose charming memorial tablet is designed in the British Arts and Crafts manner promoted by William Morris.

Anna Salai (Mount Road)

Although Anna Salai gained its present name in the 1970s, it is still generally known as Mount Road. Running diagonally south west to north east, where it ends at Fort St George, this is the most important thoroughfare in the city. Many of the better hotels, shops, restaurants and hotel facilities are located on or near it. As soon as Anna Salai leaves the city at St Thomas Mount, from which it gained its original name, the thoroughfare becomes National Highway 45 and continues to Cape Comorin, 400 miles (650km) distant.

To the north of St George's Cathedral, in the Express Estate, the run-down vestiges of the old **Madras Club** created for the relaxation of the British elite are still standing. Nearby, the **Cosmopolitan Club**, built in Ionic splendour, reflects the desire of wealthy Indians before independence to follow the habits of their rulers. Further north, at the Binny Road junction with Anna Salai, **Spencer Plaza** is an undistinguished modern replacement of Spencer's department store, once India's finest (not connected with Marks & Spencer). It was founded in 1868, prospered, and in 1895 moved to a large store of Indo-Saracenic design which burnt down a few years ago. Fortunately, Spencer's **Connemara Hotel**, in Binny Road, has survived to become the oldest hotel in Madras. Now owned by the Taj Group, its traditional ambience is maintained.

Continuing northward, as the General Patters Road junction is approached, **Higginbothams**, on the left, is the largest bookshop in India. The company was founded here in Madras in 1844, but the appearance of its building dates from 1904 remodelling: branches now exist in many Indian cities.

Government Estate is reached shortly before the River Cooum is crossed. Within its grounds, the once-splendid mansion that was formerly the residence of the British Governor of Madras is now a wreck. Well-maintained across the courtyard, however, is the old banqueting hall that was commissioned by the son of Robert Clive to commemorate his father's victory at Plassey, and the later defeat by the East India Company of Tipu Sultan at Shrirangapatam. Now called **Rajaji Hall** in honour of the only Indian to serve as Governor of Madras during British rule, the Grecian-style building still hosts important social events. It was designed by Goldingham, an East India Company Engineer

Enormous poster hoardings advertising the latest movie extravaganza are a feature of Anna Salai, reflecting the importance of Madras to the Indian film industry, the world's largest. The city has now outstripped Bombay in this field and is known as the 'Hollywood of India'. So popular is the cinema that stars have become leading political figures.

As Anna Salai reaches the man-made island in the River Cooum called, **The Island**, some may wish to inspect the equestrian statue of Sir Thomas Munro, Governor of Madras 1820-27. It was sculpted by Sir Thomas Chantrey who, in a moment of aberration, forgot to provide the Governor with stirrups. By tradition, sculptors who make such mistakes commmit suicide. Chantrey, sensibly, did no such thing, and took his commission in full. Grand schemes for The Island's open land at the east side are frequently suggested but, at present, all that stands here is a fair – between January and April. Anna Salai ends as Fort St George is reached; a right turn leads to the War Memorial.

The Victory War Memorial is a convenient spot from which to begin a tour of the Bay of Bengal fringe of Madras. As has been said, this may conveniently precede a visit to Mamallapuram or any of the beach resort hotels that lie a short distance away, to the south of Madras.

The memorial, in the form of an obelisk, was erected in 1932 on the site of the Madras Coastal battery to commemorate Indians who were killed in the First World War. It now serves as a memorial to those who died in both World Wars and the four border wars fought by India since Independence. A wreath-laying ceremony is held at the memorial every 30 January to commemorate Martyrs' Day, the anniversary of Mahatma Gandhi's assassination.

From the memorial, Kamarajar Salai (formerly South Beach Road) sweeps southward, with the great sand beach of Madras shielded by gardens to the east, and a number of impressive buildings lining its west side. Two memorial gardens have been created on the beach side of the road. Entered through a split arch designed as giant elephant tusks, a path leads to the slender column that commemorates C.N. Annadurai (Anna means 'elder brother' in Tamil), a popular chief minister. Apparently, the eternal flame survives the monsoons.

Adjacent is the memorial to M.G. Ramachandran, a popular film star who switched to politics and was voted Chief Minister of Tamil Nadu for ten years. From both memorials it is easy to explore the beach.

Marina Beach

Marina Beach stretches $2^1/_2$ miles (4 km) from Madras harbour to the San Thome quarter. When Fort St George was built in 1639, its walls were lapped by the sea at high tide – now the beach stretches almost a mile (1,300 metres) out to sea at its widest point. The build-up of sand began in 1876, after the harbour was built, increasing by an extraordinary 23 feet (7 m) each year until 1921 when a sand screen was constructed. Unfortunately, the great extent of sand has done nothing to subdue 'Big Wave', and the powerful rollers combined with sudden drops in sand levels, make any form of sea bathing a hazardous proposition: no-one, therefore, enters the water at Marina Beach. Nevertheless, balmy breezes, particularly in the late afternoon, make promenading and playing games on the sands a popular recreation, particularly on Sundays. As may

be expected, vendors proliferate, selling varieties of cheap items which include south Indian snacks as well as western-style junk food and ice cream.

An elevated strip of gardens with walkways and coloured lights borders 2 miles (3 km) of Marina Beach, a development initiated by Governor Grant-Duff in the 1880s. Family parties bring their picnics to the gardens – to avoid sand in their food – and exhausted joggers puff their way past them. Those who wish to swim in safety can choose from either the Anna Swimming Pool or the Municipal Pool further south. Non-members are permitted to dine at the Boat Club's restaurant.

Since independence, many statues have been set up facing the road in the Marina Gardens. The best known of them is the first erected, which celebrates the 'Triumph of Labour': four workmen are depicted doing something energetic with long pieces of wood – but they look more tired than triumphant!

Madras University

Madras University's buildings punctuate the west side of Kamarajar Salai, occupying land formerly the gardens of the nawabs of the Carnatic. The main campus lies between Adams and Wallajah roads, but Presidency College, the first building to be constructed, occupies the Pycrofts Road corner to the south. From the outset in 1864, Chisholm's brief was to design the first two buildings, Presidency College (1871) and the Senate House (1879) in a style that would complement the exisiting Chepauk Palace between them. From north to south, the buildings of interest in the main campus are: Chisholm's old **Main Building** (with a clocktower), the **Centenary Building** (1961) and the **Senate House**. Some consider the Senate House to be the finest of all the Indo-Saracenic buildings in Madras. Fortunately, it has been preserved intact both externally and internally. In this building Chisholm incorporated much Byzantine detail.

Chepauk Palace, which faces Kamarajar Salai was built within grounds of 117 acres for the Nawab of the Carnatic in 1768. It seems to have been responsible for inspiring the Indo-Saracenic architectural style that followed a century later. The British forced the Nawab to exchange the palace, which they wanted as a government building, for a smaller estate nearby, the Amir Mahal, in which his descendants still live. Between the two blocks of the former Chepauk Palace, Chisholm built a splendid tower which survives. The complex, now the Madras headquarters of the Post & Telegraph Office, has become somewhat dilapidated.

The red brick **Presidency College**, just south of the former palace, suffered unsuitable extensions prior to Independence. In this instance, architect

Chisholm gave a Renaissance touch to his Indo-Saracenic design.

Just after passing Besant Road, the next junction, the curved facade of **Vivekananda House** comes into view; now a women's hostel, it was built in the 19th century as an ice house. Enormous blocks of ice cut from the Great Lakes were shipped to Madras from Boston in the USA and stored here. The ice was then broken down and sold to the wealthy, primarily for preserving food, cooling drinks and making ice cream.

Ahead, in the historic quarter of San Thome, lie two important religious buildings, both of which may be entered without difficulty.

San Thome Basilica

The twin-spired Neo-Gothic building completed in 1898 as the Roman Catholic Cathedral of San Thome, was given basilica status in 1956. When the Portuguese arrived in Madras they appropriated the coastal strip of ancient Mylapore and called it San Thome (Saint Thomas). In 1525 they discovered an ancient church on the beach, which had been built by Syrian (Nestorian faith) Christians; within this, a tomb was said to be that of Christ's Apostle Saint Thomas Didymus (Doubting Thomas). The Portuguese built a cathedral near the shore to accommodate the tomb's contents, which comprised the head of a lance, a pot with blood-stained earth and some bones. The present basilica was built on the site of the earlier cathedral, which was demolished for it.

As has been said earlier, there is no hard evidence that St Thomas ever visited India, but most south Indian Christians believe the tradition that he did and that he came overland from Kerala's Malabar coast to spread Christianity on the Coromandel coast, where he was eventually martyred.

In addition to this basilica, the Descanco church, Little Mount and St Thomas's Mount are all supposed to have connections with the Saint, and may be visited. However, those who wish to follow the trail of St Thomas should bear in mind the Indian's love of creating or embellishing historical 'facts'. The pilgrimage is not for doubting Thomases!

Within the basilica, the life of St Thomas is depicted in its stained glass windows. Beneath the crossing, his tomb lies in a simple crypt, but apparently few relics of the Apostle now remain within, most bones having been removed to Ortona in Italy; the head of the lance with which the Saint is said to have been wounded does, however, remain here.

A short distance inland, the large Kapaleeswarar Temple may be entered by all.

Kapaleeswarar Temple

When the Portuguese created the San Thome quarter in the 16th century, the ancient Hindu temple dedicated to Kapaleeswarar (an aspect of Shiva) was demolished and relocated further back from the sea together with the rest of Mylapore. The original temple is known to have been in existence by 1250, but may well have been founded much earlier.

The main entrance, on the east side, is beneath a high, carved *gopuram*. In front of the flagpole is the shrine of the boy saint Gnanasambandar, in which he is depicted resurrecting a dead girl from her ashes, a miracle that he reputedly performed in this temple. Particularly appealing to Mylapore citizens is the shrine of Shiva's consort Parvati, located beneath a venerable *punnai* tree. By tradition, Shiva observed Parvati admiring a splendid peacock and, overcome with jealousy, turned her into a peacock. He eventually forgave the goddess and restored Parvati to her original form at Mylapore: the town's earlier name, Mayilapore means place of the peacock. Uniquely, since the 17th century, Muslims have been permitted to use the temple's tank for a ceremony at the end of Muharram.

West of the temple on Luz Church Road, the **Luz** (Light) **Church** was built by a Portuguese Franciscan monk in 1516, as recorded by an inscription within. It is known locally as the jungle church *Kattu Kovil*. Although small, the building has much charm.

A short distance to the south, on St Mary's Road, is an even smaller 16th century church, the **Descanco Church**, constructed by the wealthy Portuguese Madeiros family. Descanco means Rest in Portuguese and, by tradition, this is where St Thomas rested on his daily walk from his cave on 'Little Mount' to the beach, where he preached Christianity to vast numbers.

Theosophical Society

The road southward crosses the Adyar River, which almost completely dries up outside the monsoon period. Immediately on the left, the 250 acre estate belongs to the **Theosophical Society**, whose headquarters this is. The Society was founded in New York in 1875 to search for the common truth expressed by the world's many faiths. It transferred to Madras in 1882, and the present elegant headquarters building was constructed that year. The Society's premises are open to the public, Monday to Friday, 8.00 to 11.00am and 2.00 to 5.00pm; Saturday, 8.00 to 11.00am only, and many come to admire the garden's 200 year-old banyan tree, the second largest in India.

Even as recently as Independence, the Adyar River marked the southern boundary of Madras, but this is no longer the case as the great city has gradually swallowed up many of its surrounding towns and villages.

Elliot's Beach, to the south, was once reserved for British administrators of importance, but is now a playground for the local inhabitants. The sea is said to be calmer here, making bathing possible. Utilitarian apartment blocks of Besant Nagar Sagar now rear up behind the once elegant stretch of sand. Elliot Beach Road leads northward to Guindy National Park.

Guindy National Park

This is the only game reserve in the world to be located within a city's limits, and only here can be seen a herd of the almost extinct Indian antelope; also to be seen, if lucky, are the small civet cat and jackal. At the north end of the park is Raj Bhavan, the official residence of the Governor of Madras. A small fee is charged to drive through the park, which now incorporates the not very exciting **Snake Park**.

Little Mount

A short distance north of the park is Little Mount, with its **cave** in which St Thomas is said to have been grievously wounded by a Brahmin's lance whilst at prayer. A narrow 'window' provides light to the cave, and it has been suggested that St Thomas escaped from his attacker through this, thence making his way to St Thomas's Mount, where he was put to death. Beside this 'window' there is said to be a print of his palm. Next to the cave is a

Above: Arjuna's Penance is perhaps the supreme example of Pallava art at Mamallapuram.
Below left: Madras Art Gallery is a first-rate pastiche of the Mogul style, rarely found in South India. ***Below right***: The grounds of Fisherman's Cove descend to Covelong Beach.

church built by a Goan, Antonio Gonsalves de Taide, in 1612 and dedicated to **Our Lady of Health**. North of the church, St Thomas is said to have preached from the spot now marked by a cross. It is also alleged that marks in the rock to the east of the church were made by the hands, knees and feet of the Saint as he collapsed after his injury. A second church, built in 1971, commemorates the 19th centenary of St Thomas's martyrdom in 71AD.

St Thomas Mount

Those who wish to follow the St Thomas trail to its conclusion must make the 2 mile (3km)journey south-westward from Little Mount towards the airport. A road reaches the Mount's summit, or a flight of 134 steps to it may be climbed. Armenians are said to have built the first church here in 530, and Marco Polo refers to visiting a Nestorian Monastery on the Mount in 1293. The present church, dedicated to **Our Lady of Expectation**, was erected by the Portuguese in 1523, but there have been two extensions since. A stone cross on the high altar is said to have been carved by St Thomas, who knelt at it as he died. It was discovered by workmen during excavations for the present church. An inscription in Palilavi, a local Madras language, refers to the Saint's martyrdom. The Mother and Child picture was allegedly painted from life by the Apostle St Luke, who presented it to St Thomas.

Accommodation

As may be expected, India's fourth largest city boasts a tremendous number of hotels. The districts of Egmore (south of Egmore Station) and George Town (east of Central Station) specialize in budget or medium-grade hotels, whilst many of the luxury establishments are close to the central stretch of Anna Salai, in particular along the arc formed by Numgambakkam High Road, Cathedral Road and Dr Radhakrishnan Salai, which bisects it. A representative selection from the many hotels is given in the FactFile; all are popular and advance booking is recommended.

Food

South India's culinary fame rests primarily on its vegetarian cuisine, as perfected along the northern coastal region of Karnataka State where it is known as *udipi*. Other southern states adapt this to their own taste: Kerala adding coconut, Andhra Pradesh chillies and Tamil Nadu various spices. In addition to *udipi* food, Madras restaurants have become noted, in recent years, for the *chettinad* cuisine. This originated in central Tamil Nadu with the splendid banquets held by wealthy Chettiar families. The banquets were prepared by self-employed chefs who worked together in teams travelling from one

Additional Information

Useful addresses

UK High Commission, 24 Anderson Road ☎ 827 3136
British Airways, Alsanmall Khaleeli Centre, Montieth Road (Egmore)
☎ 827 4272
Indian Airlines, 19 Marshalls Road (Egmore) ☎ 855 3039

function to another. In this cuisine, fish and meat are added to the vegetarian base.

As is usual in Indian cities, the best food is to be found in hotel dining rooms, particularly those of 5-star establishments. **Dasa** in Anna Salai (near Higginbothams book shop), is a vintage record shop imaginatively converted to a south Indian fast-food restaurant of outstanding quality. Ice-cream lovers will enjoy Dasaprakesh ices.

Excellent *udipi* fare is served at **Matsya Udipi House**, 1 Halls Road (Egmore) and the **New Woodlands Hotel**, 72/75 Dr Radhakrishnan Road (Mylapore). NB credit cards are still not accepted here. The **Raintree Restaurant** of the Connemara Hotel (see FactFile accommodatio) serves *chettinad* food exclusively in a delightful garden. Enormous *thalis* (known as *thattu* in Tamil Nadu) are a speciality of the **Dakshin Restaurant** at the Welcomgroup Park Sheraton (see FactFile accommodation).

First rate North Indian Mogul and Kashmiri specialities are available at the **Minar Rooftop Restaurant** of Hotel Savera, 69 Dr Radhakrishnan Road.

Buffet meals, particularly at lunchtime, are amazingly good value in Madras – even at the most expensive hotels. Hard to beat for quality are the great spreads of the **Taj Coromandel**, where the once-a-week seafood buffet – which includes lobster and tiger prawns in profusion – is practically given away. Also at the Coromandel, the **Golden Dragon** is the finest Chinese restaurant in Madras. Renowned for the great choice offered by its buffets is the **Residency Hotel**, 49 G.N. Chetty Road, where various cuisines are always represented.

The luxury hotels of Madras are virtually the last bastion of the decoction – extremely strong filtered coffee. This is sometimes known as 'coffee by the yard', a reference to the method of cooling it by pouring the Mysore coffee from one container to another at arm's length (a yard).

Shopping

Madras is the best shopping centre in south India – in spite of

Bangalore's claims. Just about every type of Indian silk including Kanchipuram hand-woven silk can be found in a multitude of designs and colours. Although few non-Indians will wish to buy sarees, lengths of silk and cotton can be purchased by the metre, for making up by a tailor, either in India or on reaching home. Anna Salai, a convenient area, is the location for **Apsara** (no. 769), Spencers Building, who stock silk specifically designed for shirt material; **Savathai** (no. 827); **Khadi** (no. 844), where raw silk for suitings is generally available. **Handloom House,** 7 Rattan Bazaar in George Town is operated by the government and prices are fixed.

Men seeking high quality tailoring should make for **Syed Bawkher** at Gem Court 14 Khader Navaz Khan Road (near the Taj Coromandel) Tel: 826 7371. A wide selection of high-quality Bangalore-woven materials is kept in stock, and Mr Bawkher's bespoke suits will cost several hundred pounds less than the prices demanded in the west for similar quality workmanship. A fitting may usually be arranged within 24 hours and, if time is pressing, the finished garment can be reliably delivered anywhere in India before returning home.

Madras is the leather centre of India, and great bargains are to be had. Designs are at their best in the luxury hotel shops and the boutiques of the **Fountains Plaza Centre.** Cheaper items are found in the **Periamet** area of Madras, but styles here are not usually so appealing.

From Madras to Mamallapuram and Kanchipuram

If time does not permit an overnight stay at Mamallapuram, it is possible to take a day tour from Madras to the resort, stopping off at Kanchipuram to visit its main temples on the return journey. However, the tours start at 6.30am and return after 7.00pm, making a very long and tiring day.

Many, of course, will take a taxi to Mamallapuram, stopping on route at the Crocodile Bank, but there are buses also, which depart from the Tamil Nadu State Bus Stand in Prakasam Road, South George Town, facing the TTC/JJTC bus stand, which lies to its east. Buses 188 (A,B,D or K) make the journey to Mamallapuram direct in two hours; alternatively, buses 19 (A or C) and 119A stop at Covelong (Fisherman's Cove) on route.

Fisherman's Cove (Covelong)

Of all the beach resort hotels between Madras and Mamallapuram, **Fisherman's Cove**, operated by the Taj Group, is the most luxurious. Although located 24 miles (39km) south of Madras, some visitors prefer to lodge at Fisherman's Cove as it has a more relaxing atmosphere and somewhat cooler climate than the big city itself. Guests stay either in the main block or in the luxury cottages between the swimming pool and the beach. A Dutch fort once stood here, but only part of its wall remains, now serving as a children's play area. **Covelong** village, with its ancient church, is only half a mile (1km) away. Though hotel staff clean the beach daily in front of the hotel there is unpleasant evidence of the presence of fishermen further along the beach – where paddling is not advisable.

On the way to Mamallapuram, 12 miles (19 km) further south, it is worth stopping at Crocodile Bank, one of the few impressive reptile collections in south India.

Crocodile Bank

Crocodile Bank is open daily from 8.00am to 5.00pm. The word 'bank' refers to the aim of the foundation, which is to protect the Indian mugger and gharia crocodiles from extinction. Over 5000 crocodiles are kept in a relatively small area; some happily recline on the backs of their brethren, but there is very little movement: those who found *Crocodile Dundee* scary should perhaps give this a miss. Croco-facts are well presented on information boards, and one is surprised to learn that they are more closely related to birds than to lizards. Only between one and three per cent of Indian crocodiles survive to adulthood; those that do grow to an average length of 4ft

6 inches (1.4 m). This is not as long as those in some countries, and nowhere near as long as prehistoric examples which reached 17 feet (16 m) in length, but long enough not to mess with. Apart from possessing beautiful skins, why bother to protect these man-eating crocodiles from extinction one might wonder, but apparently the crocodile has a mysteriously effective immune system which enables it to live to a great age, and may hold the key to increasing our own resistance to disease.

To increase tourist appeal, poisonous snakes are milked publicly of their venom at intervals throughout the day: krate, cobra and Russells viper, the star attractions, are lured out of the 'Ali Baba' pots in which they apparently live, grabbed by the throat and forced to sink their fangs into a piece of wood, thus squeezing out the 'milk'. The venom itself gives no protection to humans against snakebite, but must be injected into a horse, which can withstand its potency. When completely immune from the poison, the horse's blood is extracted and processed to form anti-snake bite serum.

Tiger Cave

Six miles (10km) further south, at **Saluvan Kuppan**, still $2^1/_2$ miles (4km) from Mamallapuram, the first of the Pallava archaeological sites may be visited (better in the morning for photographs). The man-

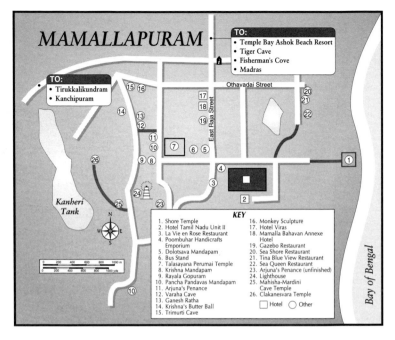

MAMALLAPURAM

TO:
- Temple Bay Ashok Beach Resort
- Tiger Cave
- Fisherman's Cove
- Madras

TO:
- Tirukkalikundram
- Kanchipuram

Othavadai Street

East Raja Street

Kanheri Tank

Bay of Bengal

N W S E

0   200   400   600   800   1000 m
0   200   400   600   800   1000 yds

KEY

1. Shore Temple
2. Hotel Tamil Nadu Unit II
3. La Vie en Rose Restaurant
4. Poombuhar Handicrafts Emporium
5. Dolotsava Mandapam
6. Bus Stand
7. Talasayana Perumai Temple
8. Krishna Mandapam
9. Rayala Gopuram
10. Pancha Pandavas Mandapam
11. Arjuna's Penance
12. Varaha Cave
13. Ganesh Ratha
14. Krishna's Butter Ball
15. Trimurti Cave
16. Monkey Sculpture
17. Hotel Viras
18. Mamalla Bahavan Annexe Hotel
19. Gazebo Restaurant
20. Sea Shore Restaurant
21. Tina Blue View Restaurant
22. Sea Queen Restaurant
23. Arjuna's Penance (unfinished)
24. Lighthouse
25. Mahisha-Mardini Cave Temple
26. Clakanesvara Temple

☐ Hotel ◯ Other

made 'cave', once thought to be a temple, was probably the stage of an open-air amphitheatre, which is now set amidst casuarina trees. Dating from the late Pallava period, the theatre was excavated for Atiranachanda, presumably an unidentified king, but something occurred to halt its completion. Framing the stage is a carved frieze of tiger (or lion) heads, hence its name; each has a different expression. To the right, smaller caves are carved with elephant heads.

Just 2 miles (3km) north of Mamallapuram stands **Ideal Beach Resort**, the first of six resort complexes. Some of the spick and span rooms are avail-

able with air conditioning and the friendly atmosphere is immediately apparent. It is possible to walk from the hotel to Mamallapuram along the beach, but not on a regular basis – two miles in the heat is just too far. Better to bus out and taxi back.

A little closer to the town is **Golden Sun Beach Resort** with more varied accommodation, some of it extremely economical for the area. **Silversands**, which follows, stretches back from the coast, only a few of its rather pricey rooms having a seafront location. Lying back from the shore, **Mamalla Beach Cottages** is the nearest to a budget hotel in the region. All rooms have private shower/ toilet and upper rooms are air conditioned. **Hotel Tamil Nadu Beach Resort**, a mile (1.5km) north of Mamallapuram, is a 25-minute stroll along the beach from the town. Considering it has a swimming pool set in a delightful, bucolic garden, the balconied rooms, all of which face the sea, are most reasonably priced. **Temple Bay Ashok Beach Resort** is the only beachfront hotel that can really claim to be located within easy walking distance of Mamallapuram, 200 yards (200 m) away. Unfortunately, this uniqueness must be paid for, and the accommodation, although pleasant enough, is somewhat overpriced. Cottages overlooking the beach – and with a view of the famous Shore Temple – have delightful balconies which pick up the cool evening breeze, a welcome feature of this part of the coast.

Mamallapuram

Although the picturesque **Shore Temple** of Mamallapuram, together with the *gopurams* of the **Madurai Temple**, are the best known sights of south India, many do not appreciate that just behind the Shore Temple, forming what is virtually an open-air sculpture museum, are some of the most exquisite examples of carving to be found anywhere in the world. Dating from the 7th century, all are the work of Pallava craftsmen; they

are to be found in profusion, and most are in an excellent state of preservation. Yet there are no luxurious hotels or restaurants in the vicinity, beach vendors are few, and it cannot be said that the town, just an hour's drive from the country's fourth largest city, is on India's main tourist circuit. Tourists there are, of course, but most are adventurous young backpackers who have heard about the wonders of this unique combination of beach resort and great art. It does not seem possible that such a situation can last long: now, before mass tourism arrives, is the time to visit Mamallapuram.

From approximately 600 to 800 this was the main port of the Pallavas, whose capital was at Kanchipuram, 40 miles (65km) inland. The Pallavas, initially followers of Jainism, were converted to Hinduism in the 7th century, and most of their existing temples are dedicated to either Shiva or Vishnu. Navasimha Varman (630 - 668) was known as Mamalla, 'the great wrestler' and the name of the town commemorates this although an alternative name, Mahabalipuram, a reference to the demon Mahabali who was defeated by Vishnu, is still used. Roman coins found in the area indicate that there was a trading post here long before the Pallavas. More than 40 bas-reliefs, *rathas* (stone chariots) and temples record not only the skill but the humanity of the

Pallava craftsmen, whose work at Mamallapuram was executed between 630 and 730. Realism, combined with the adoption of natural rather than godlike themes, singles out Pallava art from that of other Indian dynasties. A parallel with the brief Aknahatun period in Ancient Egypt might be drawn. All the carvings are executed in the hard but malleable local granite and they are monolithic, no mortar of any kind being used. It is for this reason that their condition is so exceptional, considering that all of them are around 1400 years old. Those wishing to view the monuments chronologically should begin with the famous *rathas*, to the south, which are considered to mark the birth of Dravidian architecture, but few are able to resist making straight for the Shore Temple.

Shore Temple

Now officially a World Heritage site, the Shore Temple was built by Rajasimha Narasimhavarman II (700-728). By tradition, it is only one of seven shore temples erected by this king, but no trace of others has been discovered. It is not only the beachfront location but also the double dedication to Shiva and Vishnu that makes this temple unique. Formerly, it was possible to enter the Shore Temple enclosure from any direction, but a high wall has now been built to protect it from the encroaching sea. No longer is it possible,

therefore, to obtain the romantic views as recorded in earlier photographs of the isolated temple bravely defying the waves. Something obviously had to be done, but a little more finesse in designing the wall could surely have been possible, and is there really a necessity for the broken wire fence, trim hedges and pointless signboards? Sculpted Nandi bulls which originally guarded the temple now stand on the screen wall.

The smaller of the temple's two sections, seen first, is a miniature version of the main temple and appears to have served originally as its entrance porch. Later, the passageway through it was blocked and shrines created at the west and east ends. The west shrine primarily features Shiva and Parvati, with Vishnu between them and Brahma (three-headed) to the left. Seen from the east side, the second shrine is devoted to a damaged reclining Vishnu.

The main part of the temple retains its pyramidal *vimana* tower, typical of Dravidian architecture, but there are indications that an additional superstructure was planned.

Before the sea wall was built, the black granite Shiva *lingam* in the east-facing shrine of the main temple was illuminated by the rising sun. On the back wall, two large figures represent Shiva and Parvathi, the smaller figure is their son Subramanya;

sundry figures from the Hindu pantheon are in support. A lamp pillar which faces the temple is now permanently under water, indicating how the sea has encroached since the structure was built.

The beach itself is reasonably safe for bathing, but it is also the town's toilet, one of the main reasons why Mamallapuram has not become a major tourist venue: it never will unless draconian cleaning up measures are taken.

Further south along the shore are two rocks with excavated recesses on their land-facing sides. These are embellished with carved tigers (or Asian lions) heads, a lion, a horse and the head of an elephant.

Direct exposure to the sea and the salt air has all too clearly affected the surviving beachfront sculptures of Mamallapuram, which appear to be melting in the heat, but the bulk of the town's treasures lie a short distance inland and retain much of their original crispness.

The road from the Shore Temple passes, on the left, a lotus tank with a Pallava temple in the centre. At the first road junction, beside the bus stand on the right, is the pillared **Dolotsava Mandapam**. Ahead, a walled area denotes the **Talasayana Perumal Temple**, which is faced on the main road by the **Krishna Mandapam**. Although of later date than Mamallapuram's other carvings, this is one of the most

delightful. Krishna shelters the world's inhabitants from a great deluge (the wrath of Indra) with the Govardhana mountain, which he uses as an umbrella. The naturalistic touch of a cow licking its calf while being milked is renowned.

Behind the *mandapam* rises the **Rayala Gopuram**. Further north along the road is the unfinished **Pancha Pandavas Mandapam**, followed by Arjuna's Penance.

Arjuna's Penance

Measuring 764ft x 288ft (27m x 9m), this is said to be the world's largest bas-relief and is certainly Mamallapuram's finest. A natural vertical cleft down which, by tradition, a waterfall once poured, divides the relief into two sections. On the upper part of the left section, an ascetic stands next to Shiva with arms raised. He is generally believed to represent Arjuna doing penance for Shiva by standing on one leg, and asking the god to provide him with a weapon so that he can do battle against the Kauravas. Some, however, believe that it is not Arjuna but the sage Bhagiratha who is represented, asking Shiva to bring the waters of the Ganges to the earth. Eventually, Shiva is said to have permitted the Ganges to flow through his tresses, thus slowing its descent, the impact of which otherwise would have destroyed the world.

Now dry, the cleft represents the Ganges, and has been carved with a serpent god and goddess. On both upper sections, deities, humans and animals are depicted leaning forward in their haste to reach the waters. Realistically-carved elephants approach more sedately. As with much work at Mamallapuram, this is obviously unfinished, the lower section on the left having been prepared for carving that was never to be executed. Opposite this monumental bas-relief a small open air **museum** displays Pallava objects discovered in the region.

A track ascends immediately from the bas-relief to the granite ridge behind the town. The first path on the right passes the **Varaha Cave** in which Vishnu is depicted as Varaha the boar grasping the Earth Goddess as he leaps from the sea. A tiny **Ganesh Ratha** faces **Krishna's Butterball**, the great rounded boulder on top of the ridge which provides welcome shelter for goats from the sun and the monsoons. Further ahead, the path leads to the **Trimurti** (Three-God cave) and below this a free-standing **Monkey Sculpture**; one animal is shown preening the other in a naturalistic pose typical of Pallava art.

Although some minor cave temples and rathas on this side of the ridge have not yet been seen, many will now wish to descend to the road and take an auto-rickshaw southward to the Pandava Rathas, which lie about a mile (2km) to the south. Ask the driver to stop on the way to view another, but unfinished, **Arjuna's Penance**. From here, there are good views up to the lighthouse built in 1900.

West of this is the **Mahish-amardini Cave Temple**, with its two outstanding bas-reliefs. Goddess Durga, as an amazon riding a lion, vanquishes the buffalo-headed demon Mahishasura whilst opposite, Vishnu reclines on the seven-headed serpent Adishesha.

Those seeking the best views in Mamallapuram can climb the steps nearby to the **Clakanesvara Temple**, but for some reason this is very popular with schoolchildren on outings, who can form lengthy queues.

Pandava Rathas

Built in the mid 7th century, the five **Rathas** (there are really eight in total) are named after the four Pandava brothers and their wife Draupadi, featured in the Mahabharata. Each takes the form of a temple chariot (*ratha*) and they are considered to represent the flowering of the second stage of Dravidian temple architecture – the first stage being the rock temples. All are monolithic, and it seems likely that they were cut out of a single outcrop of rock.

Set in a line from north to south are the Draupadi, Arjuna, Bhima and Dharmaraja Rathas; to the west of the Bhima Ratha is the Sahadeva Nakula Ratha.

The **Draupadi Ratha**, the smallest, has a pointed roof which was formerly surmounted by a finial. Within, the Goddess Durga (who some identify with Draupadi) is being offered his hair in supplication by a kneeling worshipper. To one side of this *ratha* stand a carved lion and an elephant, on the other a Nandi bull; it is believed that these were intended to face shrines of the deities whom they served as vehicles, respectively Indra, Durga and Shiva.

The **Arjuna Ratha** is a reproduction of a Buddhist *vihara* and heads of monks or priests peer out from the windows. Inside is a depiction of Indra, to whom the temple was presumably dedicated.

Largest of the set is the **Bhima Ratha**, but its hall has not been completed. The upper storey's roof imitates a wooden structure. To the west, the apsidal south end of the **Shahadeva Nakula Ratha** is in the form of a Buddhist chapel. The **Dharmaraja Ratha**, although similar to the Arjuna Ratha, is dedicated to Shiva.

Four other *rathas* and several cave temples will be discovered by wandering along the granite ridge above the town, from which most have been cut. A good reason for staying overnight in Mamallapuram, rather than treating the resort as a day excursion, is that the major Pallava carvings are floodlit every night.

Accommodation

Those who wish to stay in the centre of things have a reasonably wide choice, although most establishments cater primarily for backpackers. The following recommendations, in the medium range, have only double rooms. On East Raja Street, the main road, the **Mamalla Bhavan Annexe** is modern; all rooms have en-suite shower/wc and some are air-conditioned. The hotel's vegetarian-only **Golden Palate Restaurant** is rather dingy but the food is good. **Hotel Veeras**, next door, is even more recently built and has a slightly higher rating. There are both vegetarian and non-vegetarian restaurants together with a bar. **Hotel Tamil Nadu Unit II** (operated by TTDC) overlooks the south side of the lotus tank close to the Shore Temple and is set within pleasant grounds. Accommodation is in rather basic cottages, but each has its own wc/shower; there are fans but no air-conditioning. The hotel offers vegetarian and non-vegetarian food, and there is also a bar.

Restaurants

In addition to the restaurants in the above hotels, Mamallapuram, denoting its status as a resort for westerners, has a surprisingly large number of eating establishments. **Gazebo**, in the main road, is hard to beat for Indian food whilst on the beach, **Sea Shore Restaurant**'s terrace overlooks the Shore Temple which is even more attractive at night when floodlighting reduces the unfortunate visual

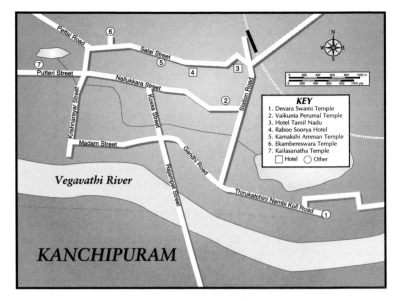

KEY
1. Devara Swami Temple
2. Vaikunta Perumal Temple
3. Hotel Tamil Nadu
4. Raboo Soorya Hotel
5. Kamakshi Amman Temple
6. Ekambereswara Temple
7. Kailasanatha Temple
□ Hotel ○ Other

Vegavathi River

KANCHIPURAM

impact of its modern wall. Just south of Sea Shore, **Tina Blue View** (with accommodation) and **Sea Queen** also benefit from sea breezes; both, naturally, specialize in seafood. Near the southwest corner of the lotus tank, on the main road, is the first floor **La Vie en Rose**, serving a good approximation of continental (usually French) food.

Carvings for sale

Tourism has led to the revival of Mamallapuram's carving skills, and craftsmen can be seen at work in numerous mason's yards. Most, but not all, of the pieces are copies of Pallava sculptures, and the quality is generally excellent. Examples can be bought from the numerous craft shops which congregate around the most popular monuments. One of these, **Poompuhar Handicrafts Emporium**, on the road to the Shore Temple, proclaims 'fixed prices', but compare prices at several establishments and bargain furiously before making a purchase.

Travel to Kanchipuram

Kanchipuram, the 'Golden town of 1000 temples' can be reached directly from Mamallapuram by bus no. 212A in around two hours. Many on route to Kanchipuram from Mamallapuram may like to stop at the Thirukkalikundram Temple, 9 miles (15km) distant, particularly if travelling by car. Buses also run from Mamallapuram to the village and make an interesting half day excursion.

230

Thirukkalikundram Temple

The village at the base of Vedagari Hill possesses a great Shiva temple with high *gopura*. However, it is the much smaller temple located on the summit of the 520 ft (160m) high hill which is the attraction. Here every day (well almost every day) between 11.00am and 12 noon, two large birds come to be fed consecrated rice by the priests. The large birds are claimed by some to be white kites, by others eagles – perhaps they take it in turns! However, the town's alternative name, Thiru Kazhukundram, literally means place of the sacred eagles, suggesting that the eagle protagonists are right. By tradition the birds, whatever their breed, are said to be an incarnation of saints who are journeying from Varanasi (Benares) to Rameswaram. There is no road to the top of the hill, and a steep flight of 565 steps must be climbed; many pilgrims as well as tourists do so. For the elderly or infirm there are strong young men who, for a small fee, will carry them up in a rattan version of a sedan chair.

Kanchipuram (or Conjeeveram)

Kanchipuram is one of India's seven most sacred cities, the others being Varanasi, Mathura, Ayodha, Ujjain, Hardwar and Dwarka; Kanchipuram, however, is sacred to both Shiva and Vishnu. This is therefore a popular pilgrimage centre, devotees being promised great happiness from their visit. In the first century BC, Kanchipuram was the capital of the early Cholas, the Pallavas followed in the sixth century, with brief occupations by the Chalukyams; in the 16th century, its last great period, the city was the capital of the Vijayanagar rajas.

By tradition, Kanchipuram, the 'Golden Town', once boasted 1000 temples; nothing however, remains from its Buddhist period when Ashok, in the third century BC, is said to have built many stupas in the region. Of the 126 temples that have survived, five are considered outstanding; a taxi or auto-rickshaw is essential to visit them and at least three hours should be allocated for an unhurried tour. As usual, the temples close between 12 noon and 3.00pm (some don't open until 4.00pm), so one must opt either for a late afternoon visit or make a very early departure from Mamallapuram for the morning session. If the midday eagle/kite feeding has been seen at Thirukkalikundram, those with cars will arrive at Kanchipuram around 2.15pm which gives time to visit the silk shops or have a meal (vegetarian only) before the first temple opens. A ticket (for car-parking outside!) purchased at any temple is valid for all five.

Devara (or Varada) Swami Temple

This temple is situated south east of the city, in Little Kanchipuram, and will be the first to be visited by those approaching from Mamallapuram. Dedicated to Vishnu, most of the temple dates from remodelling by the Vijayanagars in the 16th century. Entered from the west side, the seven-storey *gopuram* is undecorated. Facing it on the east side the higher gopuram, once the main entrance, is an older structure; both *gopura* have adjoining tanks.

Delicate pavilions in the first courtyard face a granite column which served as a lamp holder. To the north, the famous **Hall of Pillars** is one of the most beautiful *mandapa* in south India. Its 96 intricately carved columns depict scenes from the avatars of Vishnu, the Ramayana and the Mahabharata. Rearing horses with their mounts, each different, form the brackets. Damage to some of the carving is said to have been caused by Hyder Ali and his troops. Non-Hindus may not enter the second courtyard.

Vaikunta Perumal Temple

As this is located midway between the railway station and the bus stand, it will be the first temple seen by many who arrive by public transport. Built by Nandivarman II in the 8th century, this is one of the most perfect Pallava temples to survive. Its unusual *vimana* tower incorporates three tiers of shrines, one above the other, in which Vishnu is depicted standing, seated and lying. A frieze around the *vimana* relates the history of the Pallavas and their battles with the Chalukyas. The courtyard is arcaded on all sides, its columns sculpted with lions. On the east side, the *mandapam* is surmounted by an uncompleted *gopuram* erected by the Vijayanagars.

Kamakshi Amman Temple

This temple, believed to have been in existence in the 6th century, is dedicated to Parvathi 'the goddess with love in her eyes'. There are four *gopura* and several *mandapa*, of which the Amai (tortoise) *mandapam* is outstanding for its carving. Only Hindus may approach the main shrine, but its gilded superstructure can be seen by all.

Ekambereswara Temple

Although the complex covers 20 acres, much of it is open space and non-Hindus may not enter the inner section. First constructed by the Pallavas, the Ekambereswara Temple was extensively rebuilt by the Cholas and the Vijayanagars, whose king Krishna Devaraja erected the 188ft (58.5m) high cream *gopuram* in 1509, ensuring that he and his consort were depicted amongst the carvings on each of its nine storeys. This is the largest Shiva temple in Kanchipuram.

The Hall of a Thousand Pillars, on the left of the first great courtyard, has profusely carved columns (540 in reality) and friezes. By tradition, Shiva's consort Parvathi, in playful mood, momentarily covered the god's eyes with her hands, thus condemning mortals to many years of darkness. The angry Shiva made Parvati do penance, but eventually forgave her on the site of this temple. During the Carnatic Wars, the complex served as a British fortress.

Kailasanatha Temple

Visitors to Kanchipuram should ensure that they have sufficient time in which to see this temple (closing time 12.00-3.00pm), usually the last in the circuit, as it is the purest example of Pallava art in the city. Fortunately, as the temple is now managed by the Archaeology Department, non-Hindus may visit all sections of it. Narasimha Varma II built the temple in the 8th century and it is the only Pallava temple at Kanchipuram to have escaped remodelling by later dynasties. A wall divides the temple's two courtyards.

Shiva in different postures is depicted on the walls of the smaller courtyard. The eight, finely carved shrines on the east side resemble the *rathas* of Mamallapuram. The shrine in the centre of the dividing wall may be entered from both courtyards. Its exterior and interior are superbly carved.

In the larger courtyard, a series of small shrines each with a *sikhara* tower, resemble Jain work, but no Jain figures are sculpted. Each shrine was

originally occupied by a Shiva *lingam*. On the east side of the temple are pillared *mandapa* with shrines.

Traces of paintwork remain, indicating that the temple was once a riot of colour. Unfortunately, crude attempts to restore the carvings are all too obvious; apparently, the composite material used, which looks like plaster, cannot be removed.

Kanchipuram Silk

If time permits, a visit to observe the handloom weaving of silk can be arranged by the **Weavers Service Centre** 20 Station Road, Tel: 22530. Since the 16th century, Kanchipuram silk has been the finest produced in India. Prices depend on weight and the amount of gold thread incorporated. Few westerners purchase sarees, but cloth is sold by the metre and Kanchipuram suiting silk is reputedly the hardest wearing in the world. As the prices are geared to tourism, it is often more economical to purchase silk elsewhere.

Kanchipuram is very much a 'day trip' town, but those who wish to stay overnight have a choice of two medium priced hotels, the **Hotel Tamil Nadu** in Station Road, and **Baboo Soorya** in the town centre, incorporating a vegetarian restaurant rated the best in town.

Fact File

Index to FactFile

ACCOMMODATION

Southern India offers a wide range of accommodation, from basic rooms in villagers' homes to luxury resort hotels with all the expected facilities. A grading system for hotels is operated, ranging from one to five stars. All rooms in a star-rated establishment will be provided with en-suite showers and toilets, telephones and televisions. A high percentage of visitors will have pre-booked their accommodation; if not, it is best to contact the local tourist information office. When shown the room, ensure that everything functions and that all switches are understood – they can be extremely complicated. If hot water has been promised, make sure that it is connected to the shower, not just a low tap as is often the case – South Indians don't like hot showers! In December and January, prices are slightly higher in all establishments, but considerably more expensive in the upper-grade hotels. At this time, also, accommodation may be difficult to find in Kovalam. Many hotels and guest houses, particularly those in Kovalam, are described in detail, usually with colour photographs, in the brochures of tour operators that specialise in South India.

Chapter 1

Kovalam (0471)
Alitalia Beach House ☎ 481452
Aparna Guest House ☎ 480950

Apsara ☎ 480507
Ashok Beach Resort ☎ 480101
Fax: 481522
Blue Sea ☎ 480401 Fax: 451858

Fact File

Bright Resort ☎ 481210
Golden Sands ☎ 481476
Green Valley Cottages ☎ 480636
Hilton Beach Guest House
☎ 481077
Kadaloram Beach Resort
☎ 481116
Linchu Holiday Resort ☎ 481395
Moon Light Tourist Home
☎ 480375
Neelakanta ☎ 480421
Neptune ☎ 480222
Orion ☎ 480999
Palm Shore ☎ 480495
Peacock Hotel ☎ 481395
Raja ☎ 480355
Rockholm ☎ 480360
Royal Retreat ☎ 481010
Samudra ☎ 480089
Samudra Tara ☎ 480653
Sea Face ☎ 481835
Seaweed ☎ 480391
Swagath Holiday Resort ☎ 480421
Varma's Guest House ☎ 480478
Wilson's Guest House ☎ 480051

Chapter 2

Trivandrum (0471)
Hotel Pankaj, MG Road.
☎ 76 667
South Park Hotel, MG Road.
☎ 65 666
Mascot Hotel, Museum Road
☎ 43 8990
Hotel Fort Manor (with rooftop
restaurant), Power House Junction
☎ 46 2222

Bangaram Backwaters
Lagoona Beach Resort
☎ 443738

Pulinkudi
Surya Samudra Beach Garden
☎ 480413 Fax: 481124

Chowara
Somatheeram Beach Resort
☎ 481600 Fax: 480600
Manaltheeram Beach Resort
☎ 481610 Fax: 481603

Chapter 4

Madurai (0452)
Hotel Aarathy, 9 Perumal Koil
West Mada Street ☎ 31 571
Hotel Prem Nivas
Hotel Madurai Ashok,
Alagarkoil Road. ☎ 62 531
Hotel Pandyan, Alagarkoil Road.
☎ 42 470 Fax: 42 020
Hotel Supreme, 110 West
Perumal Maistry Street. ☎ 36 331
Taj Garden Retreat,
7 Thirupamkundram Road,
Pasumalai ☎ 60 2300 Fax: 88601

Chapter 5

Varkala (0472)
Government Guest House
☎ 042227
Taj Garden Retreat ☎ 403000
Fax: 0472 402296

Quilon (0474)
Government Guest House
(Tourist Bungalow)
☎ 70356
Hotel Sudarsan ☎ 75322

Alleppey (0477)
Alleppey Prince Hotel, AS Road
☎ 3752
Komala Hotel ☎ 3631

Kottayam (0481)
Anjali, KK Road
☎ 56 3661
Vembanad Lake Resort
☎ 56 4866

Kumarakom (0481)
Coconut Lagoon Resort
☎ 92491
Kumarakom Tourist Village
☎ 92258
Taj Garden Retreat ☎ 92 377

Periyar Lake/Thekkady (04869)
Aranya Nivas ☎ 22023
Fax: 04869 22282
Forest Lodge & Watch Tower
☎ 22027
Lake Palace ☎ 22023
Periyar House ☎ 22026
Spice Village ☎ 22315

Chapter 5

Kodaikanal (04542)
The Carlton, Lake Road
☎ 40 071
Hilltop Towers, Club Road
☎ 40 413
Kodaikanal Club, Club Road
☎ 41 341
Sivapriya, 45 Convent Road
☎ 41 226 Fax: 41 100
Valley View, Post Office Road
☎ 40 181

Munnar (04865)
Dassery East End, Temple Road
☎ 30 451
Isaac's The Residency
☎ 30 247

Alwaye (0484)
Hotel Periyar ☎ 25024

Chapter 6

Cochin (0484)
Casino Hotel (Willingdon Island)
☎ 66 6821
Hotel Seagull (Fort Cochin)
☎ 22 8128

Taj Malabar Hotel (Willingdon Island) ☎ 66 6811

Ernakulam (0484)
Hotel Abad Plaza, MG Road
☎ 36 1636
Hotel Joylan, Durbar Hall Road
☎ 36 7764
Metropolitan Hotel,
Caravara Road ☎ 36 9931
Paulson Park Hotel
☎ 354002
Hotel Presidency ☎ 35 5372
Taj Residency ☎ 37 1471

Bolgatty Island (0484)
Bolgatty Palace Hotel
☎ 35 5003

Lakshadweep Islands (0484)
Bangaram Island Resort
☎ 66 6821

Chapter 7

Trichur (0487)
Casino Hotel ☎ 24699
Fax: 0487 399037
Government Guest House
☎ 332300

Malampuzha (0491)
Garden House Hotel
☎ 55207
Govardhana Holiday Village,
Rock Garden Road ☎ 56010

Coimbatore (0422)
Anand Vihar, Davey & Co Lane
☎ 21 2580
Hotel City Tower, Sivasamy Road
☎ 23 0681 Fax: 23 0103
Sivakami, Davey & Co Lane
☎ 21 0271
Surya International Hotel,
105 Racecourse Road
☎ 21 7751 Fax: 21 6110

Fact File

Coonoor (4264)
Taj Garden Retreat, Church Road, Upper Coonoor.
☎ 20021 Fax: 22775

Calicut (0495)
Taj Residency PT Usha Road.
☎ 765354.
Fax:0495766448
Government Guest House
☎ 766920
Hotel Malabar Mansion,
Mananehira Square ☎ 76 014
Hotel Malabar Palace, GH Road
☎ 76 071
Paramount Tower, Town Hall Road ☎ 62 731
Seaqueen Hotel, Beach Road
☎ 36 6604

Telicherry (0497)
Paris Presidency, Logan's Road
☎ 232666
Hotel Pranam, Narangapuram
☎ 220634

Cannanore (0497)
Kamala International, SM Road
☎ 66 910
Mascot Hotel
Palm Grove Tourist Home,
152 Mill Road ☎ 503182
Government Guest House
☎ 506426

Kasargod (04995)
City Tower Hotel, MG Road
☎ 52 1324
Government Guest House
☎ 52 0666

Bakel Beach (04995)
Travellers Bungalow
☎ 502

Chapter 8

Mangalore (0832)
Taj Manjarun, Old Port Road
☎ 45 5525
Moti Mahal, Falnir Road
☎ 44 1411

Hassan (08172)
Hassan Ashok, BM Road
☎ 68731 Fax: 08172 67154

Belur (08233)
Mayura Velapuri ☎ 2209

Mysore (0821)
Lalitha Mahal Palace ☎ 27605
Sreekrishna Continental,
73 Nazarbad Road ☎ 37042
Palace Plaza, 2716 Sri Harsha Rd
☎ 30875 Fax: 520639
Metropole, 5 Jhansi Lakshmi
Bai Road ☎ 20681
Kings Kourt, JLB Road ☎ 25250
Southern Star, 13-14 Vinoba Rd
☎ 27217
Krishnaraja Sagar, Brindavan
Gardens, Belagola 22

Chapter 9

Bangalore (080)
Budget
Janardhana, Crescent Road
☎ 226 4444
New Victoria, 47 Residency Road
☎ 558 4076 Fax: 558 4945
Curzon Court, 10 Brigade Road
☎ 558 2997
Medium
Highgates Hotel, Church Street
☎ 559 7172
Luxury
Gateway, 66 Residency Road
☎ 558 4545 Fax: 558 4030
West End, Racecourse Road
☎ 226 9281 Fax: 220 0010

Oberoi, 37 MG Road
☎ 558 5858 Fax: 558 5960
Taj Residency, 41/3 MG Road
☎ 558 4444 Fax: 558 4748

Chapter 10

Madras (044)
Budget

Surat, 138 Prakasam Road
(George Town) ☎ 589236. Ask
for a room at the rear.
Sri Durga Prasad, 10 Kennet
Lane (Egmore) ☎ 825 3881
Broadlands, 16 Vallabha
Agraharam Street (North
Triplicane) ☎ 84 8131 or
84 5573. Built around court-
yards, only non-Indian guests
are welcome.

Mid range

Impala Continental, 12 Gandhi
Irwin Road (directly faces
Egmore Station) ☎ 825 0484
Chandra Towers 9 Gandhi Irwin
Road (also faces Egmore Station)
☎ 825 8171
Kanchi, 28 Cin C Road
☎ 827 1100
New Woodlands,
72/5 Dr Radhakrishnan Salai
(North Mylapore) ☎ 827 3111
Nilgiri's Nest,
58 Dr Radhakrishnan Salai (North
Mylapore) ☎ 827 5222

Upper range

Connemara, Binny Road

(Anna Salai) ☎ 8520123
Ambassador Pallava,
53 Monteith Road (Anna Salai)
☎ 826 8584
Madras International,
693 Anna Salai ☎ 852 4111
President, 16 Dr Radhakrishnan
Salai (North Mylapore) ☎ 832211

Luxury

Taj Coromandel, 17
Nungambakkam High Road
(Anna Salai) ☎ 827 2827
Fax: 825 7104. Essential to book
as this is the most luxurious of
the Madras Hotels and it's
restaurant's are the finest.
Welcomgroup Chola Sheraton,
10 Cathedral Road (Anna Salai)
☎ 828 0101 Fax: 827 8779

Mammallapuram (04113)

Ideal Beach Resort
☎ 2240 Fax: 2243
Golden Sun Beach Resort ☎ 2245
Silversands ☎ 2228 Fax: 2280
Mamalla Beach Cottages ☎ 2375
Tamil Nadu Beach Resort
☎ 2235 Fax: 2268
Temple Bay Ashok Beach Resort
☎ 2251 Fax: 2257
Mamalla Bhavan Annexe ☎ 2260
Veeras ☎ 2288
Tamil Nadu Unit II ☎ 2287

Kanchipuram (04112)

Hotel Tamil Nadu, Station Road,
☎ 22552
Baboo Soorya, 85 East Raja
Veety, ☎ 22555

CLIMATE

The south-west monsoon always hits Kerala during the last week of
May, petering out in August. Rains are very heavy from May to July,
when few holidaymakers will wish to visit. A second, somewhat
lighter monsoon, from the north-east, brings some rain to Kerala

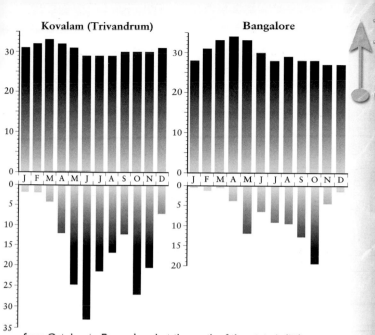

Kovalam (Trivandrum)

Bangalore

from October to December, but the north of the state is little affected. The best time to visit Kerala, therefore, is between December and May. Temperatures vary little throughout the year, but at sea level are significantly higher away from the coast. Sea temperatures are fairly constant, and the water is always slightly refreshing, rather like the Mediterranean in early summer; the 'hot bath' warmth of South-East Asian seas will not be found. Strong winds are rare throughout the dry season. Mysore and Bangalore have a much lower rainfal than Kerala, escaping the heaviest of the midsummer monsoon, as does the Madras region, which bears the brunt of the autumn monsoon.

CREDIT CARDS

Leading credit cards are accepted in most of the higher-rated hotels, restaurants and tourist agencies, but check in advance if unsure. It is always safer to carry sufficient cash for small purchases, but practically all shops accept cards for major items.

CURRENCY REGULATIONS

A maximum of 250 rupees (less than £5 at current rates) may be brought into or taken out of the country. In theory, amounts of foreign currency or travellers cheques in excess of US$1,000 should be declared on arrival in India, but in practice this appears to be unnecessary. Visitors staying more than 90 days have to apply for an income tax exemption certificate; to obtain this, currency exchange forms must be produced (see Money, below).

CUSTOMS REGULATIONS

One bottle of spirits and 200 cigarettes may be brought into India. Valuable items such as cameras, transistors, etc may have to be entered in a Tourist Baggage Re-Export form to ensure that they will not be re-sold in India, where they are extremely expensive. The form and the items concerned must be shown on departure.

ELECTRICITY

Throughout Kerala voltage is 230-240 AC. All sockets take continental plugs and most take UK two point plugs, but not always; bring a continental adaptor. Men should always take wet razors (and blades) in case of power cuts. Large hotels have their own generators, otherwise power cuts can occur at any time. However, times of cuts are published and rarely last more than half an hour.

FESTIVALS

Most Kerala festivals take place on dates which vary each year, according to religious calendars. Ascertain precise dates on arrival.

Kovalam

Great Elephant March
12 January
Gramman Village Fair
14-23 January

Trivandrum

Nishagandhi Dance Festival
21-27 February.
Music Festival in the Horse
Palace January.
Flavour Festival
5-11 April

Madurai

Tepam Festival – late January,
early February

Alleppey

The Great Elephant March,
(Snakeboat Race) 10 January
Onam – Snakeboat Races,
2nd Saturday in August (also in
Aranmula and Payipad near Haripad)

Cochin

Carnival – end of December
(Fort Cochin)

Trichur

Great Elephant March – 9 January
Pooram Festival – April/May (variable)
Ulsavom Festival – Feb/March (Guruvayoor)

FOOD

Some Keralan and south Indian specialities which are generally
unkown outside India, together with a few basic translations, are
listed below; most, but not all, are vegetarian dishes.

Adaprad- Sweet dessert of rice
haman and coconut
Aloo Potatoes
Appam Pancake-like
bread made from rice
flour and coconut milk
(sometimes toddy).
Also known as
Kallappam,
Oothappam or
Vellayappam.
Centres are soft and
white, edges crisp
and golden. The mix
is left overnight.
Avial Strips of mixed vegetables, green banana,
coconut and yogurt
prepared in masala. In
season, jackfruit seeds
and mango slices may
be incorporated.
Beer Kingfisher, India's
most popular beer, is
generally served in
restaurants (with or
without a licence) and
bars. It is not high
in alcohol and tastes
of the glycerine that is
added as a preserva-

tive (this can be
removed with careful
pouring). Stronger and
tastier is Kalyani Black
Label (6%), brewed
in Kerala.
Brinjal Aubergines
Champa Fat-grained Kerala
rice rice, red in colour
before cooking.
Channa Chick peas
Dal Lentils
(or Dhal)
Desserts In spite of the hot
climate, south Indians
prefer desserts to be
hot rather than cold:
rice 'puddings',
pancakes, porridge
and fritters being
particularly favoured.
Dosa This spectacular crisp
pancake, made from
lentil and rice flour, is
usually served as a
breakfast or evening
dish. Accompanied by
lightly curried potato
(*masala dosa*), it is
found throughout
south India. Coconut

Fact
File

241

chutney is always served.

Drumsticks Stick-like green vegetables that can be seen hanging from the branches of trees. The skin becomes fibrous with age and then only the soft centre should be eaten. An essential ingredient of *sambar* and *avial*.

Edava chicken Edava is a Kerala village from which this chicken masala and onion curry originates.

Gobi Cauliflower

Ice cream Reliable brands to look for are Lazza, Joy and Dollops (marketed by Walls). Local ice-creams, sold from carts, are not recommended.

Idli White dumplings made from rice flour and served for breakfast.

Inchi Ground mustard, ginger and coconut served as a pickle side dish.

Kaalen (or Kalan) Bananas cooked in yogurt and spices as a side dish.

Kallural Crayfish

Kingfish Fleshy, textured fish, not unlike cod.

Konchu Prawns

Koottu Curried lentil dumplings and potatoes.

Kozhi Chicken

Malayalee Pachadi Thick, yogurt-based sauce with coconut, chillis and other spices.

Manga Diced mango with chillis and curd.

Mattar Peas

Meen Fish (*kootan*, with coconut sauce; *manga*, with mangoes; *molee*, with onions; *vevichatha*, with fiery chilli sauce).

Neipathal Rice flour bread fried and cut into star shapes.

Olan (or Olen) A white pumpkin, lentils, coconut milk and chilli sauce.

Oonu This combination of rice and various separate vegetables curries is served on a metal dish. Sambar pickles and pappadums are included.

Paani Thick yogurt with syrup made from boiling toddy.

Pachade Large cucumber boiled with coconut and spices.

Palak Spinach

Paneer Cheese

Pappadums Kerala pappadums are small and made from lentil flour; they are usually cooked in coconut oil. Masala pappadums are spicy.

Pomfret Delicious, rather expensive fish with soft white meat.

Poottu Sweet dish popular at

breakfast. Rice flour and grated coconut dumplings are either sprinkled with sugar or accompanied by mashed bananas; occasionally curried chick peas are served instead.

Pradha-man (or Payasam) Sweet porridge of rice or vermicelli.

Pulisherry Pineapple boiled with yogurt: sour in flavour.

Rasam Lentil soup with *sambar* and spices, rather like a clear mulligatawny.

Sambar Thick sauce of lentils, vegetables and spices, served as an accompaniment.

Seebral A coarse flat fish

Seer fish Delicate flavoured fish with soft, white meat. One of Kerala's most popular specialities.

Syrian chicken stew A hearty dish developed by 'Syrian' Christians living in Kottayam. Brown in colour, the stew is basically a combination of chicken, potatoes, shallots and spices. It is usually accompanied by *appams*.

Thali Always served on a large, indented metal dish, this south Indian speciality comprises small portions of curried vegetables, champa rice, yogurt and sauces, which are often topped-up, at no extra charge. Meat or fish are sometimes incorporated.

Thoren Dry dish of chopped green beans and fried grated coconut flavoured with mustard seeds - there are no chillis. Meat or fish may be added.

Ulathi-yathu A dry tomato and coconut curry dish served with either mutton or prawns and squid.

Upperi Banana chips. In India these are always salted, never sweetened.

Uppu-mavu A breakfast dish of dry wheat grains, peanuts, ground coconut, raisins and diced vegetables. Served with *sambar* and mixed with water, few westerners find this south Indian dish enjoyable.

HEALTH

Currently, it is recommended that visitors to India are injected against typhoid, paratyphoid, tetanus, polio and hepatitis A. During the dry season, few mosquitoes are seen in Kerala's coastal regions, and malaria is rare, nevertheless many may wish to take precautions. Seek advice on the current situation from a pharmacy or a general practitioner some weeks before leaving. Drugs such as chloroquine and proquanil offer 70 per cent protection, but take insect repellent — and use it. If particularly worried about health dangers, specialist hospitals will give detailed advice; in the UK contact the Hospital for Tropical Diseases Travel Clinic – ☎ 0171 637 9899.

Rabies is common throughout India, and visitors are recommended not to pat dogs or hand-feed monkeys. If bitten, seek medical advice immediately.

Most stomach upsets in South India are caused by an excess of chillis, and are quickly disposed of by proprietary medicines such as Immodium. It is best that these are brought by the visitor so that action can be taken as soon as discomfort is experienced.

Tap water should be rigorously avoided outside the luxury hotels as should any fresh fruit and salad vegetables that may have been rinsed in it. Check with the establishment to ensure that the water they provide has been purified. Ice made from unpurified tap water can also be dangerous as the freezing process does not kill the microbes which cause the problems. Indians have developed immunity to them and can drink most water without fear. Bottled mineral water is readily available in tourist areas, but should be bought in advance if travelling elsewhere. It is recommended that teeth are brushed in purified or mineral water whenever possible. Purification tablets should be brought for use in an emergency.

The sun in Kerala is much stronger than in Indian cities such as Delhi and Bombay, where air pollution creates a haze, reducing its intensity. Protective creams and lotions should be brought by the visitor and liberally applied; the usual care should also be taken to increase exposure to the sun gradually. A peaked, tight-fitting cap is recommended if on a motorbike or an open boat, as the breeze will otherwise blow back the hair, exposing virgin skin to the ultra-violet rays.

While Indian pharmacies and doctors in the main towns are generally most efficient, it is preferable that any medical supplies that might be required are brought by visitors.

If worrying symptoms develop on returning home, contact a specialist hospital immediately, eg in the UK the Hospital for

Tropical Diseases, 4 St Pancras Way, London NW1 0PE
☎ 0171 387 4411. Help is also available regionally in Birmingham,
Liverpool and Glasgow.

INSURANCE

It is imperative that adequate insurance is taken out, particularly
health cover. Those travelling on package tours will be offered a
recommended policy by their operator.

MAPS

An excellent tourist map of Kerala, scale 1:180,000 is provided free
of charge by Kerala Tourism. Copies are available at all Tourist
Centres. For those travelling to other parts of India, the Nelles
Sectional series scale 1:1,500,000, is highly recommended.

MEASUREMENTS

The metric system is used throughout India. It is helpful to remember that one kilometre equals approximately $^2/_3$ of a mile and one
kilogram weighs just over 2lb. Spirits are poured in 'pecks', which
almost equal an English double measure.

MONEY

The Indian currency is the rupee, which is divided into 100 paise
(pronounced pies). Formerly, the rupee was also divided into
sixteen annas, but the anna is no longer in use. Although the rupee
was made convertible in 1993, the amount of foreign currency that
Indians may purchase in India remains strictly limited, and the black
market, therefore, continues to flourish: the most popular unit is the
British £50 note, for which a slightly higher premium is offered. It
should be remembered by all visitors that to exchange money with
non-authorized dealers is a punishable offence.

American dollars and sterling are the simplest currencies to exchange in India, whether they be in note or travellers cheque form.
Many hotels in Kerala are able to change money for their guests,
and the rate given is now very little less than that obtainable from
banks. Indian banks should be avoided whenever possible, as the
infamous red tape and form-filling involved means that a simple
transaction may take several hours. Banking hours are: Monday to

Friday 10am-2pm, Saturday 10am-12noon. Always insist on plenty of low-value notes as no-one ever has any change. Never accept torn or damaged notes, because Indians are loth to take them.

Ensure that currency exchange forms are given for each transaction, and keep them for converting any remaining rupees when leaving India, or for obtaining a tax clearance certificate if staying more than ninety days. It is best to pay a travel agent to obtain this, in order to avoid the tiresome official procedure involving a solicitor, a local Income Tax office, a main Income Tax office, and a return to visit the latter three days later. Most banks in small towns throughout India will not be able to change travellers cheques. The most welcome travellers cheques in India are those issued by American Express and Thomas Cook, either in dollars or sterling.

PACKING

As no heavy clothes will be needed in Kerala and hotels provide a fast, reliable laundry service, it is unnecessary to pack a large amount of clothing. The standard allowance permitted by most tour operators is 20kg plus hand baggage. Toiletries, a simple medical kit and camera film (particularly for colour slides) should be brought, but all clothing is relatively cheap throughout India, much of it of excellent quality particularly in the large towns. Jackets and trousers, for example, can be made to measure in a couple of days, so leave plenty of room or bring items that can be discarded.

Those staying in Kovalam will find a torch useful. Long-life batteries can be hard to find, as can deodorants, outside the large cities. If a cocktail before a meal is appreciated, a hip-flask, filled from a duty-free bottle, is recommended. Unless staying at a top class hotel, don't be surprised if there is no plug for the sink in the bathroom; take an adaptable rubber plug. Thick socks can also come in useful if temples are being visited – shoes must always be removed, and the stone can be very hot. For the beach, sandals, although generally useful, let in the burning hot sand and canvas shoes that can be adjusted easily with valcro are better.

PASSPORTS

All visitors to India must have a passport that remains valid for six months after leaving India. A visa for India is required by all visitors (see Visas, below).

POSTAGE

Stamps may be purchased at hotels or post offices, but the latter always involve long, slow-moving queues. The postal service is remarkably quick, efficient and honest. Mail sent home should arrive in one week. Never even think about sending a parcel out of India, the procedure demanded is a nightmare. Look with suspicion on offers by stores to post goods overseas; they may or may not arrive. This does not, of course, apply to state-run emporiums or shops sited within large hotels. Post offices are open Monday to Friday 10am-5pm and Saturday 10am-12noon.

TELEPHONES

Telephone calls can be made from many telecom centres, much more cheaply than from hotels. After 11pm the rate for overseas calls is reduced.

TIME

Kerala, like the rest of India, is $5\frac{1}{2}$ hours ahead of GMT.

TIPPING

Tipping (*backsheesh*) is widely practised in India, as in most Third-World countries. Only very small amounts are usually expected, so carry plenty of low-denomination notes and coins to give for minor services. It is usual for the service charge to be included in restaurant bills; if not, tip the waiter 10 per cent. Taxi drivers and auto-rickshaw operators will generally quote an inclusive price, but for good service, a small additional tip is appreciated.

GOVERNMENT OF INDIA TOURIST OFFICES:

UK
7 Cork Street, London W1X 1PB, ☎ 0171 437 3677
USA
Suite 204, 3550 Wilshire Boulevard, Los Angeles CA 90010
☎ (213) 380 8855
Suite 1808, 1270 Avenue of the Americas, New York,
NY 10020 ☎ (212) 586 4901\2\3

Canada
West Suite No 1003, 60 Bloor Street, Toronto, Ontario M4W 3B8
☎ (416) 962 3787/88
Australia
Level 2, 210 Pitt Street, Sydney NSW 2000
☎ (9) 264 4855

TRAVEL

Air

Only chartered aircraft fly direct to Kerala (Trivandrum) from abroad. Unless travelling with a tour operator the nearest airport to Kerala for overseas visitors is Madras. Holders of Indian passports are not permitted to travel to India on chartered flights.

Visitors travelling with tour operators will automatically be met at the airport by buses to take them to their resort accommodation. Others must rely on taxis or autorickshaws.

Train

Trains link many towns in Kerala and beyond, and are particularly useful if overnight travel (with a sleeping compartment) is required. Be sure to book as much in advance as possible.

Bus

Just about every town and village of any size in Kerala is linked by a bus service of sorts and the fares are usually cheaper than on the trains. Buses are often quicker for short journeys, however, night travel can be noisy and uncomfortable.

Taxis and Auto-rickshaws

In 1997, the official rate in Kerala for taxis was 3.50 rupees per kilometre, for distances over 10 kms. If a customer is dropped off the return fare must of course be paid. Those insisting on air conditioned cabs must expect to pay almost double.

Auto-rickshaw drivers, apart from those in North Kerala and Trivandrum city centre, refuse to use their metres and rip off foreigners as much as they possibly can. Do not pay any ridiculous fares they demand. Suggest they call the police – they won't.

Car & Motorbike Hire

Tourists may now hire and self-drive cars in India in addition to motorbikes, but few directions are given, roads are not numbered and the routes are littered with unpredictable animals. Throughout India, driving is on the left. It is far better, and not that much more expensive, to hire a car with a driver.

VISAS

All foreign passport holders need a visa to enter India. In the case of the United Kingdom, this measure was introduced as a tit-for-tat by Indira Gandhi, when the British government decided to require Indians visiting the UK to obtain a visa, thereby ensuring that they were not immigrating illegally.

It is advisable to make postal application for visas at least two months in advance, although personal applicants are usually able to collect their visas on the same day — after a lengthy queue and then a wait. Tourists six-month visas should specify multi-entry validity, if trips to Sri Lanka, the Maldives or Nepal, for example are envisaged. Business visas are available for a twelve-month period, but cannot be obtained on the same day. The validity of the visa now commences on the date of arrival in India. Would-be visitors to India without a valid passport and visa will not be permitted to board the plane, nor can any refunds be expected. Travel agents are able to advise on the current procedure.
In the United Kingdom, visas must be obtained from the following:
High Commision of India, India House, Aldwych, London WC2 B4NA (☎ 0171 240 2084)

Consulate General of India,20 Augustus Street, Jewellery Quarters, Hockley, Birmingham B18 6JL (☎ 0121 212 2782)
Consulate General of India, 6th Floor, Fleming House, 134 Rengrew Street, Glasgow, G3 75T (☎ 0141 331 0777)

In Eire: The Embassy of India, 6 Lesson Park, Dublin 6 (☎ 497 0843)
Three passport-size photographs are required. If a visa is needed urgently, and personal application is difficult, passport and visa courier services exist that will simplify and speed up the process for a fee; a visa can generally be obtained in seven working days by this means. One such organisation is Thames Consular, 363 Chiswick High Road, London W4 4HS (☎ 0181 995 2492).

INDEX

LANDMARK
Publishing Ltd ● ● ● ●

VISITORS GUIDES

* Practical guides for the independent traveller

* Written in the form of touring itineraries

* Full colour illustrations and maps

* Detailed Landmark FactFile of practical information

* Landmark Visitors Guides highlight all the interesting places you
will want to see, so ensuring that you make the most of your visit

1. **Britain**
Cornwall	Cotswolds & Shakespeare Country
Jersey	Lake District
Devon	Dorset
Guernsey	Yorkshire Dales & York
Scotland	Peak District
Hampshire	Edinburgh

2. **Europe**
Bruges	Black Forest
Provence	Tuscany
Italian Lakes	Gran Canaria

3. **Other**
Dominican Republic	Florida Keys
India: Goa	Florida: Gulf Coast
India: Kerala &	Florida: Atlantic Coast
The South	Orlando & Central Florida

Landmark Publishing
Waterloo House, 12 Compton, Ashbourne, Derbyshire DE6 IDA England
Tel: 01335 347349 Fax: 01335 347303

LANDMARK
Publishing Ltd ● ● ● ●

YOUTH HOSTELLER'S
WALKING GUIDES

(each title £7.99)

THE LAKE DISTRICT

YORKSHIRE DALES
AND MOORS

THE PEAK DISTRICT

This series consists of most attractive hand-drawn
walking maps of the best routes between and around
Youth Hostels in each area, together with
descriptions of these chosen routes and details of the
hostel facilities.

Titles in this series also contain a voucher entitling
the reader to one year's free membership of the
Youth Hostel Association (England & Wales),
a saving of £10.00; free accommodation at a
YHA hostel (to a maximum of £10.00); or similar.

Send for details to:
Landmark Publishing, Waterloo House, 12 Compton,
Ashbourne, Derbyshire DE6 IDA. Tel: 01335 347349

Published by:
Landmark Publishing Ltd,
Waterloo House, 12 Compton, Ashbourne
Derbyshire DE6 1DA England

1st Edition

ISBN 1 901522 16 4

British Library Cataloguing in Publication Data:
a catalogue record for this book is available
from the British Library.

Colour Origination: AD VER srl, Italy

Print: Tipolitografia Petruzzi, Corrado +C, Italy

Cartography: Samantha Witham

Design: Samantha Witham

Picture Credits:
Christopher Turner, all save for:
David Forman; front cover,6/7, 34, 83
Government of India Tourist Office; 147(U)
Richard Todd; 10(U)

Cover Pictures
Front: The Great Elephant March at Trichur
Back: Lalitha Mahal Palace, Mysore